T0334403

Buen Vivir and the Challenges to Capitalism in Latin America

This book explores the battleground between neoliberal capitalist development processes in Latin America and the challenges to these systems that can be found through innovative community-driven *buen vivir/vivir bien* initiatives.

In the current climate of worldwide capitalist development, Latin America is caught between left-leaning proposals for progressive policies towards a more inclusive form of development, and the re-emergence of harsh austerity measures, neoliberal reforms and right-wing populism. Divided into two parts, this book first provides a retrospective analysis of the advance of resource-seeking 'extractive' capital across the continent since the 1990s. The second part goes on to focus on forward-looking challenges to neoliberal capitalist development, focusing in particular on the indigenous notion of *buen vivir/vivir bien*—the concept of 'living well' in social solidarity and harmony with nature. Drawing on cases in Mexico and Venezuela, the book argues that it will be through these new approaches to social change that we will move beyond development as we know it towards a more inclusive form of 'postdevelopment'.

Looking hopefully towards this future of development, this collection offers an essential analysis of the vortex of social change currently consuming Latin America and will be key reading for advanced scholars and researchers in the fields of Development Studies, Latin America Studies, Politics, and Social Change.

Henry Veltmeyer is senior research professor in development studies at Universidad Autónoma de Zacatecas, and senior research fellow in the centre of Advanced Latin American Studies (CALAS) at the Universidad de Guadalajara. He has authored and edited over 60 books in the area of Latin American studies, the political economy of development and globalisation, and social movements in the Latin American context.

Edgar Záyago Lau is professor and researcher of the Academic Unit in Development Studies, Universidad Autónoma de Zacatecas (UAZ), Mexico, and Co-coordinator of the Latin American Network of Nanotechnology and Society (ReLANS). His research areas include the political economy of science, technology and development; development theory and public policy. He is also the author and co-author of more than 60 articles in mainstream academic journals and has co-edited nine books.

Routledge Critical Development Studies

Series Editors:

Henry Veltmeyer
Co-chair of the Critical Development Studies (CDS) network, Research Profes-
sor at Universidad Autónoma de Zacatecas, Mexico, and Professor Emeritus at
Saint Mary's University, Canada

Paul Bowles
Professor of Economics and International Studies at UNBC, Canada

Elisa van Wayenberge
Lecturer in Economics at SOAS University of London, UK

The global crisis, coming at the end of three decades of uneven capitalist development and neoliberal globalisation that have devastated the economies and societies of people across the world, especially in the developing societies of the global south, cries out for a more critical, proactive approach to the study of international development. The challenge of creating and disseminating such an approach, to provide the study of international development with a critical edge, is the project of a global network of activist development scholars concerned and engaged in using their research and writings to help effect transformative social change that might lead to a better world.

This series will provide a forum and outlet for the publication of books in the broad interdisciplinary field of critical development studies—to generate new knowledge that can be used to promote transformative change and alternative development.

The editors of the series welcome the submission of original manuscripts that focus on issues of concern to the growing worldwide community of activist scholars in this field.

To submit proposals, please contact the Development Studies Editor, Helena Hurd (Helena.Hurd@tandf.co.uk).

The Rise and Fall of Global Microcredit
Development, Debt and Disillusion
Edited by Milford Bateman, Stephanie Blankenburg and Richard Kozul-Wright

Postdevelopment in Practice
Alternatives, Economies, Ontologies
Edited by Elise Klein and Carlos Eduardo Morreo

***Buen Vivir* and the Challenges to Capitalism in Latin America**
Edited by Henry Veltmeyer and Edgar Záyago Lau

www.routledge.com/Routledge-Critical-Development-Studies/book-series/RCDS

Buen Vivir and the Challenges to Capitalism in Latin America

Edited by Henry Veltmeyer and Edgar Záyago Lau

LONDON AND NEW YORK

First published 2021
by Routledge
2 Park Square, Milton Park, Abingdon, Oxon OX14 4RN

and by Routledge
52 Vanderbilt Avenue, New York, NY 10017

Routledge is an imprint of the Taylor & Francis Group, an informa business

© 2021 selection and editorial matter, Henry Veltmeyer and Edgar Záyago Lau; individual chapters, the contributors

The right of Henry Veltmeyer and Edgar Záyago Lau to be identified as the authors of the editorial matter, and of the authors for their individual chapters, has been asserted in accordance with sections 77 and 78 of the Copyright, Designs and Patents Act 1988.

All rights reserved. No part of this book may be reprinted or reproduced or utilised in any form or by any electronic, mechanical, or other means, now known or hereafter invented, including photocopying and recording, or in any information storage or retrieval system, without permission in writing from the publishers.

Trademark notice: Product or corporate names may be trademarks or registered trademarks, and are used only for identification and explanation without intent to infringe.

British Library Cataloguing-in-Publication Data
A catalogue record for this book is available from the British Library

Library of Congress Cataloging-in-Publication Data
Names: Veltmeyer, Henry, editor. | Záyago Lau, Edgar, editor.
Title: Buen vivir and the challenges to capitalism in Latin America / edited by Henry Veltmeyer and Edgar Zayago Lau.
Description: New York : Routledge, 2020. | Series: Routledge critical development studies | Includes bibliographical references and index. |
Identifiers: LCCN 2020016937 (print) | LCCN 2020016938 (ebook) | ISBN 9780367550011 (hardback) | ISBN 9781003091516 (ebook)
Subjects: LCSH: Social change–Latin America. | Capitalism–Latin America. | Latin America–Economic policy. | Latin America–Politics and government–21st century.
Classification: LCC HN110.5.A8 B834 2020 (print) |
LCC HN110.5.A8 (ebook) | DDC 303.4098–dc23
LC record available at https://lccn.loc.gov/2020016937
LC ebook record available at https://lccn.loc.gov/2020016938

ISBN: 978-0-367-55001-1 (hbk)
ISBN: 978-1-003-09151-6 (ebk)

Typeset in Times New Roman
by Wearset Ltd, Boldon, Tyne and Wear

Contents

Illustrations

Figures

Tables

Maps

Contributors

Dario Azzellini is Senior Research Professor in Development Studies at Universidad Autónoma de Zacatecas and Visiting Fellow at the Latin American Studies Program of Cornell University. He received his PhD in political science from Goethe University Frankfurt, Germany, and his PhD in sociology from Benemérita Universidad Autónoma de Puebla, Mexico. He was lecturer for development sociology, Cornell University; assistant professor for sociology at Johannes Kepler University Linz, Austria; and fellow at the CUNY graduate center, the CUNY Murphy Institute and at the Cornell ILR School. He has published more than 20 books, numerous other writings and 11 documentary films in the areas of critical labour studies and global social change with a special focus on Latin America and Europe, including *Communes and Workers' Control in Venezuela: Building 21st Century Socialism from Below* (2017); *They Can't Represent Us. Reinventing Democracy From Greece to Occupy* (2014); *The Class Strikes Back. Self-Organised Workers' Struggles in the Twenty-First Century* (2018); and *Ours to Master and to Own: Worker Control from the Commune to the Present* (2011). Much of his work is available at: www.azzellini.net.

Jean Paul Benavides is Assistant Professor and Researcher with the Institute of Socioeconomic Research at the Universidad Católica Boliviana 'San Pablo'. Publications include *TOOLKIT for the Monitoring and Evaluation of Productive Products with Gender-based Approach* (2020), *Institutional Diversity and Local Forest Governance* (2014), Carbon Sequestration in Community Forests: Trade-offs, Multiple Outcomes and Institutional Diversity in the Bolivian Amazon (2014), and Public Policy Reforms and Indigenous Forest Governance: The Case of the Yuracaré People in Bolivia (2012).

Raúl Delgado Wise is Professor and Director of the Doctoral Program in Development Studies at the Autonomous University of Zacatecas, general coordinator of the UNESCO Chair on Migration, Development and Human Rights, and member of the advisory board of the UNESCO-MOST committee in Mexico. He is also president and founder of the International Network on Migration and Development, co-Director of the Critical Development Studies Network. He has authored and edited 30 books, and written more than 200 essays, including book chapters and refereed articles. Recent books include *Mexico's Economic Dilemma: The Developmental Failure of Neoliberalism* (2011); *Critical Development Studies. An Introduction* (2018); and *Migration, Civil Society and Global Governance* (2019).

Stefanie Garry is an Economic Affairs Officer at the United Nations Conference on Trade and Development (UNCTAD) in Geneva, Switzerland. She works in the Office of the Director, Division for Africa, Least Developed Countries and Special Programmes. She has also served as Associate Economics Affairs Officer with the Economic Commission for Latin America and the Caribbean (ECLAC) in the Subregional Office in Mexico City, and a sectoral specialist at the International Labor Organization (ILO)—with a specialised interest in economics and development, community development planning, value chains, small business development, labour market analysis, employment and labour market statistics.

Eduardo Gudynas is Director and Senior Researcher at the Uruguay-based Latin American Centre for Social Ecology (CLAES). His expertise is in the area of social ecology, sustainable development and alternatives. He has worked and continues to work closely with social movements, particularly in South America. He is also associate researcher in the Department of Anthropology, University of California, Davis (US); was Arne Naess chair on environmental and global justice at the University of Oslo (Norway), fellow at the Center for Advanced Studies at LMU Munich University (Germany), and researcher with the Uruguayan innovations and research agency. He has been listed among the 74 key thinkers in development and one of the 50 most influential intellectuals in Latin America. He has authored or edited over 30 books, including now classic textbooks on Nature's rights in Latin America (printed in six countries) and on extractivisms (two versions in Spanish, and forthcoming in English).

Efe Can Gürcan is Associate Dean of Research and Development for the Faculty of Economics, Administrative and Social Sciences at İstinye University. He is also a faculty member in the Department of International Relations, İstinye University and Research Associate at Manitoba University's Geopolitical Economy Research Group. He completed his undergraduate education in International Relations at Koç University. He received his master's degree in International Studies at the University of Montréal and earned his PhD in Sociology at Simon Fraser University. He speaks English, French, Spanish and Turkish. His publications include three books as well as more than 30 articles and book chapters on international development, international conflict and international institutions, with a geographical focus on Latin America and the Middle East. His recent book is *Multipolarization, South-South Cooperation and the Rise of Post-Hegemonic Governance* (Routledge, 2019).

Horacio Mackinlay, a sociologist and political scientist, is Professor of Sociology at the Universidad Autónoma Metropolitana, campus Iztapalapa. His work is about political and rural sociology in Mexico. He has published over 30 scholarly articles and book chapters. His new research project is about several aspects on the history of the Mexican agrarian reform (1915–1992). His most recent article is 'Well-off small-scale tobacco growers and farm workers in the Mexican agrarian reform (1972–1990)', published in the *Journal of Agrarian Change*. Most of his work is available at: http://sgpwe. izt.uam.mx/Profesor/1030-Horacio-Mackinlay.html.

Juan Carlos Moreno-Brid received his PhD in Economics from Cambridge University. For many years he served as Director of the regional centre (Mexico) of the Economic Commission of Latin America and the Caribbean (ECLAC), but now is Professor of Economics at the Autonomous National University of Mexico (UNAM), serving as lecturer and tutor in Economic Development Knowledge as well as Economic History. His many publications include *Cambio estructural y crecimiento en Centroamérica y República Dominicana* (CEPAL, 2014) and *Desarrollo y crecimiento en la economía mexicana: una perspectiva histórica* (Fondo de Cultura Económica, 2014; Oxford University Press, 2009).

Gerardo Otero, a sociologist and political economist, is Professor of International Studies at Simon Fraser University in Vancouver, Canada. His work is about political economy of agriculture and food, civil society and the state in the Americas. He has published over 100 scholarly articles, chapters and books. He is the author of *Farewell to the Peasantry? Political Class Formation in Rural Mexico* (Westvew Press 1999, re-issued by Routledge in 2018). His latest monograph is: *The Neoliberal Diet: Healthy Profits, Unhealthy People* (University of Texas Press 2018). Much of his work is available at: www.sfu.ca/people/otero.html.

James Petras is Professor Emeritus in Sociology at Binghamton University in New York and Adjunct Professor in International Development Studies at Saint Mary's University (Halifax, Canada). He is the author of over 50 books and numerous other writings on the dynamics of globalisation and Latin American developments, including *Unmasking Globalization* (2001); *The New Development Politics* (2003); *Social Movements and the State: Argentina, Bolivia, Brazil, Ecuador* (2005). A list and an actual file of his periodical writings and journal articles are maintained and can be accessed at Rebelion.org.

René Ramírez Gallegos is an economist with a PhD in Sociology (with specialisation in Labour Relations, Social Inequalities and Trade Unionism) awarded by the Faculty of Economics, University of Coimbra—Portugal. He worked as Coordinator of the III Regional Conference on Higher Education for Latin America and Caribbean (IESALC-UNESCO) in regard to the thematic axis 'Science, Technology and Innovation' (2018). He has served as Chairman of the Council of Higher Education in Ecuador (2011–2016); as Minister of Higher Education, Science, Technology and Innovation in Ecuador (2011–2017); and as Minister of Planning and Development (2008–2011). At present, he is guest professor-researcher at the Autonomous University of Zacatecas (UAZ) and researcher of the University Program of Studies on Democracy, Justice and Society (PUEDJS) at the National Autonomous University of México (UNAM), Mexico. His many writings include "La gran transición. En busca de nuevos sentidos comunes" (2016), "La vida y el tiempo. Apuntes para una teoría ucrónica de la vida buena a partir de la historia reciente de Ecuador" (2019). He is also co-editor of the Alice dictionary: http://alice.ces.uc.pt/dictionary/.

Joaquín Sánchez Gómez is Assistant Professor at the Faculty of Economics, The National Autonomous University of Mexico (UNAM). He also works as an independent consultant for international organisations and government agencies and does research on manufacturing, labour economics and international commerce.

Maristella Svampa is an Argentinian sociologist and writer. She is Senior Researcher at the CONICET (National Centre for Scientific and Technical Research), in Argentina and Professor at the Universidad Nacional de la Plata (province of Buenos Aires). She is the coordinator of the Group of Critical and Interdisciplinary Studies on the Energy Problem and a member of the Permanent Group of Alternative Development. She received the Guggenheim Fellowship and the Kónex award in Sociology (Argentina) in 2006 and 2016, and the Kónex award in Political and Sociological essay (2014), and the Platinum Kónex Award in Sociology (2016). In 2018, she received the National Award in Sociology in Argentina. Recent publications include *Debates Latinoamericanos. Indianismo, Desarrollo, Dependencia, Populismo, Del Cambio de época al fin de ciclo* (2016), *Gobiernos progresistas, extractivismo, movimientos sociales en América Latina* (2017); *La expansión de las fronteras del neoextractivismo en América Latina* (2018) and *Chacra 51. Regreso a la Patagonia en los tiempos del fracking* (2018). In English she has published *Development in Latin America, Challenges, Resistances, Future Directions* (Fernwood Publishing, 2019) and *Neo-Extractivism Dynamics in Latin America, Socioenvironmental Conflicts, Territorial Turn, and New Political Narratives* (Cambridge University Press, 2019).

Henry Veltmeyer is Senior Research Professor at the Universidad Autónoma de Zacatecas (Mexico) and Professor Emeritus of International Development Studies (IDS) at Saint Mary's University (Canada), with a specialist interest in Latin American development. In addition to holding a Senior Research Fellowship in advanced Latin American Studies at the University of Guadalajara he is co-Chair of the Critical Development Studies (CDS) network, and a co-editor of Fernwood's *Initiatives in Critical Agrarian Change* series. The *CDS Handbook: Tools for Change*, originally published by Fernwood Publications in 2011 has been translated into French and published by University of Ottawa Press as *Des outils pour le changement: Une approche critique en* *études du développement.* Both the CDS Handbook and the expanded and updated version (*The Essential Guide to Critical Development Studies*, Routledge, 2017) have also been translated and published in Spanish by the postgraduate program in development Studies (CIDES) at the Universidad Mayor de San Andrés, La Paz, Bolivia.

Horacio Vera Cossio is a Bolivian development economist, Researcher and Lecturer at the Catholic University of Bolivia working on issues of development, poverty, and inequality. Recent publications include *Cycles versus Trends: The Effects of Economic Growth on Earnings in Bolivia* (2015) and *When the Women Are the Ones Who Rule: The Role of Savings in Female Empowerment* (2014).

Fernanda Wanderley is a Brazilian-born Bolivian sociologist. She received her PhD in Sociology from Colombia University in 2005. Since 2016 she has served as Director and Senior Researcher at the Institute of Socio-Economic Research of the Universidad Católica Boliviana 'San Pablo' (IISEC-UCB). She has worked as a professor in the postgraduate program in Development Studies at the Universidad Mayor de San Andres in La Paz from 2007–2015. Her many publications include *Hacia el desarrollo sostenible en la región andina Bolivia, Perú, Ecuador y Colombia* (2018); *Los desafíos del desarrollo productivo en el siglo XXI* (2018); and *Between Extractivism and Living Well: Experiences and Challenges* (2017).

Edgar Záyago Lau is Professor and Researcher of the Academic Unit in Development Studies, Universidad Autónoma de Zacatecas (UAZ), Mexico, and Co-coordinator of the Latin American Network of Nanotechnology and Society (ReLANS). His research areas include political economy of science, technology and development; development theory and public policy. Currently he is the academic administrator of the Doctoral Programme in Development Studies at UAZ. He has been a visiting research scholar at the Transdisciplinary Doctorate for the Scientific and Technological Development of Society (DCTS) of the Centre for Research and Advanced Studies of the National Polytechnic Institute (CINVESTAV—IPN) (2016–present) and at the Federal University of Paraná in Curitiba, Brazil (2014). He is also the author and co-author of more than 60 articles in mainstream academic journals and has been co-editor of nine books. He is a member of the National System of Researchers (Tier II) and a member of the Mexican Academy of Science (AMC).

Introduction

Henry Veltmeyer and Edgar Záyago Lau

Latin America in the current neoliberal era of worldwide capitalist development has turned into a veritable laboratory of different alternative pathways to development. The region, it could be said, is caught up in the vortex of conflicting forces of social change, some pulling or pushing towards the left (with proposals for progressive policies in the direction of a more inclusive form of development), and others to the right (in the form of a restoration of harsh neoliberal reforms and austerity measures, the emergence of right-wing populism).

The turn into the twenty-first century was accompanied by a number of momentous changes in both the international arena (the rise of China and a reconfiguration of economic power) and in domestic politics (the rise of anti-neoliberal social movements), which ushered in a cycle of progressive policies and level-leaning political regimes in Latin America. Barely a decade in the making (from 2002 to 2015), this cycle came to an end in the wake of a 'primary commodities boom', a cycle of high prices for the commodities (natural resources with little to no processing) that dominated Latin American exports. With the collapse of this commodities boom the capacity of the progressive regimes to finance programs of poverty reduction was dramatically reduced, resulting in a pendulum swing of electoral policies to the far right, putting in power a series of regimes committed to turning the clock back towards an early cycle of neoliberal policies.

This book explores the development and resistance dynamics generated by the forces of change mobilised in this process. The context for this development process, and for the forces of resistance that it generated, was the advance of what has been described as resource-seeking 'extractive' capital—foreign direct investments by multinational corporations in the extraction of natural resources such as fossil fuels, oil and gas and agro-food products, for the purpose of exporting them in a primary commodity form so as to maximise windfall profits made possible by the high prices for the products on capitalist markets. The dynamic inflows of resource-seeking 'extractive' capital over the course of the 1990s and the past two decades not only released powerful forces of social change but created an entirely different context in the search for different economic models and development pathways, and alternative realities.

Part I of the book explores salient features of the capitalist development process in the Latin American context. The central focus of the chapters in Part I is on a retrospective analysis of the forces of change that have been mobilised in the capitalist development process. In contrast, Part II focuses on forward-looking challenges, particularly as relates to the worldview and indigenous cosmovision of alternative realities embedded in the indigenous notion of *buen vivir* or *vivir bien* (*sumak kawsay*), which is to 'live well' in social solidarity and harmony with nature. This concept has radically transformed the thinking about 'development', which has always revolved around the policy and institutional dynamics associated with the evolution of capitalism as a world system. In Part II the book turns away from an analysis of the development dynamics associated with the advance of industrial and extractive capital over the past six 'development' decades to an analysis of diverse forces of change that have emerged in the current context of capitalist development in the region—forces that have been mobilised in the direction of postdevelopment, i.e. an alternative post-capitalist society. In this regard, Chapters 7–10 (Eduardo Gudynas, Maristella Svampa, Fernanda Wanderley and associates, René Ramírez Gallegos) take us beyond the world of development as we know it, i.e. as circumscribed by the epistemology of Western thought and the associated idea of economic progress as capitalist accumulation and economic growth. The focus and central concern of these chapters is on what we might consider to be 'another world', an alternative reality based on an indigenous worldview—what Eduardo Gudynas, for one, understands as 'postdevelopment'. The indigenous concept of *buen vivir*, or *vivir bien* (living well in social solidarity and harmony with nature) captures the sense of this alternative worldview.

A chapter-by-chapter synopsis

The first chapter provides a contextual framework and sets the stage for an analysis of the forces of change that have swept across the political landscape in Latin America in recent years. The focus is on the development and resistance dynamics of these forces of change. The chapter is organised as follows. First, it reviews the dynamics of what might be understood as the new geoeconomics of capital in Latin America and the corresponding politics and realities. The aim here is to provide a theoretical framework for the subsequent analysis and for the chapters that follow. The chapter then turns to and elaborates on certain dynamics associated with the advance of resource-seeking 'extractive' capital (productive investments in the extraction of natural resources and the export of these resources in primary commodity form). At issue in this development process is the political economy of two types of capitalism, extractive and industrial, with reference to the particular way in which these two forms of capital(ism) are combined in the current context. The third part of the chapter provides a brief review of the economic and political dynamics that led to the emergence of a 'progressive cycle' of left-leaning policy regimes—a so-called 'pink tide' of regime change. The chapter ends with a brief discussion of the forces implicated in what appears to be the end of this progressive cycle. The conclusion is that the answer to this question should be sought and can be found in the fundamental contradictions of capitalism and what might be described as the antinomies of the development process.

The second chapter analyses the dynamics of class struggle and resistance on the new frontier of extractive capital. In the context of these dynamics some parts of the rural population in the region have been mobilised in protest against the advance of extractive capitalism. They have undertaken a variety of collective actions against the destructive operations and negative impacts of large-scale foreign investments in agroextraction—the acquisition of land and the extraction of natural resources for export. The chapter analyses the conflict dynamics of these forces of resistance that have emerged on the frontier of extractive capital in the rural areas, forces that pit the multinational corporations in the extractive sector, as well as the governments that have licensed their operations, against the rural communities that are most directly impacted by these operations.

The following chapter (3) analyses the development dynamics that have unfolded in the agricultural sector of the extractive frontier. The focus here is on the 'agrarian question' of the twenty-first century, namely: what is the impact of the forces of change generated by the capitalist development of agriculture in the current development context? Until recently and throughout the twentieth century, the main role of agriculture in the capitalist development process had been to constitute a proletariat in the form of a wage-labouring working class and to replenish the industrial labour force in the form of a reserve army of surplus labour. In the current context of extractive capitalism, however, the role of agriculture has changed.

The purpose of the chapter is to analyse the development and resistance dynamics of these forces of change. As for the forces of resistance mobilised in this development process, forces mobilised by the peasantry and what the World Bank chooses to call 'the rural poor' (the mass of dispossessed and semiproletarianised rural landless rural workers), they have been mobilised to protest against the advance of extractive capitalism. The rural poor of peasant farmers and landless workers in this context have undertaken a variety of collective actions against the destructive operations of large-scale foreign investments in agroextraction—the acquisition of land, or 'landgrabbing, and the extraction of natural resources for the purpose of exporting them in primary commodity form to maximise profits. The chapter analyses the conflict dynamics of these forces of resistance, which pit the multinational corporations in the extractive sector, as well as the governments that have licensed their operations, against the rural communities that are most directly impacted by these operations.

The chapter argues that, in addition to the dynamics of extractive capital, we need to understand those dynamics associated with the concentration of capital in the agricultural sector, as well as developments wherein intellectual property and ownership of *patents* has become a key component of the imperial(ist) system of domination under the aegis of neoliberal capitalism.

In Chapter 4 the authors critically engage the Latin American literature on the politics of developments with a focus on two main strands of political practice since the neoliberal turn in the 1980s, but especially after the 1994 Zapatista insurrection. These two main strands are the autonomists or the 'social left' that has taken form primarily as a complex of nongovernmental organisations that make up 'civil society', and a symbiotic or 'political left' that is fundamentally concerned with electoral politics. The focus of the chapter is on the case of Mexico, where the left-leaning MORENA (National Regeneration Movement) party, with Andrés Manuel López Obrador (AMLO) as its presidential candidate, won the presidential elections by a landslide in 2018. What is particularly interesting and highly relevant about López Obrador's electoral victory is that Mexico did not participate in the 'progressive cycle' of left-leaning regimes formed in the so-called 'pink wave'—a cycle that paralleled the primary commodities cycle of 2002–2012. While Mexico in this case turned towards the left, virtually all of the regimes that were part of the progressive cycle (particularly Argentina and Brazil, Bolivia and Ecuador) have succumbed to forces of change mobilised by the far right, resulting in the restoration of neoliberal austerity measures and authoritarian politics in the region. In this context, López Obrador's electoral victory has revived hopes on the left of another progressive cycle.

At issue in the recent swing of the pendulum politics first to the left and then to the far right is the most effective strategy for bringing about progressive change: whether progressive forces would focus on gaining state power 'from above' (via elections) or 'from below' (via social movement mobilisation from within civil society). In this context, the authors argue that those social movements that supported electoral transitions were demobilised or coopted by the social-assistance policies of the state, while autonomist movements that refused to engage with the state were mostly marginalised. In effect, both strategies failed their popular constituencies. The authors conclude that the way forward for progressive social movements is to engage with the state while staying mobilised in order for movements to retain their independence from the state and autonomy from political parties. This, according to the authors is, in fact, the challenge for MORENA and sympathiser social movements in Mexico: how can they support each other while advancing in a popular-democratic agenda of sustainable development?

In Chapter 5 the book turns away from the forces of change associated with the advance of extractive capital towards the problem of constructing a new industrial policy in the context of the turn of many countries towards an extractivist approach to national development. In the context of state-led development from the 1950 to the 1970s national development was equated with industrialisation and an endogenous industrial policy was deemed to be an essential drive of the engine of economic growth. However, the installation in the 1980s of a 'new world order' based on the principles of neoliberal globalisation radically changed the prospects for further industrial development of countries and regions on the periphery of the world capitalist system. In the forced compliance to the rules of the new neoliberal world order, and the dictates of global capital and the governments and international organisations that advanced these dictates (integration into the globalisation agenda), these countries were prevented or deprived of their capacity to pursue an active independent industrial policy and become 'a global manufacturing power'.

This was a turning point in the capitalist development process on the periphery of the system—a turn towards the advance of extractive capital in the development process. The focus of Chapter 5, which addresses this problematic is on Mexico, which led the push in the region towards the development of capitalism and modern industry in the pre-neoliberal era. Most development thinkers either argue or assume that both extractivism (the extraction of natural resources) and industrialisation (industrial development) are required conditions for expanding the forces of production and bringing about a modern form of capitalist development, or modernisation. The problem, however, is how to combine industrialism and extractivism in a way that avoids the destructive socioenvironmental impacts of both—a problem that has surfaced and taken form in the notion of neoextractivism and, according to the authors, in the revival of the search and efforts to construct a new industrial policy. The problem, they argue, is that in the context of the new (neoliberal) world order, Mexico, together with other governments in the region, has been prevented from implementing an independent and endogenous industrial policy, resulting in the destruction of forces of production built up over several decades of state-led industrial development based on an industrial policy designed to build up domestic industries.

Rather than building up an industrial sector to process the region's wealth of natural resources, the neoliberal macroeconomic agenda of the governments formed within the institutional and policy framework of this agenda favoured and promoted the advance of extractive capital, leading to an affluence of resource-seeking extractive investments that reinforced the orientation of the economies in the region towards a reliance on natural resource extraction and the export of these resources in primary commodity form, with all of the attendant contradictions and conflicts discussed in other chapters.

To situate and provide additional context for the discussion of Mexico's industrial policy in Chapter 5, it is important to understand that the 1980s provided a major turning point of developing countries away from a state-led approach to development based on a strategy of import-substitution industrialisation towards 'reprimarisation' and an associated return to extractivism as a development strategy. This turn towards primarisation and extractivism had its origins in several trends. One was the advance of resource-seeking 'extractive' capital (investments in the extraction of natural resources) to meet and satisfy the strong demand for 'primary commodities' on capitalist markets. Another is the long commodities boom of 2002–14, which spurred the interest of those governments formed in the search for a more inclusive form of development in the extraction of natural resources in the region as a source of fiscal resources to finance their social development (poverty reduction) programs. This concern for additional fiscal resources led these governments to open up the economy to foreign investment and provide the bearers of this investment, the large multinational corporations in the extractive sector, greater access to long-term contracts, concessions to explore for oil and gas, and mining licences.

A third cause was more indirect—the turn against industrial policy in the region, which opened up political and economic space for extractivism. This was most evident in Mexico. Its relatively advanced industrial sector was incorporated into global value chains through the maquiladora program and then the entry in NAFTA and the subsequent USMCA. The defining characteristic of the latter were their neoliberal emphasis on 'free trade', an economic policy that would see Mexico compete on a continental and global scale on the basis of its relatively low labour costs. As noted by the authors of Chapter 5, the emphasis on 'horizontal' and 'sector neutral' policies marked a departure from earlier attempts to build national industries through the use of selective policy interventions. This turn away from industrial policy led to a change in mindset in which industry was no longer necessarily seen as the growth-facilitating leading sector of economic development and a policy stance that no longer privileged the sector. Both of these national level changes enabled extractivism to return as a viable development strategy. Furthermore, part of the reason for the turn against industrial policy was its perceived failure; a failure to spur national innovation and now more difficult within a changing global production system within which global value chains dominated and developing countries were able to access only parts of those chains.

Developing countries such as Mexico and Brazil, in this context, could try to insert themselves into those chains on the basis of their 'strategic advantages' but national industrial policies were for a bygone era. The authors challenge this conventional wisdom by focusing on sub-national policies in the aeronautical and software industries in Mexico. They argue that while national industrial policy was abandoned, it lived on in interesting ways at the sub-national level and with some success. In arguing for this, they present the case for continued industrial policies as economic development policy instruments.

With Chapter 6 the book turns away from Part I and the dynamics of capitalist development towards the problem of constructing a socialist path towards development, a path fraught with obstacles and failed experiments. The chapter focuses on the complex and contradictory dynamics of socialist development in Venezuela—a project designed to bring about the socialism of the twenty-first century, which is to say, 'from above' (with the agency of the state) and 'from below' (with the agency of community-based organisations and institutions). While the concept of *buen vivir* (see the discussion in Part II of the book) breaks with capitalism and rejects it as a system for bringing about an alternative reality, another world of more inclusive and more sustainable form of national development, most proposals for alternative development are predicated on one form or other of capitalism, and seek a more human form of development achieved by reforming the system, In Venezuela, however, and to some extent in Bolivia under the presidency of Evo Morales (2006–19), the project of alternative development referenced or was predicated on socialism—not the state-led 'actively existing socialism' of the twentieth century based on the agency of the state, but on communalism, a new form of community-based socialist development.

In this context, from the year 2000 onwards in Venezuela, popular organisations, communities and even the government itself advanced various local self-government initiatives and promoted the formation of worker-managed cooperatives. In 1998, when Chávez was first elected to state power there existed fewer than 800 cooperatives; by August 2005 there were almost 84,000. On the basis of this development and associated initiatives and experiences in 2005 the Communal Council was formed in 2005 as a form of self-administration at the neighbourhood level; this was followed in 2007 by the construction of the Commune as a tier of self-government above that. Both of these institutions were formed with substantive grassroots organisation, although their rapid expansion was undoubtedly due to formal support by the state under the project *The Socialism of the 21st Century* formulated by Hugo Chávez in the context of his reelection in December 2006 (Chávez, 2007).

In January 2005 at the World Social Forum, Chávez explicitly called for the reinventing of socialism in a form that was different from what had existed in the Soviet Union. 'We must reclaim socialism as a thesis, a project and a path, but a new type of socialism, a humanist one, which puts humans and not machines or the state ahead of everything.' Six months later, Chávez argued the importance of building a new communal system of production and consumption—in which there is an exchange of activities determined by communal needs and communal purposes ... not just what Marx described as the 'cash nexus' or the profit motive, the incentive to make money, accumulate capital. 'We have to help to create it, from the popular bases, with the participation of the communities, through the community organisations, the cooperatives, self-management and different ways to create this system.'

Out of the different experiences and initiatives advanced with reference to this project, there emerged what Chávez termed 'the communal state', which subsequently became the political and social project of both the government and the popular movements in Venezuela. At the base of this state as Chávez understood and tried to construct it were the communal councils that were identified as the fundamental cell of Bolivarian socialism. As Chávez declared: 'All power to the communal councils', which would bring about an 'explosion in communal power', designated as the fifth of 'five motors' driving the path toward socialism.

The chapter explores the complex dynamics associated with the struggle to build socialism in the context not only of the powerful forces of internal right-wing opposition and reaction mobilised by the US state ('US imperialism'), but also the project and institution of representative democracy. As the author observes, the communal councils are constantly engaged in struggle resulting from a complex relationship of cooperation and conflict with these institutions. The chapter explores the complex dynamics associated with this political development. This includes a transition from the notion of a communal state in the transition towards socialism, a project pushed forward by the government, towards a rank-and-file chavista project of direct democracy based on communist, anarcho-syndicalist, indigenous and afro-Venezuelan ideas and experiences.

With Part II the book turns away from a retrospective analysis of the dynamics of capitalist development to the dynamics of what might be understood as 'post-development'—the challenge of constructing an alternative reality to capitalism, neoliberalism and extractivism. Chapter 7 in this connection presents the key concepts that informs a critical political economy and social ecology perspective on the development process unfolding in Latin America, namely, neoextractivism, a commodity consensus and developmentalist illusion. The chapter also established several lines of continuity and rupture between the concepts of extractivism and neoextractivism. Neoextractivism here refers to an analytical category that has a great descriptive and explanatory power in regard to contemporary developments, as well as a denunciatory character and strong mobilising power. The author elaborates on these developments in the Latin American context. Insofar as the author alludes to the unsustainable development patterns and asymmetries associated with the advance of extractive capital in the development process, the chapter warns of a deepening in the logic of dispossession and the multiscale problems that define different dimensions of the current crisis.

With Fernanda Wanderley and colleagues' contribution in the form of Chapter 8 the book turns towards the diverse and complex dimensions of the social and environmental crisis associated with the advance of capitalism in a period of epochal change. The main point of reference for the authors' discussion are the forces of change generated by the latest advances in the capitalist development process as well as the COVID-19 pandemic, which has exposed the fundamental contradictions of the capitalist system and accentuated its propensity towards crisis. At issue in this crisis that has truly assumed global and even planetary proportions is the close relationship between, on the one hand, the persistence of social exclusion, poverty and social inequalities, and, on the other hand, climate change, biodiversity loss and soil, water and air pollution. At the same time, beyond the life-threatening dimensions of a global health and economic crisis the COVID-19 pandemic exposed a fundamental contradiction of the capitalist development process: economic, social and political inequalities between and within countries.

A fundamental political truism regarding capitalism is that each phase and advance in the development process—the capitalist development of the forces of production—has activated and activates forces of resistance, which in the current context of a multifaceted global crisis have assumed the form of a global class struggle, an eco-territorial struggle of indigenous and non-indigenous communities against the ravages of extractive capitalism, and diverse citizen mobilisations that are united in the demand for answers to today's great dilemma: how to meet the needs of the present without compromising the needs of future generations in a democratic and social and environmental justice framework. This chapter articulates the social, environmental and economic outcomes of this resistance in the Andean highlands of South America and parts of the Amazonian basin: Bolivia, Colombia, Peru and Ecuador, to be precise.

Why focus on these Andean-Amazonian countries beyond the fact that they share a wealth of natural resources and a mega-diverse biozone with an exceptional environmental heritage? For one thing, despite the enormous development potential of the reservoir of natural resources shared by these countries, and several decades of a concerted strategy of extracting this wealth and exporting these resources in primary commodity form—extractivism, as we understand it—none of these countries have managed to realise the development potential of this wealth of natural resources or overcome what some economists have described as the 'resource curse' associated with extractivism. At the same time both the operations of extractive capital in these countries and the extractivist strategy and policies implemented by the governments in this subregion—both those that have opted for a progressive neoextractivist strategy (Bolivia, Ecuador) and those that continue to hoe the neoliberal policy line (Peru, Colombia)—generated forces of popular resistance whose mobilisation warrant a closer look and careful study.

Chapter 9 moves beyond the development and resistance dynamics on the extractive frontier to expand on a number of issues associated with the concept of *buen vivir*, which lies at the heart of radical societal proposals advanced in Bolivia and Ecuador to move beyond both neoliberalism and capitalism, as well as beyond the mainstream vision of development and associated concepts. The main argument advanced by the author, who has served as Ecuador's Minister of Development and Planning, is that an alternative social order such as *buen vivir* (utopia), needs first of all to be reimagined via the uchronia of a different temporal order (uchronia understood as a hypothetical alternative universe). Beyond the current hegemonic structuration of life where 'time is money', which serves as an engine for the accumulation of capital, this chapter reclaims 'time for living well' as the pillar of an alternative form of society and development. This dispute regarding 'the commonsense of time' is described by the author as a dispute of the sense of existence. This chapter argues that the utopia of living well proposed by a 'collective social intellect' (Ecuadorian society through its Constituent Assembly) needs to be re-constructed in terms of an uchronia in which time is recovered as life—not any kind of life, but life understood as living well (in solidarity and harmony with nature). For this purpose, based on a critique that exposes the limitations of using hegemonic monetary indicators of a good life, the chapter questions the socioeconomic realities in force today by reference to an alternative index for measuring *time for living well*. This new index, based on the concept of the quality of time, puts at the heart of the debate not the accumulation of money but the flourishing of life. In effect, the chapter introduces what could be called a *political socioecology of time*, a set of theoretical and methodological tools that facilitate analysis and proposes action alternatives to advance the construction of a society predicated on living well (*buen vivir*).

Eduardo Gudynas in the concluding chapter provides an overview of the diverse experiments with 'alternative development' in Latin America in the current context of a post-neoliberal transition. On the one hand, he discusses the rhetoric associated with diverse discourses on capitalism, criticisms of capitalism and possible alternatives, including what Hugo Chávez conceived of as twenty-first-century socialism. On the other hand, he goes beyond political speechmaking and the discourse on capitalism and alternative development to analyse the concrete actions taken by diverse economic actors, particularly the governments that make up what has been described as the 'progressive cycle' of Latin American politics.

The chapter analyses the concrete actions taken by these governments in the direction of progressive change, inclusive development and extractivism, with a particular concern with, and an analytical focus on, the contradictions between the development and extractivist strategies and policies of these governments. At issue in these strategies and policies are different varieties of capitalism and development. The chapter establishes the utility of the concept of *varieties of capitalism*, with reference to diverse experiments in the region in the search for an alternative development pathway. One of these alternatives is neodevelopmentalism, a model constructed by theorists associated with ECLAC and put into practice most consistently in Brazil under the administration of Luiz Inácio 'Lula' da Silva.

Because the idea of 'development' since its invention and subsequent construction in the post-Second World War period has been associated with capitalism—taken by most theorists and development practitioners as the most appropriate if not the only system that would satisfy its requirement—the concept of 'development' in theoretical discourse is closely associated with capitalism. Indeed, throughout this volume of essays the contributing authors have used the term 'capitalist development' to define the central problematic of critical development studies. Gudynas, however, in advancing the notion 'varieties of capitalism' and different forms and pathways of development, argues for and defends the position that capitalism and development should not be equated—that 'development' as a concrete social formation both precedes and will likely follow capitalism. Therefore, developments such as Cuban socialism or the socialism of the twenty-first century, and even living well (*buen vivir*), include both capitalist and non-capitalist and post-capitalist varieties. In this context, the chapter discusses and dissects the disputes in the region regarding the diverse forms taken by both capitalism and development. The chapter also establishes the meaning and delimits the use of the notion 'alternatives to development' and the relevance of what René Ramírez Gallegos in Chapter 9 describes as the uchronia of *buen vivir*.

Reference

Chávez, Hugo R. (2007). "El socialismo del siglo XXI," in Néstor Kohan (ed.), *Introducción al pensamiento socialista*. Bogotá: Ocean Sur.

1 In the vortex of social change

Henry Veltmeyer

The purpose of this chapter is to both provide a contextual framework for the other chapters in this book and to advance an argument that might be used to explain the dynamics of recent political developments in the region. The argument is constructed as follows. First, I review the dynamics of the new geoeconomics of capital in Latin America and the corresponding politics. The aim is to provide a theoretical framework for the subsequent analysis. The chapter then elaborates on certain dynamics associated with the political economy of two types of capitalism, with reference here to the particular way in which these forms of capital are combined in the current context of capitalist development in the region. The third part of the chapter provides a brief review of the economic and political dynamics that led to the pink tide of regime change in South America. Subsequently, we provide a brief review and analysis of the policy dynamics of the governments formed in the wake of this seatide of regime change and the associated progressive cycle in Latin American politics. The chapter then turns towards the recent pendulum swing of electoral politics towards the hard right of neoliberal policy reform. The chapter ends with a brief discussion of the forces engaged in what appears to be the end of the progressive cycle—forces mobilised by the advance of resource-seeking 'extractive' capital and various contradictions of capitalist development.

The new geoeconomics and geopolitics of capital

By the 'new geoeconomics of capital' reference is made to the confluence and interaction of two types of capitalism, two modalities of accumulation: (i) industrial capital(ism) based on the exploitation of the 'unlimited supply of surplus labour' generated by the capitalist development of agriculture, what we might regard as 'normal capitalism' or 'capitalism as usual'; and (ii) the advance of extractive capital based more on the exploitation of nature (extraction of its wealth of natural resources) as well as the exploitation of labour (Giarracca and Teubal, 2014; Gudynas, 2009, 2011; Svampa and Antonelli, 2009; Svampa, 2015; Veltmeyer and Petras, 2014). These two modalities of accumulation—one based on the advance of industrial capital and the other of extractive capital—do not exist in isolation, and in many conjunctures of the capitalist development process are combined in one way or the other. The point is that each form of capital, and both modalities of accumulation, has its distinct development and resistance dynamics that need to be differentiated and clearly distinguished for the sake of analysis and political action.

A second dimension of the geoeconomics of capital has to do with reconfiguration of global economic power over the past three decades, with the advent of China's voracious appetite for natural resources and commodities, in particular industrial minerals and metals, and fossil fuels. This 'development' implicates not just rapid economic growth and the Chinese demand for natural resources but also the 'emerging markets' of the BRICS, which helped fuel the growth of a demand for these resources on capitalist markets and a primary commodities boom. This boom in the demand for natural resources, and an associated decade of rapid economic growth in Latin America,[1] fuelled by record commodity prices spurred by Chinese demand and consumer demand in the BRICS, coincided in Latin America with a progressive cycle of governments formed in the wake of a pink (and red) tide of regime change … governments oriented towards the 'new developmentalism' (a social policy of 'inclusive development', or poverty reduction) as well as an extractivist economic development strategy.

As for the geopolitics of this development process the chapter brings into focus the progressive cycle of postneoliberal policy regimes formed in this changing of the political tide. The policy regime of these 'progressive' or left-leaning governments has been described as neoextractivism, with reference to the use of the fiscal revenues derived by these governments from the export of raw materials to finance their poverty reduction program (Gudynas, 2009; Svampa, 2017). In short, the economic model used by these progressive governments to make public policy in the area of development has two pillars: neodevelopmentalism, or the post-Washington Consensus on the requirement of a more inclusive form of development based on poverty reduction, and an extractivist strategy of capital accumulation.

The political economy of extractive capitalism

An extractivist strategy based on the export of natural resources in primary commodities form has long been the dominant approach of governments in the region towards national development, an approach that is reflected in the emergence of an international division of labour in which countries on the periphery of the world system serve as suppliers of raw materials and natural resources with little to no value added processing or industrialisation.[2]

Turning to the question of the geoeconomics and geopolitics of capita in the current context of neoliberal globalisation, it can be traced back to the 1980s, to conditions and forces generated by the establishment of a then 'new' world order of free market capitalism, designed to liberate the 'forces of economic freedom' from the regulatory constraints of the development state. This world order entailed a series of policy guidelines or 'structural reforms' in macroeconomic policy such as *privatisation* of the means of production), *deregulation* of markets and the *liberalisation* of trade and capital flows. Implementation of these reforms resulted in the destruction of forces of production in both agriculture and industry that had been built up in previous decades under the aegis of the development state. It also unleashed a massive inflow of capital in the form of foreign direct investment (FDI), particularly resource-seeking extractive capital, which by the end of the 1990s dominated the flows of capital into the region.[3]

Although the service sector at the turn into the new millennium still accounted for almost half of FDI inflows, this dominance of extractive capital in FDI inflows either held steady or trended upwards in the years 2002 to 2008 of the commodities boom (ECLAC, 2012). Despite the global financial and economic crisis at the time, FDI flows towards Latin America and the Caribbean in 2008 reached a record high (US$128.3 billion), an extraordinary development considering that FDI flows worldwide at the time had shrunk by at least 15 per cent. This countercyclical trend signalled the continuation of the primary commodities boom and the steady expansion of extractive capital in the region—until 2012, when the prices of many key commodities began to fall or collapse, heralding the beginning of the end of the boom (Harrup, 2019; Wheatley, 2014).

In 2009, barely a year into what has been described as a 'global financial crisis',[4] Latin America received 26 per cent of the capital invested globally in mineral exploration and extraction. And according to the Metals Economics Group, a 2010 bonanza in world market prices led to another increase of 40 per cent in investments related to mineral exploration, with governments in the region, both neoliberal and post-neoliberal, competing fiercely for this capital. In 2011, on the eve (the year before) of an eventual collapse of the primary commodities boom, South America attracted 25 per cent of global investments related to mining exploration, the production of fossil and bio-fuels, and agro-food extraction (Kotze, 2012).

Large-scale investment in the acquisition of land and the extraction of natural resources (in the form of metals/minerals, fossil fuels and agro-food products) was a defining feature and a fundamental pillar of the model used by the progressive regimes formed in the pink wave to make public policy in the area of development. The other pillar was extractivism, or to be precise, neoextractivism, which led to a process of rapid economic growth, averaging 5–6 per cent over the progressive cycle, which coincided almost precisely with the progressive policy cycle and a process of primarisation (Cypher, 2010)—or, to be more precise, reprimarisation, inasmuch as the exports of most of the countries in the region long involved the export of commodities in primary form (on this see Table 1.1)—but this fundamental long-term structural trend, as well as the commodities boom-bust cycle, was accentuated in a new development-resistance cycle that emerged with the advance of extractive capital in the Latin American development process.

The policy dynamics of the pink tide and the associated or resulting cycle of development and resistance—NB each cycle in the capitalist development process generates a corresponding development in the forces of resistance—has

Table 1.1 The structure of Latin American exports, 1990–2011

	1990	2000	2004	2006	2008	2011
Argentina	70.9	67.6	71.2	68.2	69.1	68.0
Bolivia	95.3	72.3	86.7	89.8	92.8	95.5
Brazil	48.1	42.0	47.0	49.5	55.4	66.2
Chile	89.1	84.0	86.8	89.0	88.0	89.2
Colombia	74.9	65.9	62.9	64.4	68.5	82.5
Ecuador	97.7	89.9	90.7	90.4	91.3	92.0
Mexico	56.7	16.5	20.2	24.3	27.1	29.3
Peru	81.6	83.1	83.1	88.0	86.6	89.3
Venezuela	89.1	90.9	86.9	89.6	92.3	95.5
Latin America	**66.9**	**40.9**	**46.2**	**51.3**	**56.7**	**60.9**

Source: ECLAC (2004, 2012).

been analysed at length if not in depth. Besides, and in addition to the question as to the fundamental pattern and dynamics of capital inflows in the form of FDI, at issue in this analysis are problems—to which I will make only brief reference—such as:

1   The policy outcomes of the economic development model used to formulate policy in the area of development ... a combination of *neodevelopmentalism* (the quest for inclusive development ... a strategy formulated in the Post-Washington Consensus formed in the 1990s) and *extractivism*. One of the main policy outcomes, which relates to both this consensus and a protracted war fought by the World Bank and the United nations since at least the mid-1970s, is the dramatic reduction in the rate of poverty achieved by these governments over the course of the decade-long cycle of progressive policies ... up to 40–50 per cent in the case of a number of progressive regimes formed in the wake of the pink tide (see the discussion below).

2   The contradictions of extractive capitalism (see the discussion below), when added to the fundamental contradiction of labour and capital and the secondary contradiction of centre-periphery relations within the world capitalist system, introduces an entirely new dynamic into the forces of resistance to the advances of capital in the development process. This dynamic relates particularly to the contradiction between the strategy pursued by the progressive postneoliberal regimes in the region, which, in the case of Ecuador and Bolivia, implicates the sought-for condition of *vivir bien*, or *buen vivir* (living well in solidarity and harmony with nature)—and the destructive and negative impacts of extractive capital.

3   The forces of resistance and the class struggle formed in response to the advance of extractive capitalism: a struggle of indigenous and non-indigenous communities on the extractive frontier to reclaim their territorial rights to the commons of land, water, resources for production and subsistence), and in protest against the negative socioenvironmental impacts of extractive

capital and its destructive operations. On the complex and diverse social and political dynamics of this resistance see, inter alia, Barkin and Sánchez (2017); Bebbington and Bury (2013); Bollier (2014); and Dangl (2007).

The contradictions of capitalism

Marx's theory regarding capitalism is that it is beset by contradictions that are reflected in a propensity towards crisis and class conflict (Marx, 1975 [1866]). The source of this conflict is an economic structure based on the capital-labour relation and the exploitation of workers (Labour) by capitalists (Capital). The capitalist class, it is argued, is driven by the need to accumulate—to profit from the labour power of workers. The developmental dynamics of this relation of capital to labour—the driving force of capitalist development—are both structural and strategic. The structural dynamics of the system are manifest in conditions that are, Marx argued, 'independent of our will' and thus not of our own choosing and objective in their effects—an objectivity that accords with each individual's class position. The strategic or political dynamics of the capital–labour relation, the foundation of the social structure in capitalist societies, are reflected in class consciousness, basically a matter of workers becoming aware of their exploitation and acting on this awareness. In this context, each advance of capital in the development process generates forces of resistance and social change.

Marx's theory of Capital, as well as most studies by Marxist scholars on the contradictions of capitalism, is predicated on the capital–labour relation and the capitalist development of agriculture—the dispossession and proletarianisation of the direct producers, the peasantry of small-scale peasant farmers, and the exploitation of the 'unlimited supply of surplus labour' generated by the capitalist development process (Araghi, 2010). As mentioned above each advance of capital in the development process generates forces of resistance, social relations of conflict and contradictory outcomes in which Capital appropriates the social product of cooperative labour. The result, at the level of the capital–labour relation, is a protracted class struggle over land and labour—a struggle that dominated the political landscape in the twentieth century—and a propensity towards crisis. At the level of international relations this fundamental contradiction has manifested itself in the uneven development of the forces of global production and a relation of dependency between the centre and the periphery of the world system—between the imperial state in its quest for hegemony over the system and the forces of anti-imperialist resistance (Borón, 2012).

The 1970s can be viewed as a decade of diverse structural and strategic responses to a systemic crisis, which put an end to what some historians have dubbed 'the golden age of capitalism'. One of these responses was the construction of a 'new world order' based on the belief in the virtues of free market capitalism and the need to liberate the 'forces of economic freedom' from the regulatory constraints of the development state. The installation in the 1980s of this new world order by means of a program of 'structural reforms' in macroeconomic policy (globalisation, privatisation, deregulation and the liberalisation of the flow of goods and capital) gave rise to a new development dynamic on the Latin American periphery of the system—the advance of extractive capital—and with it new forces of resistance that brought to the fore what we might conceive of as the 'contradiction(s) of extractive capitalism'.

The advance of extractive capital in the form of large-scale foreign investment in the acquisition of land—'landgrabbing', in the discourse of Critical Agrarian Studies (Borras et al., 2012)—and the extraction of natural resources took the form of a primary commodities boom from 2002 to 2012, and what Maristella Svampa describes as the 'commodities consensus' and what others (for example, Gudynas, 2009) understand and have described as 'neoextractivism' (the combination of neodevelopmentalism and extractivism)—the export of natural resources in primary commodity form to capitalist markets and the use of the resource rents appropriated in the process to finance a program of inclusive development or poverty reduction.

The fundamental contradiction of extractive capitalism is manifest in a pronounced tendency for the accumulation process to exceed the ecological limits of sustainable development (O'Connor, 1998; Redclift, 1987). This contradiction takes a number of forms, including what some economists have described as a 'resource curse'—that resource-rich economies tend to be poor and underdeveloped, while many resource-poor countries have managed to achieve high levels of economic and social development (Acosta, 2009, 2011; Berry, 2010). Dimensions of this resource curse include what has been described as the 'Dutch disease' (with reference to the negative effect of commodity exports on other export sectors) and what Latin American economists in the structuralist tradition have described as 'dependency'—a reliance on the export of unprocessed raw materials and primary commodities in exchange for value-added processed and industrialised goods produced in the centre of the system.

A fundamental dimension of the contradictory nature of extractive capitalism is an exaggerated form of the capital–labour relation of economic exploitation. Extractive capital typically employs relatively little labour—relative to capital and technology. As a result, while the share of labour in national income for a regime based on industrial capital might be as high as 40 to 60 per cent in a regime based on extractive capital (particularly in the mining sector), the share of labour typically oscillates around 10 per cent. With the state appropriating another 10 per cent in the form of resource rents (royalties, export taxes), well over 60 per cent, up to 80 per cent, of the value of the social product on capitalist markets is appropriated by Capital (foreign investors, multinational corporations, Commodity Traders),[5] while the brunt of the destructive and negative socioenvironmental impacts of the operations of extractive capital are borne by the indigenous and non-indigenous communities contiguous to the sites of extraction. Needless to add, this feature of extractive capitalism has generated powerful forces of resistance and relations of conflict between the companies and the communities, with the governments—even the most progressive ones such as Ecuador under Correa and Bolivia under the presidency of Evo Morales—more often than not taking the side of capital against the communities in this conflict. This is a fundamental dimension of the contradictory nature of extractive capitalism, which in the current context on the extractive frontier is taking the form not of a class struggle but a territorial struggle—in the demand of communities to reclaim their fundamental human and territorial rights to the global commons, as well as the rights of nature.

Another fundamental contradiction of extractive capitalism in the current Latin American context is manifest in the actual policies in the area of economic development that some progressive governments formed in the pink wave of regime change have pursued in contradiction with the constitutionally defined aim of bringing about a social condition of *buen vivir* (living well in solidarity and harmony with nature).

Resource nationalism, left-wing populism and poverty reduction

The progressive governments that came to power in the pink—and red in the case of Bolivia, Ecuador and Venezuela—tide of regime change have been widely criticised for the failure to use the additional fiscal revenues derived from resource exports to bring about lasting structural change and sustainable development, particularly as regards the possibility of moving the population towards a social condition of *buen vivir* (Acosta and Machado, 2012). And these criticisms might be warranted, at least as regards the contradictions of an extractivist model of economic development. However, these criticisms should not lead to a failure to acknowledge the considerable progress made by these so-called 'populist' regimes in the direction of poverty reduction, the principal policy instrument of a neodevelopmentalism strategy oriented towards the goal of bringing about a more inclusive form of development based on a social redistribution of income, the hallmark of progressivism.

The evidence is clear enough. All of the governments formed in the pink and red tide of regime change, in the context of the primary commodities boom, pursued a neoextractivist strategy of channelling additional fiscal revenues derived from commodity exports into programs of poverty reduction. Table 1.2 provides a graphic representation of the results of this strategy, which revolved around the policy of 'conditional cash transfers'—transferring to poor households, on condition that children of the households would be sent to school and clinics to attend to their healthcare, sufficient income to automatically lift them out of a condition of extreme poverty as defined by the World Bank's measure of $1.25 a day ($37.50/month). The table also suggests that the downward trend in the rate of poverty has stalled and to some extent has been reversed in the post-boom/progressive cycle context.

Taking Bolivia, as an exemplar of the policy that was subsequently pursued by up to 19 governments in the region, including some like Mexico, which, until the recent election of AMLO, had continued to pursue a neoliberal policy line, the percentage of people living in poverty fell or was reduced from 59.9 per cent in 2006, when Morales came to power, to 34.6 per cent in 2017. Extreme

Table 1.2 Latin America: poverty and extreme poverty rates, 2002–2015 (Percentages)

	2002	*2008*	*2010*	*2012*	*2014*	*2015*
Poverty	43.9	33.5	31.1	28.2	28.2	29.2
Extreme poverty	19.3	12.9	12.1	11.3	11.8	12.4

Source: ECLAC (2015). Preliminary data.

poverty, in the same timeframe according to government figures (validated by CEPAL) was reduced from 38.3 to 15.2 per cent. The reduction in Bolivia's poverty rate and the associated drop in inequality in the distribution of national income tallied with a trend that held across all the regimes formed in the progressive cycle—the average reduction in the poverty rate somewhere between 40 and 50 per cent. This trend was in stark contrast with the situation in countries like Mexico that continued to toe the neoliberal policy line throughout this progressive cycle. In the case of Mexico, the poverty rate in 2017 continued to oscillate between 47 and 54 per cent, depending on the data source (Lomeli, 2013).

The association between the policy regime of the progressive governments and the reduction in poverty help up though the entire policy cycle, as did the trend towards economic growth and the primary commodities boom, which ended somewhere around 2012, coinciding with the end of the growth trend. A dramatic instance of this association was Brazil, where an average growth rate of over 5 per cent per annum throughout the boom—and the progressive cycle at the level of politics—was reduced to, creating conditions, it would seem, for the end of the progressive cycle and the return to state power of the neoliberal hard right. Radical right regimes currently rule in Argentina, Brazil, Colombia, Paraguay, Peru, Guatemala, Honduras and Chile. In several countries the extreme right regimes have already instituted abrupt changes, reversing the progressive policies instituted by their progressive predecessors, while in others they build on incremental changes constituted over time. The changes instituted in Argentina and Brazil represent examples of extreme regressive transformations directed at reversing income distribution, property relations, international alignments and military strategies. The goal is to redistribute income upwardly, to reconcentrate wealth and property ownership, and to subscribe to imperial doctrine. These proto-populist or kleptocratic regimes are run by men who openly speak to and for very powerful domestic and overseas investors and are generous in their distribution of subsidies and state resources—a kind of 'populism for the plutocrats'.

One of the few governments to resist the pendulum swing in electoral political to the hard or extreme right in the wake of a retreating commodities boom was Bolivia, but Bolivia again confirming the correlation between the commodities boom and the progressive cycle in politics. It turns out that Bolivia was one of very few countries in which the rate of resource export driven economic growth driven by the demand for resources continued past the collapse of the commodities boom in 2012. The regime formed by Evo Morales was the only pink tide government able to sustain the commodities boom driven average growth rate of 4.9 per cent, perhaps explaining in part the failure of a right-wing opposition forces to take power. Export revenues grew sixfold during Evo's first term in office, from an average of $1.14 billion a year over the previous two decades to $7 billion. Another partial explanation of Morales's continued popular support, despite several scandals and opposition from indigenous groups concerned about his government's extractivist strategy vis-à-vis the stated goal of *vivir bien*, is continued support from the social base of the regime in the social movements, particularly the cocaleros, once led by Evo Morales.

Today, there are cocaleros in support and in opposition to the government, but Morales has managed to contain opposition from this source and to manage the fraught relationship between the government and the social movements. This is in sharp contrast to other progressive regimes such as Correa's regime in Ecuador where once the centre-left regime was consolidated the social movements whose dynamics helped propel into state power were pushed aside.

The relationship between the regime and the social movements, including the cocaleros'—the social base of Morales' political leadership and power base in MAS (Movement Towards Socialism)—has not all been rosy, however. It has required a process of active strategic 'management' and tactical manipulation. In its early years in power, the unions had gained control of the state apparatus and their members were appointed to new institutional positions, including many parliamentary and civil-service roles. The opposition was a neoliberal right determined to block the functioning of Bolivia's Constituent Assembly. Until 2009, MAS managed to maintain a popular unity not seen since the struggles against military dictatorships in the 1970s and 1980s. But this ended with the December 2009 referendum that approved Bolivia's new constitution. Though the right was crushingly defeated at the polls, the left's internal divisions resurfaced. Even so, Morales since then has managed to contain these opposition forces both within the neoliberal hard right and within his own social base. And this is no small part due to both Morales' ability to manage or manipulate the social forces ranged in his social movement base, but also the government's macroeconomic success and the ability of the regime to deliver on a promise of progressive development in the direction of socialism (or communalism, as Morales defines it).

Bolivia, under Evo Morales, has demonstrated an exceptional capacity for sustaining growth, securing re-election and neutralising the opposition by combining a radical left foreign policy with a moderate, mixed public–private export economy. In this connection while Bolivia continues to condemn US imperialism, major oil, gas, metals and lithium multinationals continue to invest heavily in Bolivia, Evo Morales has moderated his ideological posture, shifting from revolutionary socialism to a local version of liberal democratic cultural politics.

Evo Morales' embrace of a mixed economy neutralised any overt hostility from the US and the new far-right regimes in the region. Thus, while remaining politically independent, Bolivia has integrated its exports with the far-right neoliberal regimes in the region. President Evo Morales's moderate economic policies, diversity of mineral exports, fiscal responsibility, incremental social reforms and support from well-organised social movements has led to political stability and social continuity despite the volatility of commodity prices. No doubt this helps explain the ability of Evo Morales to avoid the fate of his fellow progressives.

Even the professional groups and other segments of the country's middle class, a clear beneficiary of the policies pursued by the regime, have struggled to contest the proposition that life has become demonstrably better over the past decade. As reported by *The Guardian Weekly* (15 March 2019), Morales' policies have not only resulted in greater social equality in the distribution of income, or at least reduced poverty as well as improvements in conditions of work and the minimum wage, but also in conditions of greater concern and interest to the country's growing middle class—a stable currency, subsidised petrol, asphalt highways, shopping centres, access to affordable housing and university education (Lewis, Clarke and Barr, 2019).

The end of the progressive cycle? The swing to the right of the pendulum of electoral politics

It would seem—particularly in the cases of Bolivia and Venezuela, but also Argentina and elsewhere—that the origins of the progressive cycle in Latin American politics, i.e. the pink wave, can be attributed to the political activism of the social movements in the 1990s, which was directed against the neoliberal policies of the governments at the time. In contrast, the social movements in the 1960s to 1970s were oriented towards the demand for land and labour, and the movements formed on the extractive frontier were oriented towards reclaiming their territorial rights and the right of access to the commons (Bollier, 2014; Bollier and Silke, 2012).

In recent years there have been diverse attempts at explaining the end of the progressive cycle. Theories have ranged from structural explanations (the contradictions of extractive capitalism, and the consequent loss of an important segment of progressive forces), the collapse of the commodities boom and/or the fall in the international prices of oil, and the resulting loss of fiscal revenues to finance social and development programs), to widespread corruption as well as fundamental mistakes in designing and executing development policies (particularly in the case of Venezuela), as well as shifts in the correlation of class power at the level of electoral politics. But whatever the reason or the forces involved, there is no doubt that the pendulum of electoral politics has swung back towards the right—restoring to power regimes oriented towards what might well be described as 'authoritarian neoliberalism'. In this regard recent political developments in Latin America reflect what appears to be a global.

The beginnings of this trend—a change in the correlation of force in the class struggle at the level of electoral politics—can be traced back to the ascension of Mauricio Macri to political power in the case of Argentina, and the 'soft coup' perpetrated against the PT regime of Dilma Rouseff)[6] and then the election of Bonsanori in March 2019). In addition to these two cases, there have been a number of other electoral contests—in the years 2018–2019 up to 14 presidential schedules have taken place or has been scheduled to take place.

The one major exception to this pattern has been the election in December 2018 of Andrés Miguel López Obrador (AMLO) in Mexico, which did not participate in the progressive cycle but continued to toe the neoliberal line in alignment with the US throughout the cycle. As for the progressive regimes, most of them, including Ecuador under the post-Correa regime established by Lenin Moreno, succumbed to the forces of electoral change. The one exception—apart from Venezuela, which is a special case of a progressive regime (in not having its origins in the activism of the social movements)—is Evo Morales, whose survival against the opposition forces ranged against it, can also be attributed to the social movements. In other cases, where the social movements were directed against the state the government's neoliberal policies, but on the centre-left's ascension to state power were to all intents and purposes sidelined or demobilised, the policies of the progressive regime lost its social base in the movement, thus rendering it vulnerable to forces of reaction. In the case of Bolivia, however, the movements were neither demobilised nor shunted aside. Rather, Evo continues to mobilise the movements in continuing support of his progressive policies.

Conclusion

Although the populist social programs of the postneoliberal compensatory states constructed in the wake of the pink tide of regime change managed in a number of cases to significantly reduce the incidence of poverty, they did not anywhere lead to structural change. In effect, the resulting improvement in income redistribution did not fundamentally alter the class structure and the social inequalities associated with it. The poverty reduction and social development programs implanted by these 'progressive' regimes merely compensated the least well-off strata with resource rents derived from the export of natural resources within the context of a short-lived commodity boom on capitalist markets. Even so, there were undeniably positive outcomes of the pink wave and progressive cycle. One the one hand, there is much to admire in the progressive policies and accomplishments of these postneoliberal compensatory states. See, for example, the discussion by René Ramirez Gallegos in Chapter 9 of the case of Ecuador, or the discussion by Fernanda Wanderley and colleagues in Chapter 8 of the case of Bolivia. Poverty in these two and other cases was reduced by as much as 40 to 50 per cent, lifting millions out of poverty as well as incubating an incipient middle class. Behind this accomplishment these progressive regimes or postneoliberal compensatory states—especially Venezuela, Bolivia and Ecuador, countries that represented a more radical form of regime change oriented towards socialism conceived of in one form or the other—were able to capture the surplus from the export bonanza, and by means of a New Social Policy (NSP) designed for 'inclusive development' (conditional cash transfer programs accompanied by state investments in healthcare and education), achieve significant social gains. But an assessment of these gains must be balanced against the limits of progressive change under regimes tied to extractive capital and rentier capitalism. For example, social compensation provided an internal momentum for economic expansion based on the expansion of the consumption capacity of the popular classes—what economists associate with the growth of a 'middle class'—but the underlying structure of social inequality and power, as well as the associated rights and privileges, as already mentioned remained fundamentally unchanged.[7]

The improvements in income redistribution and the few benefits flowing to the bottom or poorest strata in the current context are a function of a model that allowed and has led to a disproportionate appropriation of the wealth generated by the model by foreign investors, obliging the indigenous and peasant farming communities that make up what the World Bank describes as the 'rural poor' to bear the exceedingly high social and environmental costs of the extractive model. This is to say, the social gains of the progressive policies implemented by some governments in recent years are limited by the contradictions of extractive capitalism and global markets tied to rentier capitalism.

This is one conclusion drawn by the collaborators in the construction of this book from their research. Another is that the apparent end of the progressive cycle in a pendulum swing in the arena of electoral politics towards the neoliberal hard right can be explained in large part in terms of what some economists (e.g. Acosta, 2009, 2011; Berry, 2010) have described as a 'resource curse' but that we understand as the contradictions of extractive capitalism. That is, the erosion in popular support suffered by left-leaning pink-wave governments such as Argentina and Brazil that combined extractivism with neodevelopmentalism, and by governments such as Ecuador under the presidency of Rafael Correa committed to a more radical form of post-neoliberalism, can be attributed to the pursuit and commitment of these governments to an extractivist development strategy—a strategy fraught with contradictions.

These 'contradictions' include a dependence on large-scale foreign investments in the extraction and export of natural resource wealth. Conditions of this dependence—the 'new dependency' according to some theorists (Borón, 2008; Martins, 2011; Sotelo, 2000, 2009)—implicate:

1   a reliance on these foreign investments and associated resource rents to finance the government's poverty reduction and development programs, subjecting the domestic economy to the boom–bust cycle of commodity exports on capitalist markets;

2   consolidation of an export structure with a built-in tendency towards uneven development, with a resulting 'underdevelopment' of the region's forces of production;[8]

3   externalisation of the benefits of economic growth, leading to a decapitalisation of domestic production and the national development process, and a degradation in the conditions of social existence of communities on the extractive frontier, forced to bear all of the negative socioenvironmental costs and destructive impacts of extractivism while being virtually totally excluded from its questionable economic benefits;

4   dependence of the state on access to global capital, resulting, inter alia, in these states (including those formed in the pink tide of regime change) taking the side of Capital in the struggle of local communities on the extractive frontier to resist the destructive forces of capitalist development; and, at the level of electoral politics,

5   the propensity of rentier regimes on both the Left and the Right towards endemic corruption, resulting in widespread deception and disillusionment among the electorate with politics as usual by the political class.

This disillusionment was undoubtedly a factor in the correlation of force in the class struggle and the pendulum swing in electoral politics towards the right. But the evidence, which includes the demonstrated ability of Evo Morales in the particular case of Bolivia to resist the rightward turn in the tide of political change, suggests that the most recent change in the pendulum swing of electoral politics can be found in the contradictions of extractive capital as well as the inability of the regimes formed in the pink wave to hold onto a social base for their progressive policies.

A dramatic illustration of this point is Venezuela, where the urban and rural poor, the social base of the regime's progressive or socialist policies, continues to support the socialist regime despite the enormous pressures placed on the regime in the current economic and political crisis and by the heavy hand of US imperialism. Under Chávez and Maduro's radical populist policies and socialist regime not only were millions lifted out of poverty but over two million houses were built for the shantytown dwellers; and over two dozen universities and educational centres were built for the poor—all free of charge. Public hospitals and clinics were built in poor neighbourhoods as well as public supermarkets that supplied low-cost food and other necessities that sustain living standards despite subsequent shortages. How did the regime manage to survive such pressures and these conditions when the other regimes formed in the recent progressive cycle succumbed to them, and the Chávez-Maduro regime was also a clear and obvious victim of at least one of what we have described as the contradictions of extractive capitalism (dependence on the boom-bust cycle of commodity markets)? The answer is not unambiguously clear, but it might well include the fact that unlike the other pink wave governments the regime did not pursue a policy of class conciliation; and in regard to the urban and rural poor the regime went well beyond the new developmentalist model by including the poor themselves in decision-making in the form of cooperativism and community development, and popular militias and community councils, that mobilised and gave voice to the mass of the poor and facilitated their active participation as well as their representation. It turns out (see Chapter 6 for a discussion and details) that the state-led project initiated by Chávez to bring about the socialism of the twenty-first century has effectively been transformed into a communitarian socialist project advanced by a broad popular Chavista movement. The capacity of this and other instances of an emerging popular movement in the region to resist the advance of capital in the development process, and to take over from the state the responsibility and project of constructing and alternative from of society, is one of several lessons that the Left can draw from an analysis of the vortex of social change in which the region is currently embroiled.

Notes

1 From 2002 to 2012 Latin America experienced a decade of rapid economic growth at an annually averaged rate of at least 5 per cent (Ocampo, 2007). Over this period—dubbed by some as the 'decade of Latin America'—the region almost doubled its share of world economic output to 8 per cent (Rathbone, 2013). The IMF estimated that the windfall from the commodity boom, which began in 2002, was equivalent to an extra 15 per cent of output a year. At the same time, the middle class grew by an estimated 50 million while inequality in the distribution of income (i.e. the rate of poverty) shrank from 40 to 50 per cent (ECLAC, 2012).

2 A generation of structuralist and dependency theorists in the 1960s–1970s described this approach as the structural source of uneven capitalist development or the 'development of underdevelopment'. The same economic structure was taken by Lenin as a defining feature of what he described as 'imperialism', the highest stage of capitalism as he understood it at the time.

3 The 'real FDI boom in Latin America and the Caribbean', according to ECLAC (2012: 72) took place in the second half of the 1990s when many state-owned assets were privatised and many sectors, which until then had received little FDI, were opened up and deregulated. It was during this period that transnational corporations began to expand their role in the region's economies. The 1990s it saw a six-fold increase in the inflow of capital in the form of FDI in the first four years of the decade and then another sharp increase from 1996 to 2001, which in less than ten years tripled the foreign capital accumulated in the region (ECLAC, 2012: 71). As a result of these trends from 2002, at the beginning of the commodities boom, to 2008, barely six years in, the share of natural resource extraction in total FDI inflows increased from 10 to 30 per cent (Arellano, 2010).

4 By a number of accounts, unlike a series of financial crises in the 1990s that primarily hit economies on the periphery, including Latin America, the 2008 financial crisis primarily affected economies at the centre rather than the periphery of the system (Veltmeyer, 2010). ECLAC economist Porzecanski (2009), with specific reference to Latin America, even raised the question 'Crisis, what crisis?'

5 As for the financial returns to external entities and interests, foreign investors, etc., the *Financial Times* on 18 April 2013 published an article (Blas, 2013) that documented the fact that traders in commodities have accumulated large reserves of capital and huge fortunes in the context of the primary commodities boom and the financialisation of capitalist development. As the author of the article observed: 'The world's top commodities traders have pocketed nearly $250bn over the last decade, making the individuals and families that control the largely privately-owned sector big beneficiaries of the rise of China and other emerging countries'—and, we might add, beneficiaries of the turn towards extractivism and export primarisation.

6 Note the irony in that Temer, who, as Dilma Rouseff's second in command took power as the result of machinations focused on removing her from office, and ensuring the imprisonment of Lula, who undoubtedly would have won the election, because of corruption, has just been charged and imprisoned (April 2019) for reasons of high crimes of corruption.

7 Machado and Zibechi (2016), for example, point out that although progress in the pink wave was made in reducing poverty through the implementation of redistribution policies, the same did not happen in terms of inequality. They distinguish two types of inequality—structural and conjunctural—and argue that during the decade of progressive governments there were improvements in terms of the second type of inequality but that the indicators of structural inequality were not modified. On this see also Dávalos and Albuja (2014) in regard to Correa's Ecuador.

8 López Segrera (2016), for example, analyses the weaknesses that remain despite the progress made based with respect to the policies implemented by the post-neoliberal governments, with particular reference to the dependence of the region's economies on the price of raw materials and associated problems. In this regard he points out that in addition to the dependence generated by the economy being linked to the international prices of exported goods, many of these sectors depend on the importation of technologies and products from the central countries. At the same time, they have a social impact in terms of the devastation of some regional economies, the expulsion of populations and the impact on the health of those exposed to the destructive and negative socioenvironmental impacts of extractive capital and its operations.

References

Acosta, A. (2009). *La maldición de la abundancia.* Quito: Ediciones Abya-Yala.

Acosta, A. (2011). "Extractivismo y neoextractivismo: dos caras de la misma maldición," in M. Lang and D. Mokrami (eds). *Mas allá del Desarrollo.* Quito: Fundación Rosa Luxemburgo/Abya Yala.

Acosta, A. and D. Machado (2012). "Movimientos comprometidos con la vida. Ambientalismos y conflictos actuales en América Latina," *Revista Colección OSAL.* Buenos Aires: CLACSO. http://lalineadefuego.info/2012/10/01/ambientalismos-y-conflictos-actuales-en-america-latinamovimientos-comprometidos-con-la-vida-por-alberto-acosta-y-decio-machado/

Araghi, F. (2010). "Accumulation by Displacement, Global Enclosures, Food Crisis and the Economic Contradictions of Capitalism," *Review*, 32(1): 113–146.

Arellano, M. (2010). "Canadian Foreign Direct Investment in Latin America," *Background Paper*, Ottawa, North-South Institute, May.

Barkin, D. and A. Sánchez (2017). "The Collective Revolutionary Subject: New Forms of Social Transformation," Unedited Paper for *Revolutions: A Conference*, University of Manitoba, Winnipeg, September.

Bebbington, A. and J. Bury (eds). (2013). *Subterranean Struggles: New Dynamics of Mining, Oil and Gas in Latin America.* Austin, TX: University of Texas Press.

Berry, B. (2010). "The Natural Resource Curse in 21st Century Latin America," *Canada Watch*, Fall: 23–24.

Blas, J. (2013). "Commodity Traders Reap $250bn Harvest," *Financial Times*, April, 14.

Bollier, D. (2014). "The Commons as a Template for Transformation," *Great Transformation Initiative*, April. www.greattransition.org/publication/the-commons-as-a-template-for-transformation.

Bollier, D. and H. Silke (2012). *The Wealth of the Commons: A World Beyond Market and State.* Amherst: Levelers Press.

Borón A. (2008). "Teorías de la dependencia," *Realidad Económica*, 238, August–September: 20–43.

Borón, A. (2012). *América Latina en la geopolítica del imperialism.* Buenos Aires: Ediciones Luxemburg.

Borras Jr S., J. Franco, S. Gomez, C. Kay and M. Spoor (2012). "Land Grabbing in Latin America and the Caribbean," *Journal of Peasant Studies*, 39(3–4): 845–872.

Cypher, James (2010). "South America's Commodities Boom. Developmental Opportunity or Path Dependent Reversion?" *Canadian Journal of Development Studies*, 30(3–4): 635–662.

Dangl, B. (2007). *The Price of Fire: Resource Wars and Social Movements in Bolivia.* Oakland CA: AK Press.

Dávalos, P. and V. Albuja (2014). "Ecuador: Extractivist Dynamics, Politics and Discourse," pp. 144–171 in Veltmeyer, H. and Petras, J. (eds), *The New Extractivism: Post-Neoliberal Development Model or Imperialism of the Twenty-First Century?* London: Zed Press.

ECLAC—Economic Commission for Latin America and the Caribbean (2004). *Statistical Yearbook for Latin America and the Caribbean.* Santiago: ECLAC.

ECLAC (2012). *Capital Flows to Latin America and the Caribbean. Recent Developments.* Washington, DC: ECLAC.

ECLAC (2015). *Social Panorama of Latin America.* Santiago: ECLAC.

Giarracca, N. and M. Teubal (2014). "Argentina: Extractivist Dynamics of Soy Production and Open-Pit Mining," pp. 47–79 in H. Veltmeyer and J. Petras (eds), *The New Extractivism.* London: Zed Books.

Gudynas, E. (2009). "Diez tesis urgentes sobre el nuevo extractivismo. Contextos y demandas bajo el progresismo sudamericano actual," in *Extractivismo, Política y Sociedad.* Quito: CLAES/CAAP.

Gudynas, E. (2011). "Más allá del nuevo extractivismo: transiciones sostenibles y alternativas al desarrollo," in Fernanda Wanderley (ed.). *El desarrollo en cuestión. Reflexiones desde América Latina.* La Paz: Oxfam /CIDES-UMSA.

Harrup, A. (2019). "South America Suffers from the End of Commodities Boom," *The Wall Street Journal*, May 17.

Kotze, C. (2012). "South American Mining Sector to Continue as Resource-Based Economy," *Mining Weekly*, 15 June. www.miningweekly.com/article/south-american-mining-sector-to-continue-as-resource-based-economy-2012-06-15.

Lewis, P., S. Clarke and C. Barr (2019). "People Power: Do Populist Leaders Actually Reduce Inequality?" *The Guardian Weekly*, 15 March.

Lomeli, E. (2013). "Conditional Cash Transfers Asocial Policy: Limitations and Illusions," pp. 163–188 in H. Veltmeyer and D. Tetreault (eds). *Poverty and Development in Latin America.* Sterling, VA: Stylus.

Machado, D. and R. Zibechi (2016). *Cambiar el mundo desde arriba. Los límites del progresismo.* La Paz: Centro de Estudios para el Desarrollo Laboral y Agrario (CEDLA).

Martins, C.E. (2011). *Globalizacao, Dependencia e Neoliberalismo na América Latina.* Sao Paulo: Boitempo.

Marx, K. (1975[1866]). *Capital*, Vol. 1. Mexico: Siglo XXI.

Ocampo, J.A. (2007). "The Macroeconomics of the Latin American Economic Boom," *CEPAL Review*, 93.

O'Connor, J. (1998). *Natural Causes: Essays in Ecological Marxism.* New York/London: Guilford Press.

Porzecanski, A. (2009). "Latin America: The Missing Financial Crisis," *Studies and Perspectives*, No. 6, Washington, DC: ECLAC.

Rathbone, P. (2013). "Doubts Come to Surface about 'the Decade of Latin America'," *Financial Times*, May 12.

Redclift, M. (1987). *Sustainable Development: Exploring the Contradictions*. London: Methuen.

Sotelo A. (2000). "¿Globalización: estancamiento o crisis en América Latina?" *Problemas de Desarrollo*, 120 (January–March).

Sotelo, A. (2009). *Neo-imperialismo, dependencia e novas periferias." A América Latina e os desafíos da globalizaca*. Rio de Janeiro: Boitempo.

Svampa, M. (2015). "Commodities Consensus: Neoextractivism and Enclosure of the Commons in Latin America," *The South Atlantic Quarterly* 114(1): 65–82.

Svampa, M. (2017). *Del cambio de época al fin de ciclo: gobiernos progresistas, extractivismo, y movimientos sociales en América Latina*. Buenos Aires: Edhasa.

Svampa, M. and M. Antonelli (eds) (2009). *Minería transnacional, narrativas del desarrollo y resistencias sociales*. Buenos Aires: Biblos.

UNCTAD (2012). "Investment Trend Monitor," No. 8, New York, United Nations, 24 January.

Veltmeyer, H. (2010). "The Global Crisis and Latin America," in M. Konings (ed.) *Beyond the Subprime Headlines: Critical Perspectives on the Financial Crisis*. London: Verso.

Veltmeyer, H. and J. Petras (2014). *The New Extractivism in Latin America*. London: Zed Books.

Wheatley, J. (2014). "Emerging Markets Adapt to 'New Normal' as Markets Adapt to 'New Normal' as Commodities Cycle," *Financial Times*, 5 October.

Part I

Development in the neoliberal era

2 Extractive capitalism

Development and resistance dynamics

James Petras

This chapter analyses the class dynamics of capitalist development and the resistance on the new frontier of extractive capital that has opened up with the primary commodities boom at the turn into the new millennium. In this analysis we make reference to and use the concept of 'accumulation by dispossession' popularised by David Harvey in recent years.[1] In the temporal and spatial context of these dynamics, parts of the rural population have been mobilised in protest against the advance of capital. Indigenous and farming communities on the extractive frontier have undertaken a variety of collective actions against the destructive operations and negative impacts of large-scale foreign investments in the acquisition of land and the extraction of natural resources for export. The forces of resistance engendered in this process have targeted the policies of governments that have facilitated the foreign investments in land and the operations of extractive capital. The class struggle and conflicts associated with this resistance have taken various forms but generally pit the multinational corporations in the extractive sector and the governments that have licensed their operations against the rural communities that are most directly impacted by these operations. At issue in these conflicts and struggles are various conditions and forces that compel some or many members of these communities to abandon their communities and to separate them from the land and their means of production—what David Harvey (2003) conceptualises as 'accumulation by dispossession'.

In some cases (Bolivia, for example) accumulation by dispossession has taken the form of a government policy to privatise access to productive resources (in this case, natural gas and water), turning over to foreign investors and the agents of global extractive capital the right to market these resources, and denying members of the communities affected open access to what had been for millennia the commons. In effect, we have a new form of the enclosures that helped bring about capitalism in nineteenth century England. In other cases, multinational corporations in the extractive sector have been granted a concession on a long-term (30-year) lease to explore for and exploit natural resources—oil and gas, or minerals and metals—that might be found in these concessions, which in some cases includes anywhere from 23 per cent of the national territory (the case of Mexico) up to 70 per cent (the case of Peru). And more recently a number of countries in the region, like their counterparts in

Africa and Asia, have been subjected to the large-scale inflow of foreign investments in the acquisition of land—'landgrabbing', in the discourse of critical agrarian studies (Borras et al., 2012). To purchase the tracts of land for the purpose of what might be described as 'agroextractivism' (the extraction of agro-food or biofuels for export) or gain privileged access to the region's sub-soil mineral resources, multinational corporations in the extractive sector have taken maximum advantage of their 'economic opportunities' provided by these purchases, signing lucrative agreements with state officials that allow them to appropriate up to 60 per cent of the value of the exported and traded commodities. In many cases, the land and ancestral territorial rights of the population and indigenous communities who live and work the land involved in these concessions, and that have customary use of water and elements of the commons, were or have been violated. In most cases, the rural population affected by the operations of extractive capital have been dispossessed and forced to abandon their communities and way of life.

Agrarian change as a lever of capital accumulation

In the context of seventeenth-century England, which Marx used as a benchmark to construct his theory of capitalist development, the separation of the direct producers from their means of production—'primitive accumulation' in Marx's formulation—marked the origins of capitalism. However, a number of Marxist scholars, including Rosa Luxemburg and more recently David Harvey, have argued that the dynamics of what Marx conceived as the 'primitive' or 'original' accumulation is not only found at the outset of the capitalist development process but throughout the history of capitalism—as a permanent condition, or as Harvey (2003: 144) argues, in times of crisis such as at that which precipitated the neoliberal era.

In Marx's day the basic mechanism of 'primitive accumulation' was the enclosure of the commons, denying thereby access of direct producers to vital resources for subsistence and forcing them to abandon their way of life and their communities, in the process creating a proletariat (i.e. a class dispossessed of their means of production, in possession only of their capacity to work, their labour power), which they are compelled to exchange for a living wage. However, as Harvey argues, this dynamic and situation is by no means limited to the beginnings of capitalism. For one thing, in its propensity towards crisis, capitalism creates forces of change similar to those that materialised in other periods in the capitalist development of the productive forces, resulting in a similar process of proletarianisation and productive-social transformation. An example of this is the capitalist development process that unfolded in the 1970s in the midst of a systemic crisis. This crisis led to the transition from one form of capitalism (state-led development) to another (free market capitalism).

The advance of capital in these conditions—including the submission of the state to the dictates of capital and a 'structural adjustment' of macroeconomic policy to the new world order—resulted in the massive destruction of productive forces in both agriculture and industry, and a massive inflow of capital in the form of foreign direct investment.[2] It also led to an acceleration of a long-term process of productive and social transformation in which large masses of prole-tarianised peasant farmers (rural landless workers, or the 'rural poor' in the jargon of World Bank economists) were forced to emigrate, to abandon both their source of livelihood (agriculture) and their rural communities (Delgado Wise and Veltmeyer, 2015).

A key issue in the debates that have surrounded and still surround this process was what Marxists and other scholars in the field of Critical Agrarian Studies conceived as the 'Agrarian Question' is whether the peasantry can survive the transition to capitalism in agriculture and industry. But David Harvey, with his contributions regarding capitalism in the 'neoliberal era' on the periphery of what is now a global system, has opened up a new line of debate regarding the contemporary dynamics of capitalist development in the process of productive and social transformation. At issue in this debate are the forces of change generated in this process and the precise mechanisms of 'accumulation by dispossession'.

Here we engage Harvey's concept of accumulation by dispossession. The argument is that the advance of extractive capital on the Latin American peri-phery of the system can be viewed as a contemporary form of what Marx had described as 'primitive accumulation'. Further, this implies a new form of 'enclosures'—enclosing the global commons—and a new dynamic of resistance and class struggle. The argument can be summarised as follows.

First, the territorial advance of capital and capitalism requires the separation of direct producers from the land and their means of production. Second, the mechanism for doing this is through the enclosure of the commons—land, water and other resources necessary for the subsistence of the direct producers. Third, in the current context of a system of neoliberal policies—privatisation, market deregulation and the liberalisation of goods and capital flows—conditions are created that allow for and facilitate the accumulation and the advance of capital. Fourth, the same conditions generate a new proletariat disposed towards sys-temic transformation. Finally, the new proletariat consists of diverse social classes, including a mass of semiproletarianised peasants and landless rural workers, that are adversely affected by the destructive operations of extractive capital and the policies of the neoliberal regimes formed in this context. The forces of resistance mobilised in this struggle derive from the social relations of capitalist production and are directed against the advance of capital as well as the social and environmental depredations of extractive capital, and the policy measures of the regimes formed in these conditions.

This argument is as follows. First we outline and briefly describe the dynamics of a transition from the Washington Consensus on the virtues of free market capitalism towards a new consensus regarding the need to bring the state back into the development process in order to secure a more inclusive form of development (Infante and Sunkel, 2009). We then go on to describe what might be understood as the new geoeconomics of capital in the region. Third, we outline the contours of a new model under construction, a model characterised by what has been described as 'inclusionary state activism'. The model is constructed on two pillars, with reference to the post-Washington Consensus regarding the need for a more inclusive form of national development—*new developmentalism*, as understood by economists at ECLAC (Leiva, 2008; Bresser-Pereira, 2006, 2007)—and *extractivism*, which, when combined with the inclusionary state activism prescribed by the theorists of the new developmentalism, has been described as 'progressive' or 'neoextractivism' (Gudynas, 2009). The argument is made with reference to the experiences of Bolivia and Ecuador, paradigmatic cases of a post-neoliberal model of social change and post-development oriented towards a system conductive of social solidarity and harmony with nature. Fourth, I discuss the different forms taken by the assault of capital on the commons and the diverse mechanisms of accumulation by dispossession involved. The chapter ends with a brief review of the dynamics of struggle and resistance against capitalism in its extractive and neoextractive form.

From the Washington Consensus to neodevelopmentalism

No economic model has had much influence on public policy regarding development in Latin America over the past three decades as the Washington Consensus model of free market capitalism and 'structural reform'. The consensus took the form of an argument regarding the virtues of free market capitalism and the need to liberate the 'forces of economic freedom' (the market, private enterprise, foreign investment) from the regulatory constraints of the welfare-development state. On the one hand, proponents of the Washington Consensus lauded a neoliberal policy regime for the benefits that it would bring. On the other hand, there is the harsh reality that of the benefits that did materialise most accrued to capital. Public policies of structural reform facilitated corporate entry and expansion, while both the rural and urban proletariat were excluded and further marginalised, and those elements of the peasantry that retained some access to the land were forced to abandon their livelihoods and communities. Under these conditions the widespread destruction of the forces of production caused by neoliberal politics led to a new round of capital accumulation in the region—inflows of a large volume of profit- and resource-seeking foreign direct investments, and with them an upsurge of the resistance against the new capitalist world order and neoliberal policies (Gaudichaud, 2012; Petras and Veltmeyer, 2013; Svampa and Antonelli, 2009; Zibechi, 2012).

The Washington Consensus was put into practice in the early to mid-1980s as a set of 'structural reforms' in macroeconomic policy imposed on governments via the mechanism of debt repayment and as a conditionality of 'aid' (debt payment negotiation). It was given official form and was codified by the economist John Williamson (1990). The irony is that this codification of the basic principles of 'structural reform' was made precisely at the point when the architects of these reforms, including the World Bank, came to the conclusion that they were dysfunctional and that they had 'gone too far' in the direction of free market capitalism and that what was needed was a more inclusive form of development based on the agency of the state.

The neoliberal model was constructed with reference to three fundamental principles/policy prescriptions: macroeconomic equilibrium and discipline, liberalisation of trade and the flow of capital (foreign direct investment), and market deregulation. The combination of these three policy prescriptions was expected to reactivate the capital accumulation process and stimulate economic growth. But the results were disastrous—a decade lost for development, an increase of poverty and inequality without economic growth—resulting in the formation of powerful forces of resistance in the form of social movements with their social base in the indigenous communities and peasant organisations. Another result was a new consensus regarding the need to bring the state back into the development process.

Whither the Washington Consensus? On the one hand, the guardians of the new world order, and the architects of neoliberal reform, came to the conclusion that the Washington Consensus was too simplistic and paid insufficient attention to issues of equity, poverty, the environment and cultural diversity. On the other hand, the prescribed labour reforms—deregulation of the labour market and the flexibilisation of labour—worked to the advantage of Capital, opening up economic opportunities for multinational corporations via the provision of an abundant supply of cheap and docile labour for the maquila, a new sector of manufacturing firms based on the assembly operations. However, liberalisation of trade and foreign private investment, and the deregulation of the labour market, did not lead to economic growth or create more jobs and improved working conditions. On the contrary. The failure of the neoliberal model to deliver on its promise of economic growth, and the host of problems associated with the destruction of forces of production in both agriculture and industry, led policy analysts to the conclusion that what was needed was to achieve 'a better balance between state and market' (Ocampo, 2005), which would lead to a more inclusive form of capitalist development.

The new paradigm and policy agenda based on this post-Washington Consensus was defined by the following measures implemented by many, if not most, Latin American governments in the 1990s. First, governments needed to stay the course of 'structural reform' to ensure an effective process of productive transformation and modernisation. Second, to ensure that the poor would receive some of the benefits of economic growth there was the need for a new social policy focused on poverty reduction. Third, inclusive development required a more democratic form of governance and local development based on a policy of administrative decentralisation and social participation, i.e. incorporation of civil society into the development process (Fine and Jomo, 2006).

In the 1990s practically all governments in the region conformed to this new consensus and implemented some version of the new social policy of poverty reduction based on a neostructural model of inclusive development—the 'new developmentalism' as understood and formulated by Bresser-Pereira (2009).

The new geoeconomics of capital: the dynamics of foreign direct investment inflows

Tracing the flow of productive capital or foreign direct investment over the past two decades is a good way of understanding the new geoeconomics of capital in the region today as well as the associated development dynamics.

A good starting point in tracing the dynamics of productive capital in the region is the transition from the era of the developmental state into the new world order of neoliberal globalisation in the 1980s. The neoliberal policy regime of structural reform—privatisation, liberalisation, decentralisation and deregulation—facilitated a massive and historically unprecedented inflow of capital in the form of FDI.[3] According to UNCTAD the inflow of private capital in the form of FDI increased from around 8.7 billion dollars in 1990 to 61 billion in 1998 (1998: 256, 267–268, 362; 2002).

It has been estimated that up to 40 per cent of this capital was invested in the purchase of the shares of privatised state enterprises in the strategic sectors of the economy such as the telecommunications industry and the industry. By sector, up to 50 per cent of this capital was invested in services, including banking, while the manufacturing sector absorbed 25 per cent and the extractive sector only 10 per cent (Arellano, 2010). However, certain forces of change in the world economy, including the ascent of China and the emergence of a 'commodity boom', radically changed the geoeconomics of capital in the region. First, in the first decade of the new millennium the volume of FDI flows to Latin America exploded. Second, by the end of the decade the share of the services sector in FDI flows had been reduced from 60 to 47 per cent, while the share of the extractive sector in these annual flows grew from 10 to 30 per cent (Arellano, 2010).

In 2011, FDI in the region experienced a growth rate of 34.6 per cent, well above that of Asia, which grew by only 6.7 per cent (UNCTAD, 2012). A critical datum: the inflow of resource-seeking capital in South America, the main recipient and destination point for extractive capital in this period, reached and was valued at 150 billion dollars in 2011, 15 times greater in volume than in the early 1990s (Zibechi, 2012). In absolute numbers the inflow of FDI in the region for the first time exceeded the flows to the US and was only surpassed by FDI flows to Europe and Asia.

The expansion of extractive capital in Latin America in the new millennium is reflected in the composition of exports, i.e. in a process of '(re)primarization—a growing trend to export the social product in the form of' commodities (natural resources and raw materials, unprocessed with little to no value added) (ECLAC, 2010: 17). This is evidenced by data provided by ECLAC that show a decrease in the degree of primarisation in the 1990s but then a process of reprimarisation in the first decade of the new millennium. The data also indicate a more pronounced reprimarisation trend in countries such as Brazil and Colombia that are the major recipients of FDI flows in the region. Brazil, for example, received 32.8 per cent of regional flows of FDI in 2000 but in 2008, a year of global financial crisis (and the largest inflow of FDI flows over the decade), Brazil received 45 per cent of total regional inflows of FDI (CEPAL, 2012: 50).

The flow of productive capital towards Latin America over the past decade has been driven by two factors: commodity prices, which remained high during most of this period, and the strong economic growth of the South American sub-region, which encouraged market-seeking investment. This flow of FDI is concentrated in four countries of South America—Argentina, Brazil, Chile and Colombia—that represent 89 per cent of total FDI inflows in the subregion. The extractive sector in these countries, especially mining, has absorbed most of these flows. For example, in 2009 Latin America received 26 per cent of global investment in mining exploration (Seine-Fobomade, 2011). And with the expansion of oil and gas projects, mineral extraction is the most important source of export earnings for most countries in the region.

The explosion of foreign direct investment in the extractive sector responded to a growing demand on the world market for commodities (natural resources such as metals and minerals, energy in the form of fossil- and biofuels, and agricultural products).[4] The commodity boom was not only the driving force of a rising tide of extractive capital but encouraged the election of progressive centre-left governments that were oriented towards a combination of extractivism and the new developmentalism.

A new economic model: new developmentalism and extractivism

Capitalist development in the 1990s not only caused a large inflow of foreign investments but the formation of powerful social movements that engaged in collective action against the neoliberal policies of governments that subjected the people to the dictates of Capital. By the end of the decade the uprisings and actions of these forces of resistance had managed to halt the advance of Capital and the neoliberal policies of governments in the service of Capital, provoking the formation of a political movement concerned with 'going beyond neoliberalism' in the search for 'another world'.

Another result of the dynamics of resistance in the popular sector was a left turn in electoral politics and the rise of political regimes seeking ways of exploiting (capitalising on) the forces of change generated by the social movements. Analysts and observers of this trend spoke and wrote of a sea change—a 'red' wave of regime change (reference here to regimes such as Venezuela, Bolivia and Ecuador, with a resource nationalist and radical populist or socialist orientation) and a 'pink' of post-neoliberal regimes with a more pragmatic approach to social change and capitalist development (Grugel and Riggirozzi, 2012; Levitsky and Roberts, 2011; Macdonald and Ruckert, 2009).[5]

Notwithstanding the distinction between policy regimes with a radical populist complexion (presented as the 'socialism of the twenty-first century') and those with a more pragmatic orientation, the 'progressive' post-neoliberal regimes that emerged in the space generated by the activism of the social movements share several features. They include deployment of a new economic model constructed on the base of two pillars: (i) new developmentalism (including what has been described as 'inclusionary state activism') and (ii) a new more progressive form of extractivism in which the state regulates the operations of extractive capital and uses fiscal revenues/resource rents (derived from the extraction and exports of natural gas, oil, metals and minerals) to finance social programs of poverty reduction (Dávalos and Albuja, 2014).

In this conjuncture two countries—Bolivia and Ecuador—driven by the political and intellectual activism of the indigenous communities and organisations, have sought to go beyond both neoliberalism and the new developmentalism in constructing not an alternative form of development but an alternative model—a post-development form of social change expressed in the notion '*vivir bien*': to live well in social solidarity and harmony with nature (Acosta, 2013; Huanacuni, 2010; Prada, 2013). The idea of this *vivir bien* model of social change and entrenching it in a new constitution that recognises not only the identity and territorial rights of the indigenous peoples in the country but also the rights of nature has led to a great debate on the construction of another possible world: another development or post-development (Gudynas, 2017)?

This debate has several axes. One has to do with the viability of a model and policy regime based on the notion of living well in social solidarity and harmony with mother earth. Another has to do with the policies actually implemented in recent years and the model underlying these policies. Alberto Acosta, an economist who helped draft the government's development model and national development plan (*Para Vivir Bien*) but today is one of the government's fiercest critics, has argued that the extractivist strategy pursued by the government, and the policies that it has implemented based on this strategy, is in irreconcilable contradiction with the concept of *vivir bien* (living well).

As Dávalos and Albuja (2014) argue in their discussion of the contradictory features of the government's actual policies regarding economic development, Correa has emerged as one of the strongest and ardent supporters of both 'new developmentalism' (inclusionary state activism) and 'extractivism' (the use of resource rents to achieve poverty reduction). Correa's position on this is that the extraction and export of natural resources of the country in a partnership with foreign investors signifies an 'economic opportunity' that the country and government cannot afford to not take advantage of. This is despite the forces of resistance that this policy has generated in the indigenous movement and the communities most directly affected by the destructive operations of extractive capital. A manifest form of this resistance is the fight led by CONAIE, an organisation of indigenous peoples that has led the opposition to the neoliberal policy agenda of Ecuadorian governments since 1989, against the government's extractivist policies in recent years. More recently, CONAIE has called for an 'indigenous and popular uprising' and a 'national strike' against the government on August 11, 2015 (CONAIE, 2015).

As for the indigenous movement and the opposition to extractivism in Bolivia the government's recent announcement of its intention to resume its project to build a road through the national park TIPNIS, and to continue with the policy of allowing oil exploration in the protected areas of this park, has sparked a revival of indigenous protests against the policy of allowing the invasion of capital in indigenous territories (*Hoy Bolivia*, 2015; IBCE, 2015).[6]

As Dávalos and Albuja have argued in the case of Ecuador, Correa's policies exemplify all the contradictions and pitfalls of the new extractivism and submission to foreign capital. This includes the enclosure of the commons; the commodification of land, natural resources and water; the violation of the territorial rights of indigenous peoples and communities, and their marginalisation or integration into the circuits and global dynamics of capital accumulation. It also includes the expansion of the extractive frontier—the exploration and exploitation of the country's oil reserves—in the country's pristine glacial waters and tropical forests as well as the open sea and significantly in nature reserves such as Yasuni-ITT and in the indigenous territories (the 'political ecology of territorial transformation'). The resistance and the struggle against the depredations of extractive capital further also encompasses bituminous shale industrialisation; open pit mining; corporate agroextractivism, including the use of pesticides, seeds/genetically modified organisms and plantation monoculture; the privatisation of public services (including water, carbon markets and picturesque landscapes of the tourism industry); and the use of biotechnology and geotechnics in the conversion of farmland for the production of biofuels.

In 2007 President Rafael Correa launched the Yasuni-ITT project by means of which the government proposed permanent suspension of oil extraction in the Yasuni Ishpingo-Tambococha-Tiputini National Park (ITT) in exchange for payments of 3.6 billion dollars by the international community. The project was received with enthusiasm by environmentalists, post-developmentalists and the indigenous movement and supporters. The Yasuni-ITT park has around 846 million barrels, or 20 per cent of the country's proven oil reserves. The aim of the initiative was the conservation of biodiversity, protection of indigenous peoples that are living in voluntary isolation, and prevention of the release of CO_2 emissions. The Yasuni-ITT Trust Fund was officially launched on 3 August 2010, but by 2012 only 200 million dollars had been committed, prompting a 180-degree turn in the Yasuni-ITT project. 'The world has failed us', Correa announced, and spoke of the rich countries as hypocrites because they emit the most greenhouse gases while expecting poor nations like Ecuador to sacrifice their economic progress to preserve the environment (Watts, 2013).

As with the TIPNIS controversy in Bolivia[7] Correa's abandonment of the Yasuni-ITT project shed light on the contradictions of government policy, particularly in regard to the insurmountable contradiction between the government's post-development *Plan para el bien vivir* and the government's economic development policies based on capitalism and extractivism (Acosta, 2012).

The plan to extract oil from the Yasuni-ITT reignited a debate on the appropriate development strategy for Ecuador (Chimienti and Matthes, 2013). Many economists and environmentalists, as well as advocates for indigenous territorial rights, have pointed towards a serious defect in the logic of government policy, namely, that the aim to generate economic growth and reduce poverty through extractivism implies a fatal contradiction with the *Plan Nacional Para Vivir Bien*.[8]

Since his election in 2007 Correa has embarked on a process of aggressive negotiations with mining companies in order to secure for Ecuador a greater share of the value of the product, and thus increase the government's fiscal revenues in service of a strategy aimed at a more equitable distribution of the country's social product. And it appears that the Correa's strategy bore fruit. According to the UNDP's 2014 *Human Development Report* from 2003 to 2013 Ecuador's poverty rate was reduced by 50 per cent over the course of Correa's administration. Needless to say, this success in meeting the UN's Millennium Development Goal regarding poverty reduction was attributed by the government to the government's policy of expanding expenditures on social welfare programs.[9] But at what cost was this achieved? This is one of the core issues of the debate.

Correa's economic development strategy demonstrates the extraordinary importance of the extractive sector in contemporary Ecuador. With the abandonment of banana production for export, oil revenues have come to account for almost one third of the national budget, although Dávalos and Albuja (2014) argue that resource rents from the extraction of oil contributed next to nothing to the revenues used by the government to reduce poverty. Moreover, under Correa, Ecuador has not only experienced the negative socioenvironmental impacts of expanded oil production, but an expansion of the palm oil sector and large-scale mining projects that are notoriously destructive of both the environment and livelihoods. Moreover, in the context of the government's efforts to justify its extractivist policies by reference to the overriding need to combat both underdevelopment and poverty, Correa's concern for the environment and the rights of Mother Earth have been reduced to vague rhetoric. In this context, Acosta points out, Correa has been unable or unwilling to recognise the ecosystem—and political—limits to the dependence on natural resource extraction. In fact, Correa continues to invoke the importance of exploiting the country's wealth of natural sources:

> Our way of life is unsustainable if we do not use our oil and minerals in the next 10 or 15 years while developing alternative energy sources. Those who say that we should not exploit our resources put at risk programs designed to place Ecuador in the forefront of Latin American nations. They would have us return to the status of being a poor nation without a future.
>
> (Correa, 2013)[10]

A new enclosure of the commons?[11]

David Harvey has argued that the policy of privatisation (turning public assets over to the private sector) has served as the principal mechanism to enclose the commons (land, water and other natural resources needed for subsistence or sustainable livelihoods) and sacrifice biodiversity on the altar of extractive capital. Enclosure in this and other forms has served as a lever for capital to jumpstart or activate a process of accumulation—an 'accumulation by dispossession' as Harvey has it—in the neoliberal era of capitalist development.

The dawn of this era can be traced back to the early 1980s in the context of a conservative counter-revolution, construction of a new world order of free-market capitalism in conditions of a systemic crisis, and a consensus on the need to free the 'forces of freedom' (private property, capital and the market) from the regulatory constraints of the welfare-development state. The 'new economic model' constructed in this context included privatisation of the means of production, a policy of liberalising international trade and the flow of foreign investment, as well as deregulation of the market. The stated aim of these policies was to reactivate the process of capital accumulation and stimulate economic growth by creating favourable conditions for investors and the expansion and operations of capital. Privatisation, in particular, according to Harvey (2003: 149), played a crucial role in this process by serving as a mechanism of accumulation by enclosing the commons.

This argument of Harvey's was used by Spronk and Webber (2007) in their analysis of the revolutionary struggle associated with the water and gas wars in Bolivia between 2000 and 2005. Spronk and Webber used Harvey's concepts of 'accumulation by dispossession' and 'enclosure of the commons' in analysing the dynamics of resistance (against neoliberal policies of the government) and a struggle that brought together indigenous and peasant communities as well as workers and the urban poor. As they see it, these dynamics exemplified the connections made by Harvey between the neoliberal policy agenda of the state, capital in the form of FDI and the multinational corporation, and organised resistance in the form of social movements formed to challenge the enclosure of the commons and the privatisation (and commodification) of vital and productive resources (gas and water in the cases analysed by Spronk and Webber). A key aim, and mobilising force, of the Resistance was to 'reclaim the commons'.

We conclude from this and our own research into the contemporary dynamics of the class struggle that privatisation as a mechanism of accumulation by dispossession (AbyD) is an undeniable importance in the analysis of both the dynamics of capital expansion in the region and the dynamics of resistance and the struggles that they generate. To illustrate this point, we can point to the case of Mexico in the electricity sector, where in June 2015 the project to strip commoners of their land and property so as to gain access to oil and gas reserves was extended to the power plants in the electricity sector (Beceril, 2014).

Another dimension of the same problem, which anticipated by decades the neoliberal policy of privatising the commons, is manifest in the policy of constructing dams and other infrastructure mega-development projects (García Rivas, 2014). In the cases studied by Garcia Rivas related to the construction of three hydroelectric dams in the state of Nayarit, the collusion of the political class with foreign capital and investors for mutual benefit was well documented and analysed as an example of the state as a facilitator of a process of enclosing the commons and a mechanism of accumulation by dispossession.

Privatisation has long been used by 'international financial institutions' such as the World Bank and the IMF as a mechanism of accumulation by dispossession (AbyD). However, it is by no means the only one. Our own research has led us to identify other mechanisms as discussed below.

In addition to the extraction of oil and gas, mining for industrial minerals and precious metals (gold and silver) has proven to be a useful lever of capital accumulation in recent years. At issue here are the gold and silver mines worked by Canadian mining companies that dominate foreign investments in this sector, as well as the open pit mines (*minas a cielo abierto*) created to extract coal, iron ore, copper and other minerals and metals. These open pit mines, which use much less labour per unit of capital invested than the underground mines of earlier years, are notorious for their enormously destructive and devastating impact on both the environment—raping the land and polluting the water needed by nearby communities and those downstream both for their livelihoods and their very existence—and the conflicts and resistance movements that they have generated within the communities affected by the destructive operations of extractive capital. Giarracca and Teubal (2014) have documented and analysed in detail the way in which these open mines in the case of Argentina have served both as a lever of capital accumulation and as a means by which the local population and entire communities have been violently dispossessed, forced to abandon their communities and way of life.

Another mechanism of accumulation by dispossession that has proven to be particularly useful for foreign investors in the agriculture sector (the agroextractivism) is landgrabbing, termed 'large-scale foreign investments in the acquisition of land' in official development discourse (Borras, et al., 2012). According to Borras and his colleagues in the Critical Agrarian Studies (ICAS) network, since 2007 this process of landgrabbing encompasses a vast expanse of land estimated at 220 worldwide million hectares worldwide, with significant consequences for the livelihoods of affected populations and communities.

In Latin America, this landgrabbing process has been driven by the world market demand for energy and the search for alternatives to fossil fuels. In response to this demand in the southern cone of Latin America (Argentina, Brazil, Bolivia and Paraguay) there has emerged a rapidly growing economy based on the conversion in the use of land from the production of grains and food for local consumption and exports into the production of biofuels for export. Not only has this economy of large-scale agribusiness and agroextractivism come to threaten the local economy of family farmers and peasants but it has accelerated a process of forced outmigration.

The scale of this phenomenon—landgrabbing, natural resource extraction, environmental degradation and violent expulsion of local inhabitants from the land and their communities—is enormous. In the case of Argentina, an important destination for extractive capital in the form of open pit mining and the production of soy-based biofuels, it is estimated that nearly 30 million hectares of the best land and fertile soil, water basins and natural reserves, including strategic reserves of minerals, in 23 provinces, are now foreign-owned, and

13 million hectares are currently for sale (http://laangosturadigital.com.ar). On reviewing the data for other countries in the region it is clear that even with the emergence of resource nationalist regulatory regimes such as Bolivia, Latin America in recent years has ceded much of its territory for exploration and the exploitation of its natural wealth, and an increasing part of its extractive industries has fallen under the sway of transnational companies based in the imperial centres.

Land (and water) grabbing has served capital in the form of multinational agribusinesses and 'commodity traders' not only as a means of facilitating access to marketable agro-food resources but also to energy in the form of biofuels based on soy and sugarcane, which is in great demand and has more value in the world market. Recent years have seen the expansion of different lines of research in this area. They include research into the dynamics of biofuel production based on a process of land-grabbing, environmental degradation and dispossession in which the big landowners and the agents of foreign capital have managed to further enclose the commons and commodify natural resources needed by local inhabitants and the communities affected by the operations of extractive capital for their social existence.

Norma Giarracca and Miguel Teubal (2014) among others have researched extensively the political economy of soya production (*soyazicación de la agricultura*) and the enclosure of the commons in the form of landgrabbing. As described and explained by Borras and his colleagues, the land at issue or in dispute in many cases is considered 'empty' and 'ownerless'—the property or territorial rights based on customary or traditional use ignored or disrespected.

Landgrabbing and the eviction of the villagers who have customary usage of the land but do not have legal title, and who are therefore vulnerable to being evicted either by legal means (when the invaders turn to the state) or violent confrontations, have begun to assume the form of a class struggle. That is, they are generating not only protests and disputes over territory but broader movements organised to mobilise the forces of resistance against the operations of extractive capital and the neoliberal policies that facilitate these operations (Giarracca and Teubal, 2010, 2014).

Until the recent collapse in the price of oil, the dominant movement of extractive capital had been in the direction of fossil fuels. And, as discussed above, another major destination point for extractive capital has been mining— the production of metals and minerals for industry or middle class consumption. The conditions to facilitate the accumulation of this capital included a neoliberal policy of structural reforms—privatisation, liberalisation, deregulation—as well as financialisation. According to studies undertaken by Evans, Goodman and Lansbury (2002), the global mining industry experienced a systemwide process of privatisation, deregulation and financialisation in conditions promoted by the World Bank and other agents of global capital and the imperial state. Warhust and Bridge (1997: 1–12) note that 'more than 90 countries … reformed their laws mining investment and mining codes in the past two decades', i.e. the 1980s and 1990s. These reforms included the abolition of royalties to encourage FDI inflows. Mexico and Peru, for example, in the 1990s fully complied to this dictate of the World Bank. With no royalty regime in the mining sector, and according to the Auditor General of Mexico an extremely lax regulatory system and an effective tax rate that is below 2 per cent, Mexico's policy regime for the extraction and exportation of minerals and metals functions not only as a lever of capital accumulation but as a system designed for looting the country of a precious resource—a haemorrhaging or deep bleeding, in the colourful language of Galeano—with an absolutely minimal compensation for the heavy environmental and social costs that the extraction of these minerals and metals represent (Bárcenas, 2012).[12] Moreover, instead of integrating these reforms into a national development plan, they are designed as a sectoral approach designed to favour corporate interests (Canel, Idemudia and North, 2010: 5–25).

In some cases we should recognise that the strategy of the mining companies is not to separate the direct producers from their means of production, forcing them to abandon their communities and their way of life or their ancestral territory. Strictly speaking, this cannot be argued in that mining companies in the extractive sector are evidently willing to negotiate a mutually beneficial agreement with residents and the communities affected by their operations. However, the problem for these companies is that many if not most of those affected are not willing to negotiate with them. Understandably, given what is at stake for them—their very survival as well as their ancestral and territorial rights—they invariably choose or have chosen the path of resistance, thus entering into a relationship of conflict with companies and capital (Bebbington and Bury, 2013).

Resistance on the extractive frontier

Harvey argues that accumulation by dispossession has led to multifaceted forms of struggle that have some new features. One is that these struggles do not come under the banner of labour or a trade union, or the leadership of the working class, but rather of 'civil society' broadly understood as all manner of associative forms of organisations that inhabit the wide expanse between families and the state. This excludes class-based organisations such as the social movements formed within the same expanse. Given the wide range of interests and groups involved in these struggles, it is postulated that they involve 'a political dynamic less focused on social action' (Harvey, 2003: 168). It is possible to argue that they also lead to more social but less political forms of collective action, a 'non-power approach towards social change', as argued by Holloway (2002). Some political analysts have gone further in stating that given that these movements are rooted in civil society rather than a class structure based on social relations of production, they therefore do not engage a class struggle but rather a multifaceted struggle with a broader and more heterogeneous base.

This conception of the social movements that emerged in the context of resistance against the neoliberal policies of governments in the 1990s has its origins in a postmodernist theory of social change that can be traced back to the 1980s but that has lost its relevance in contemporary times in that it does not and cannot explain the dynamics of the anti-extractivist movements that have emerged in recent years . Although it resorts to some ideas advanced in this failed theory of 'new social movements', a more relevant line of research has been elaborated by Raul Zibechi in terms of the notion of 'subterranean struggles' (Zibechi, 2012). Zibechi, together with the authors presented in a recent book by Bebbington and Bury (2013), argues that these struggles are an integral part of the new extractive economy in Latin America. But the reference here is not to the movements that have emerged on the new frontier of extractive capital, but rather the everyday struggles and cries of 'the excluded', those seeking to adapt their livelihoods to the conditions generated by mining and other extractive operations in the spaces available to them. These analysts argue that these struggles are an integral part of the new extractive economy in Latin America, and have a basic flaw. These struggles are documented and described in considerable detail but without adequately theorising their dynamics and their structural and political roots in the functioning of capitalism as a system. That is, they see these localised struggles and movements as anti-extractive—and, indeed, anti-neoliberal (in terms of government policy and the agribusiness corporate model—but not as anti-capitalist or anti-imperialist).

Conclusion

Today we are in a new phase in the capitalist development of the forces of production, with a corresponding transformation in the social relations of production and the dynamics of class struggle. In terms of the type of capital involved in the process we can conceive of this stage as extractive capitalism. This does not mean that it has replaced the classical form of capitalism theorised by Marx, with its base in the capital–labour relation. This relation undoubtedly remains the basis of the capitalist mode of production. Reference to a new phase of capitalism implies a combination of different forms of capital, including industrial capital, which dominates the global production system, and financial capital, which dominates the structure of power relations within this system. The advance of extractive capital in the 1980s and 1990s was facilitated by a neoliberal program of 'structural reforms', but in recent years and in the current conjuncture has relied on the progressive policies of the neoliberal state.

The advance of capital on the extractive frontier is facilitated by four main mechanisms, each working to accumulate capital by dispossessing the direct producers from their means of production, forcing them to abandon their livelihoods and their rural communities. One is the neoliberal policy of privatisation, which is to turn over the means of production in the strategic sectors of the economy to the so-called 'private sector', i.e. the CEOs of the multinational corporations that dominate the global economy, or the 'international capitalist class'—or, as some have it, the global ruling class. The second is the mechanism of landgrabbing, which allows capital and foreign investors—and governments such as China in search of food security or energy—direct access agro-food products, agrofuels and other sources of energy and natural resources. The third mechanism, which operates in the mining sector (mining and metals) and the extraction of carbohydrates (oil and natural gas), takes the form of concessions of large tracts of land and territorial space extended to foreign investors and mining companies on long-term contracts to allow them to explore for and exploit the valuable resources of the subsoil. The fourth major mechanism of accumulation by dispossession is also found in the extractive sub-sector of mining. It works by means of destroying the ecosystem on which the economy of small-scale producers and peasant farming depends.

The institutions and policies that permit the functioning of these diverse forms of accumulation lead to an enclosure of the commons that breeds new forces of resistance, creating conditions of political conflict on the frontier of extractive capital. In these conditions the advance of extractive capital generates new forces of resistance. In the current juncture of the capitalist development process this struggle assumes a very particular form, resulting in the formation of a new proletariat and an anti-extractive sociopolitical movement—a socioenvironmental movement of those negatively impacts by the operations of extractive capital. These movements have demonstrated considerable dynamism in the struggle against capitalism in the current conjuncture of its historical trajectory.

Notes

1 As Gudynas (2015) points out, notwithstanding the repeated invocation of David Harvey's concept of 'accumulation by dispossession' in literally hundreds of studies on Latin America and by Latin American scholars themselves, the idea advanced by this concept is nothing new. On the contrary, it has been formulated in different ways by many Latin American scholars over the years. Although I am in total agreement with Gudynas' criticism of the concept as often applied to capitalism in the current Latin American context, I nevertheless believe that although not new or any advance on Marx's original formulation, the concept has some analytical utility and relevance for understanding the contemporary dynamics of capitalist development.

2 In the 1990s Latin America was the recipient of a massive wave of private capital in the form of FDI, increasing from about 8.7 billion dollars in 1990 to 61 billion dollars in 1998 (UNCTAD, 2007). This invasion was facilitated by the neoliberal 'structural reforms' in 'macroeconomic policy' (privatisation, liberalisation, deregulation …) mandated by the Washington consensus in the new world order established in the early 1980s.

3 This capital was both unproductive—viz. the purchase of the assets of privatised state enterprises, reflected in a process of 'acquisition and mergers' that is estimated to have consumed up to 40 per cent of the capital invested in the 1990s—and productive in the transfer of new modern technologies.

4 The region remains the world's leading source of metals: iron (24%), copper (21%), gold (18%), nickel (17%), zinc (21%), bauxite (27%) and the silver (Campódonico, 2008; UNCTAD, 2007: 87). Oil made up 83.4 per cent of total exports of Venezuela from 2000 to 2004, copper accounts for 45 per cent of Chilean exports, nickel 33% of Cuba's exports, and gold, copper and zinc 33 per cent of Peru's exports. Along with agricultural production, extraction of oil, gas and metals remains essential for the region's exports. From 2008 to 2009 exports of primary products accounted for 38.8 per cent of total exports from Latin America (ECLAC, 2010).

5 For an analysis of these post-neoliberal regimes see Ciccariello-Maher (2013), Gaudichaud (2012) and Katz (2008).

6 The indigenous movement both in Bolivia and Ecuador continues to urge Presidents Morales and Correa to be faithful to the principles of their national development plan

(designed for living well) and to make way for a postextractivist strategy. http:// hoybolivia.com/Noticia.php?IdNoticia=155750&tit=5_leyes_autorizan…; http://ibce. org.bo/main-news-Bolivia/news-national-deta. Also www.elmundo.es/internacional/ 2015/08/12/55c21ad7268e3ec5218b457e.html.

7 On Evo Morales' controversial project to build a road through a national park that contains one of the largest reserves of natural biodiversity in the world, against the resistance of the indigenous communities that inhabit the reserve, see Prada (2012) and Achtenberg (2012).

8 The Plan Nacional Para Vivir Bien 2009–2013 emphasises the importance of redeployment and reduction of inequality, in addition to environmental protection.

9 Dávalos and Albuja (2014) dispute this claim with substantive empirical evidence.

10 This comment is from President Rafael Correa's weekly broadcast to the nation in April and was translated by Ecuador Digest. www.cuencahighlife.com/post/2013/ 04/11/ECUADOR-DIGEST3cbr3eCorrea.

11 For an elaboration of the 'commons' paradigm see Bollier (2014).

12 According to the Auditor General (Bárcenas, 2012: 31), Mexico receives only 1.2 per cent of the value of the metals extracted in the country to sell on the world market.

References

Achtenberg, E. (2012). "Bolivia: TIPNIS Communities Plan National March and Resistance to Government," *Rebel Currents*, 23 March.

Acosta, A. (2012). *Buen Vivir. Sumak kawsay. Una oportunidad para imaginar otros mundos*. Quito: AbyaYala.

Arellano, M. (2010). "Canadian Foreign Direct Investment in Latin America," Background Paper, North–South Institute, Ottawa, May.

Bárcenas, F. (2012). "Detener el saqueo minero en México," *La Jornada*, 28 February. www.jornada.unam.mx/2012/02/28/opinion/023a1pol

Bebbington, A. and J. Bury (eds) (2013). *Subterranean Struggles: New Dynamics of Mining, Oil and Gas in Latin America*. Austin: University of Texas Press.

Beceril, A. (2014). "Buscan legalizar despojo de tierras también en el sector de electricidad," *La Jornada*, 14 June.

Bollier, D. (2014). "The Commons as a Template for Transformation," Great Transformation Initiative, April 2014. www.greattransition.org/publication/the-commons-as-a-template-for-transformation.

Borras, S.M., C. Kay, S. Gómez and J. Wilkinson (2012). "Land Grabbing and Global Capitalist Accumulation: Key Features in Latin America," *Canadian Journal of Development Studies*, 33(4): 402–416.

Bresser-Pereira, L.C. (2007). "Estado y mercado en el nuevo desarrollismo," *Nueva Sociedad* 210(July–August): 110–125.

Bresser-Pereira, L.C. (2009). *Developing Brazil: Overcoming the Failure of the Washington Consensus*. Boulder, CO: Lynne Rienner Publishers.

Campodónico, H. (2008). *Renta petrolera y minera en países seleccionados de América Latina*. Santiago: CEPAL.

Canel, E., U. Idemudia and L. North (2010). "Rethinking Extractive Industry: Regulation, Dispossession, and Emerging Claims," *Canadian Journal of Development Studies*, 30(1–2): 5–25.

CEPAL. (2012). *Anuario estadístico de América Latina y el Caribe*. Santiago: CEPAL.

Chimienti, A. and S. Matthes (2013). "Ecuador: Extractivism for the Twenty-first Century?" *NACLA*, 46(4), Winter.

Ciccariello-Maher, G. (2013). *We Created Chávez. A People's History of the Venezuelan Revolution.* Durham NC: Duke University Press.

CONAIE. (2015). "Porque nuestra lucha histórica es junto a las comunas, pueblos y nacionalidades. Vamos todos al levantamiento indígena y popular!" Quito: CONAIE. www.pueblosencamino.org/index.php/asi-si/resistencias-y-luchas-sociales02/1425-ecuador-conaie-vamos-todos-al-levantamiento-indigena-y-popular.

Dávalos, P. and V. Albuja (2014). "Ecuador: Extractivist Dynamics, Politics and Discourse," in H. Veltmeyer and J. Petras (eds), *The New Extractivism: A Post-Neoliberal Development Model?* London: Zed Books.

Delgado Wise, R. and H. Veltmeyer (2015). *Agrarian Change, Migration and Development.* Halifax: Fernwood Publications/London: Practical Action.

ECLAC—UN Economic Commission for Latin America and the Caribbean. (2010). *Time for Equality: Closing Gaps, Opening Trails.* Santiago: ECLAC.

Evans, G., J. Goodman and N. Lansbury (eds) (2002). *Moving Mountains: Communities Confronting Mining and Globalisation.* London: Zed books.

Fine, Ben and K.S. Jomo (eds) (2006). *The New Development Economics: After the Washington Consensus.* London: Zed Books.

García Rivas, M.A. (2014). "El proyecto hidroeléctrico en Nayarit como una manifectación de la acumulación por diposesión," Doctoral thesis, Estudios del Desarrollo. Zacatecas: Universidad Autónoma de Zacatecas.

Gaudichaud, F. (2012). "El volcán latinoamericano. Izquierdas, movimientos sociales y neoliberalismo en América Latina," Otramérica. http://blogs.otramerica.com/editorial/.

Giarracca, N. and M. Teubal (2010). "Disputa por los territorios y recursos naturales: el modelo extractivista," ALASRU, 5, América Latina, realineamientos políticos e projetos em disputa. Brazil, December.

Giarracca, N. and M. Teubal (2014). "Argentina: Extractivist Dynamics of Soy Production and Open-pit Mining," pp. 47–79 in H. Veltmeyer and J. Petras (eds), *The New Extractivism: A Post-neoliberal Development Model?* London: Zed.

Grugel, J. and P. Riggirozzi (2012). "Post Neoliberalism: Rebuilding and Reclaiming the State in Latin America," *Development and Change*, 43(1): 1–21.

Gudynas, E. (2009). "Diez tesis urgentes sobre el nuevo extractivismo. Contextos y demandas bajo el progresismo sudamericano actual," pp. 187–225 in *Extractivismo, Política y Sociedad.* Quito: CLAES/CAAP. http://extractivismo.com/documentos/capitulos/GudynasExtractivismoSociedadDesarrollo09.pdf.

Gudynas, E. (2015). "La necesidad de romper con un colonialismo simpatico," *Rebelión,* 30 September.

Gudynas, E. (2017). "Postdevelopment as Critique and Alternative," in H. Veltmeyer and P. Bowles (eds), *The Essential Critical Development Studies Guide.* London: Routledge.

Harvey, D. (2003). *The New Imperialism.* Oxford: Oxford University Press.

Holloway, J. (2002). *Change the World without Taking Power: The Meaning of Revolution Today.* London: Pluto Press.

Hoy Bolivia. (2015). "Cinco leyes autorizan actividad petrolera en un parquet," 6 August.

Huanacuni Mamani, F. (2010). *Buen vivir/vivir bien: Filosofía, políticas, estrategias y experiencias regionales andinas.* Lima: Coordinadora Andina de Organizaciones Indígenas—CAOI.

IBCE. (2015). "Indígenas del tipnis vuelven a reactivar movilizaciones," 10 August. Available at: http://ibce.org.bo/principales-noticias-bolivia/noticias-nacionales-deta.

Infante, R. and O. Sunkel (2009). "Chile: Towards Inclusive Development," *CEPAL Review*, Issue 97, April: 133–152.

Katz, C. (2008). *Las disyuntivas de la izquierda* (The Dilemmas of the Left in Latin America). Buenos Aires: Luxemburg Editions.

Leiva, F. (2008). *Latin American Neostructuralism. The Contradictions of Post-Neoliberal Development*. Minneapolis: University of Minnesota Press.

Levitsky, Steven and Kenneth Roberts (eds) (2011). *The Resurgence of the Latin American Left*. Baltimore: Johns Hopkins University Press.

Macdonald, L. and A. Ruckert (2009). *Post-Neoliberalism in the Americas*. Basingstoke, UK: Palgrave Macmillan.

Ocampo, J.A. (2005). "A Broad View of Macroeconomic Stability," *DESA Working Paper* No. 1 (ST/ESA/2005/DWP/1). www.un.org/esa/desa/papers/2005/wp1_2005.pdf

Petras, J. and H. Veltmeyer (2013). *Social Movements in Latin America: Neoliberalism and Popular Resistance*. Basingstoke, UK: Palgrave Macmillan.

Prada Alcoreza, R. (2012). "Misería de la geopolítica: Crítica a la geopolítica extractivista," *America Latina en Movimiento*, 18 October, 2. www.alainet.org/es/active/58901.

Prada Alcoreza, R. (2013). "Buen Vivir as a Model for State and Economy," pp. 145–58 in M. Lang and D. Mokrani (eds), *Beyond Development: Alternative Visions from Latin America*. Amsterdam: Transnational Institute.

Spronk, S. and J. Webber (2007). "Struggles against Accumulation by Dispossession in Bolivia: The Political Economy of Natural Resource Contention," *Latin American Perspectives*, 34(2), March: 31–47.

Svampa, M. and M. Antonelli (eds) (2009). *Minería transnacional, narrativas del desarrollo y resistencias sociales*. Buenos Aires: Editorial Biblos.

UNCTAD (2007). *World Investment Report. Transnational Corporations, Extractive Industries and Development*. Geneva: United Nations.

UNCTAD (2012). *World Investment Report*. Geneva: United Nations.

Warhust, A. and G. Bridge (1997). "Economic Liberalization, Innovation and Technology Transfer: Opportunities for Cleaner Production in the Minerals Industry," *Natural Resources Forum*, 21(1): 1–12.

Watts, J. (2013), "Ecuador approves Yasuni national park oil drilling in Amazon rainforest," *The Guardian*, 16 August. www.theguardian.com/world/2013/aug/16/ecuador-approves-yasuni-amazon-oil-drilling.

Williamson, J. (ed.) (1990). *Latin American Adjustment. How Much Has Happened?* Washington, DC: Institute for International Economics.

Zibechi, R. (2012). *Territories in Resistance: A Cartography of Latin American Social Movements*. Oakland, CA: AK Press.

3 Capitalism on the frontier of agroextractivism

Raúl Delgado Wise

Today we are witnessing a new phase in the national and global development of the productive forces where intellectual property and ownership of *patents* has become a key component of the imperial(ist) system of domination[1] under the aegis of neoliberal capitalism (Rodriguez, 2008). This phenomenon is taking place within the institutional and policy framework of a system set up in the 1980s to liberate the 'forces of economic freedom' (capital, the market, private enterprise, globalisation) from the regulatory constraints of the welfare-developmental state and a system of 'global governance' where the concentration and centralisation of capital has reached unprecedented levels. The diverse and multifaceted dynamics of this process have been extensively studied and analysed in different regional and national contexts. However, a relatively understudied aspect of this process is the profound restructuring undergone by the system of technological innovation at the heart of the capitalist development process over the last two and a half decades, where the concentration and the private appropriation of the means of knowledge creation and technological innovation—what Marx defined as the *general intellect*—has reached major proportions. Far from favouring a progressive or revolutionary development of society's productive forces (in the direction of both development and socialism) this trend has placed a number of countries on the periphery of the world system on a regressive path in the advancement of knowledge, exacerbating the propensity of the world system towards crisis.

The aim of this chapter is to unravel some fundamental features of this restructuring and capitalist development process in what David Harvey (2005) has described as the *neoliberal era* and Samir Amin (2013), from a world systems and monopoly capital perspective, has termed the *era of generalised monopolies.* With reference to the systemic dynamics and forces at work in these conditions this chapter is concerned with, and has a dual focus on, the expansion of corporate capital in the agricultural sector and the advance of resource-seeking, or extractive, capital in this sector. Unlike the system whose dynamics were theorised and analysed by Marx, extractive capitalism[2] is based not so much on the exploitation of labour as the looting and pillage of natural resource wealth. Needless to add, these two forms of capitalism are not exclusive one of the other, and at every stage in the evolution of capitalism they are normally combined and coexist, as do the diverse forms of resistance that capitalist development in any and all of its diverse forms inevitably gives rise to.

Historically, capitalist development of the forces of production has always hinged on the exploitation of surplus labour traditionally or most often supplied by the agricultural sector, as well as the process of productive and social transformation associated with it. But, as emphasised by Marx in *Capital*, the truly revolutionary pathway towards the accumulation of capital and capitalist development is scientific knowledge and its technological application to production, a process of technological innovation and internal restructuring of the production apparatus in response to conditions of crisis (Marx, 1981, Chap. 10). As Marx saw it, the development of science and technology, or, more generally, knowledge production and technological innovation, not only is the best antidote to the propensity of capitalism towards crisis but it is a revolutionary pathway towards progressive development (Marx, 1977).

The challenge therefore is to establish the intersection of these two dynamics—the exploitation of agricultural labour, the origin and basic source of surplus value; and technological innovation, a fundamental means of increasing the productivity of labour and thus intensive growth based on the generation of surplus value. Another challenge, which we take up in the chapter, is to analyse the intersection of these two dynamics with the economic and policy dynamics of natural resource extraction, which include the generation and extraction of ground rent and technological rent with the advance of extractive capital on the periphery of the system.

On these points we advance our argument in four parts. First, we establish the relevance of what we describe as the imperial innovation system and its implications for the agricultural sector. We then briefly discuss the advance of capital on the extractive frontier in the form of agribusiness, with reference to what we view as the imperialist innovation agenda (the appropriation of scientific knowledge and control of production technology) as it plays out in a global context. Third, we bring up and briefly discuss the new geoeconomics of capital, with reference to what in the Latin American context might be viewed as the new political economy of agriculture: agroextractivism. Fourth, we make a brief detour into what could be described as the political economy of biofuels capitalism on the extractive frontier. We end the chapter with a brief discussion of the dynamics of the resistance to capitalism and extractivism, highlighting the Zapatista initiative and proposals regarding the possible construction of another world—a world that in their words 'encompasses many worlds'.

The central argument advanced in this chapter is that the political economy of agriculture as well as the new geoeconomics of capital in Latin America can best be understood in terms of the globalising dynamics of forces released in an ongoing capitalist development process. In these terms the capitalist development process in the region has resulted in the evolution of extractive capitalism, a new phase in the evolution of Capital characterised by the extraction of natural resource and technology rent, and the construction of an 'innovation system' within a global economy based on monopoly power and the exploitation of accumulated 'brain power'—what we conceive of as an *Imperial Innovation System.*

The emergence of Silicon Valley's imperial innovation system[3]

A critical dimension and complex issue of capitalist development in the contemporary era relates to how large multinational corporations in the sector of communications and information technology, many of them headquartered or with venture capital posts in Silicon Valley, have managed to place at their disposal the 'human capital'[4] and knowledge production capacity formed in different countries across the world in both the centre and the periphery of the world system. This development—the accumulation of knowledge and skills as a productive resource and a crucial force of production[5]—has undergone a similar process, and subjected to the same conditions, as capital in other sectors. This includes the concentration and centralisation of capital, a process that works to reduce labour costs, transferring associated risks to non-capitalist producers, and capitalising on the appropriated benefits through the mechanism of patenting, the ownership of patents on the knowledge or social technology embodied in the production process (Delgado Wise, 2015; Delgado Wise and Chávez, 2016; Míguez, 2013).

This capitalist development process over time has resulted in the construction of an 'innovation system'[6] within a knowledge-based global economy—what could be conceived of as an *Imperial Innovation System*, a system that has five characteristic features.

1. *The increasing internationalisation and fragmentation of research and development activities* by means of the organisation and promotion of collective forms innovation such as a crowd-sourcing economy through what can be viewed as *open innovation*. In contrast to the traditional innovation processes that normally take place 'behind closed doors' in Research & Development departments internal to large multinational corporations, this trend includes the opening up and spatial redistribution of knowledge-intensive activities with the participation of external partners, activities such as *start-ups* that operate as privileged cells of the new innovation architecture and the supply of risk capital, head-hunters, firms of lawyers, subcontractors, universities, research institutions, etc., to create complex 'ecosystems' of innovation (Chesbrough, 2008).

This new modality of organising this *general intellect* has given rise to a permanent configuration and reconfiguration of innovation networks that interact within an institutional complex commanded by the large multinational corporations and the imperial state and that, in the particular case of Silicon Valley, transcends with increasing complexity and dynamism at compulsive rhythms hitherto available forms of technological transformation.

2. *The creation of scientific cities*—such as Silicon Valley in the US and the new 'Silicon Valleys' established in recent years in peripheral areas or emerging

regions, principally in Asia, where collective synergies are created to accelerate innovation processes. As conceptualised by Annalee Saxenian (2002, 2006), this development embodies a new geo-referenced paradigm of innovation based on flexibility, decentralisation and the incorporation of new stakeholders that simultaneously interact in local and transnational spaces. Silicon Valley stands as the central pivot of a new global innovation system surrounded by a constellation of scientific maquilladoras that are allocated to peripheral spaces.

3. *The development of new methods of controlling Research & Development agendas* (through venture capital, partnerships and subcontracting, among others) and appropriating the products of scientific endeavours through the *acquisition of patents* by large multinational corporations. Indeed, the rhythm of patenting has increased exponentially over the last two decades. Between 1991 and 2011 an overflowing dynamic of patenting has taken place in the US, where more patents were registered than in 200 years of previous history.

4. *A rapidly expanding highly-skilled workforce*—particularly in the areas of science and engineering *formed in the global south* is being tapped by multinationals for Research & Development in countries on the periphery of the system through recruitment via partnerships, outsourcing and offshoring (Batelle, 2012). In fact, this spatial restructuring of R&D has crystallised into a new geography of innovation, in which R&D—following the pattern of industrial production— is shifting towards peripheral economies. In fact, this trend can be conceived of as a higher stage in the development of the global networks of monopoly capital, as the New International Division of Labour moves up the value-added chain to R&D, and Monopoly Capital moves to capture the productivity gains and knowledge of a highly skilled workforce in the global south (Arocena and Sutz, 2005). This trend can be traced out in different sectors of the global economy, including agriculture—biotechnology and biohegemony in transgenic crops, and the appropriation of indigenous knowledge regarding seed technology (Gutiérrez Escobar and Fitting, 2016; Lapegna and Otero, 2016; Motta, 2016).

And, most importantly,

5. *the creation of an* ad hoc *institutional framework* aimed at the concentration and appropriation of products created by the *general intellect* through *patents*, embodied in the World Intellectual Property Organization (WIPO) and the World Trade Organization (WTO) (Delgado and Chávez, 2016). Since the late 1980s, a trend towards ad hoc legislation has been initiated in the US, in line with the strategic interests of large multinational corporations regarding intellectual property rights (Messitte, 2012). Through regulations promoted by the WTO this legislation has broadly expanded. Through negotiations for the signing and implementation of the Free Trade Agreements, these negotiations have been carried out through the Office of the US's Trade Representative, who in turn has protected and represented the interests of industries that are intensive in the use of intellectual property. Because of its multilateral nature, intellectual property disputes within the WTO tend to become more complex, so the US strategy also includes bilateral FTA negotiations as a far-reaching means to control markets and increase corporate profits. The regulations established by

the Patent Cooperation Treaty—modified in 1984 and 2001—in the framework of WIPO–WTO have contributed significantly to fostering this trend.

All of this has led to the unprecedented appropriation of knowledge, as intangible common goods, giving rise to an abundant expansion, concentration and private appropriation of the products of *general intellect*, which—far from promoting a progressive path to development in productive forces—has inaugurated a regressive phase in the advancement and application of knowledge. Moreover, sometimes patents are acquired by monopoly capital to prevent or postpone its application with the aim of controlling and regulating markets, giving rise to what Guillermo Foladori (2014) conceives of as 'fictitious science' given its speculative character—echoing the notion of fictitious capital coined by Marx.

It is worth adding that in line with the nature and characteristics of the Imperial Innovation System described above, the US features as the world's leading innovation capitalist power, accounting for 28 per cent of all patent applications through the WIPO system from 1996 to 2010. Taking the total number of OECD countries together (excluding Mexico, Chile and Turkey), they account for 90 per cent of global patent applications.

Agribusiness in the imperialist innovation agenda

Over the last two and a half decades, multinational corporations in the agricultural sector (food and farming) have achieved impressive levels of concentration and centralisation worldwide. This process has been led by the so-called *big six*: Monsanto, Dow, BASF, Bayer, Syngenta and DuPont. The principal areas of investment by these corporations have been: pesticides, seeds, and biotechnology.[7]

Rather than competing among themselves the *big six* engage in 'cooperative strategies and collusive practices between the few major competitors, notably through the establishment of elaborate cross-licensing structures' (Pesticide Action Network, 2011). Moreover, '[c]ooperative strategies include licensing, cross-licensing agreements, subcontracting, and other contractual structures that frame patterns of inter-company alliances'. These are, the authors point out, current practices in agricultural biotechnology. Indeed, 'because of the cumulative nature of the genetics and biotechnologies embodied in transgenic varieties, the next innovation is likely to "stack" traits upon those developed in the previous innovation'.

To avoid encroaching upon each other's patent entitlements, companies are obliged to enter into licensing and cross-licensing deals. All the leading firms in agricultural biotechnology (including Monsanto) are themselves licensed under various patents, which expire from time to time, covering many products, processes, and product uses. Under a cross-licensing agreement, two parties grant a license to each other for the exploitation of the subject matter claimed in patents. In some cases, cross-licensing is the mutual sharing of patents between companies without even payment of royalties if both patent portfolios are deemed equal in value (UNCTAD, 2006: 33–34).

The big six also promote: '[v]ertical integration upward along the food chain, with the establishment of food chain clusters that combine agricultural inputs with the grain handlers' extensive processing and marketing facilities' (Pesticide Action Network, 2011).

The unprecedented power secured by the *big six* allow them to: (i) hegemonise the agricultural research agenda; (ii) appropriate the fruits of technological advance and production knowledge in the agricultural sector; (iii) exercise command over trade agreements and agricultural policies; (iv) position their technologies as the 'science-based' 'solution' for increasing crop yields, feed the hungry and 'save the planet'; (v) extend the value chain of corporate capital and corporate control over land, agricultural production and territories; (vi) avoid 'democratic' and regulatory controls over their activities and the accumulation process; (vii) undercut the counterhegemonic and anti-imperialist agenda and struggle for food sovereignty and agroecology advanced by Via Campesina and other forces of resistance in the agricultural sector; and (viii) subvert any possibility of promoting competitive markets in line with the hidden neoliberal agenda.

The monopolistic power exerted by the large multinational corporations in the agricultural sector has far-reaching implications regarding 'the speed of concentration in the agricultural input sector, associated with the privatisation and patenting of biological resources, raises serious competition issues. Further, it raises concerns over social justice and food security' (UNCTAD, 2006: 38). We might add here the fundamental concern for environmental justice and food sovereignty, not to mention territorial rights and the private appropriation of nature, technological innovations and the 'wealth of nature' or the 'global commons' (Barkin, Fuente and Rosas, 2009; De Castro et al., 2016; Porto Goncalves and Leff, 2015; Leguizamón, 2016; Rosset, 2011).

According to PCT–WIPO statistics in 2015–2016, the number of patent applications by Dow, Bayer, Dupont, BASF, Monsanto and Syngenta were: 804, 761, 758, 714, 290 and 108, respectively. This accounted for 22 per cent of the total PCT–WIPO patent applications in this period (Miguelez and Fink, 2012).

There are many examples of investments by venture capital groups of Monsanto, Dupont, Dow and Bayer in cutting-edge start-ups in Silicon Valley. Below are a few quotes that show the increasing connection of these corporations to the Silicon Valley innovation ecosystem.

> Based in San Francisco, Monsanto's venture capital group invests in cutting-edge Silicon Valley start-ups and sometimes acquires them … Acquired in 2014 by Climate Corp., the technology subsidiary of Monsanto, 640 Labs soon will be doing business in Europe—an ancillary result of Climate's recent acquisition of VitalFields, an Estonia-based software company.
>
> (www.chicagotribune.com/business/ct-monsanto-growth-ventures-1209-biz-20161209-story.html)

> The Palo Alto R&D Center hosts nearly 200 scientists and engineers conducting enzyme research in biochemistry, molecular biology, protein

chemistry, and chemical engineering as well as senior executives, business and regulatory leaders, and intellectual property team members … It is a central site for protein engineering enzyme production systems and pathway engineering for chemicals, and home to applications teams in grain processing, biomass conversion, fabric and household care, and textiles processing.

(www.dupont.com/corporate-functions/our-approach/innovation-excell
http://fortune.com/2015/07/15/dow-chief-chemical-science/ence/science/
dupont-research-development-centers-worldwide/palo-alto-
california-dupont-research-development-center.html)

The Bayer LifeScience iHUB in Silicon Valley is one of several initiatives in order to make sure Bayer leverages digital technologies for its Life-Science businesses. Digital technologies are very important to the future success of Bayer. Bayer is therefore building up competencies in digital technologies, especially with external partners https://stanford.applysci.com/sponsor/bayer/.

(Dow Chemicals is 'catching up to Silicon Valley' http://fortune.com/2015/07/15/dow-chief-chemical-science/)

These quotes, and our analysis as to how big capital in the agricultural sector features in a trend towards the concentration of the means of production and the private appropriation of the 'wealth of nature' as well as indigenous knowledge, raise a number of questions for closer study and further research, some of which we address below. But one tentative conclusion that can be drawn from this glimpse into these development dynamics is that in many ways the agricultural sector is at the forefront of the contradictions that characterise innovation (and the control and appropriation of knowledge) in the neoliberal era of generalised monopolies.

The new political economy of agriculture: extractive capital and agroextraction

Silicon Valley is a visible representation of the concentration and centralisation of human capital (scientific knowledge applied to production) in the form of what we term an imperial innovation system, and the appropriation of production-based technologies and patents. However, Silicon Valley and the innovation system of communications and information technologies is not the only centre of human capital formation and scientific knowledge applied to production. As noted above, the cluster of firms that form the 'big six' in the agricultural sector constitutes another centre of human capital production, formed in a dynamic process of mergers and acquisitions that characterised the development process in the 1990s and the first decade of the new millennium (UNDP, 2009).

This monopoly capital dynamic—the concentration and centralisation of capital—is particularly evident in the international trade in grains. But it is also a dominant feature of what might be described as the new political economy of agriculture based on the expansion and advance of resource-seeking, or extractive, capital. This relates in particular to the formation and expansion of the soy economy in the south-west of Brazil and the north of Argentina, as well as more recently in Bolivia, Paraguay and Uruguay—the so-called Soya Republic (Leguizamón, 2016; McKay and Colque, 2016; Ezquerro-Cañete, 2016).

The formation of this economy on the frontier of extractive capital in South America reflects a pronounced trend towards the expanded flow of resource-seeking foreign investments in the acquisition of land and access to resources in high demand on the world market. This dynamic—the new geoeconomics of capital in the region[8]—is also reflected in a trend towards land-grabbing as a means of gaining direct access to raw materials to supply the market for both agro-food products and biofuels for the production of oil in the food industry, feedstock for animals, and a renewable source of energy (Borras and Franco, 2012). In Latin America this dynamic, and an associated concentration and centralisation of capital, is particularly evident in the formation of a soy complex in Argentina, Brazil, Bolivia, Paraguay and Uruguay. First, large tracts of arable land have come under ownership of firms in the agroextraction sector and used to either supply the market for feedstock and edible oil or converted from the production of food to supplying the demand for energy in the form of biomass and other biofuels. On average since around 2008 an additional two million hectares of land in the southern cone, mostly in central-west Brazil and North Argentina but also in Bolivia and Paraguay, is being brought into production each year.

Already in 2008 Brazil and Argentina respectively had 21.3 million and 16.4 million hectares of land under soya cultivation—representing 38.8 percent of the total global area under soya cultivation and for the production of soybean oil, and 46 percent of total global soya production (FAO, 2010, based on FAOSTAT data). In recent years other countries in the subregion have also significantly increased their production capacity, driven by the global demand for soybean oil (for use in the food sector), soybean meal (mainly as a source of animal feed protein), but increasingly as feedstock for the production of bio-diesel and first-generation biofuels (Schoneveld, 2010). Brazil, in this context, exports most of its soybean in unprocessed seed form while Argentina processes more than 80 per cent of soybean seeds domestically into meal and oil. Currently approximately 16 per cent of total soybeans harvested in Brazil is used for energy purposes, while approximately 3.5 per cent of the soybean harvest is used to produce biodiesel—most of it exported (Van Gelder and Dros, 2002).

The production for export of agrofuels, like international trade in grains and foreign investments in land and agroextraction, is highly concentrated and dominated by a small cluster of firms that have acquired an oligopoly in the marketing and sale of their production. This cluster of monopoly or oligopoly capital in the sector of agroextraction intersects with the Big Six in Cargill, the largest privately owned corporation in the US, but it also includes other firms, and various clusters of capital, that have combined in a process of mergers and acquisitions or more flexible arrangements such as partnerships, contracts or joint ventures, to form a 'real cluster of firms' that could monopolise the global trade in grains and soy-based biofuels. Together, this 'real cluster of firms'—a cartel in the judgement of economists at the UNDP (2007/08)—together control 52 per cent of the global trade in staple grains, cereals and oilseed. And more importantly, they have a commanding control of seed patents and agricultural production technologies.

This cartel, known as ABCD (Bunge, Cargill ...),[9] currently finances from 60 to 85 per cent of soybean producers in Brazil, offering farmers credit as well as a technological package that effectively converts them into their agents in the new agricultural economy formed by companies that effectively control conditions for production in the Southern cone territory.

Apart from its role as a supplier of surplus labour and cheap wage goods to hold down the cost of labour in the industrial sector the important role of agriculture in the capitalist development process had been largely overlooked for the five decades prior to the current turn to—or return towards—agroextraction and a policy of primary commodity exports.[10] In this context, instead of capitalising on the region's relatively abundant resource endowment and resultant comparative advantage, policymakers used the agricultural sector as a cash cow to be milked in order to subsidise relatively more inefficient firms in the industrial sector.

There is nothing novel or new about this development; it is well known and has been extensively studied and theorised over the years. Policymakers in this context pursued a strategy of export-led development—exporting primary products—thereby sustaining their assigned or self-assumed role as suppliers to industrial countries. The negative consequences of this strategy have been extensively theorised and analysed, most often from a dependency theory perspective. But in the new millennium—in conditions of the new geoeconomics of capital, i.e. the phenomenon of large-scale foreign investments in land and resources)—the role of agriculture for development has significantly changed. For one thing, many multinational corporations in the agroextraction sector, to guarantee a supply of raw materials and resources, shifted away from direct investments in the acquisition of assets to contract farming (UNCTAD, 2009: 110). For another, with the growing demand for biofuels and the resulting conversion of land from the production of food to energy, the much debated built-in barriers to the expansion of capital into the agricultural sector have been pushed back within the limits of environmental degradation in the agricultural sector,[11] leading to the increased subsumption of agricultural labour as well as another cycle in the expulsion of the direct producers to fuel the growth of a global reserve army of surplus labour and a global labour force available to monopoly capital for its expansion into its various redoubts of industrial capital, located mostly in the heartland of the world system. It would seem that here at least agriculture has been pushed back towards its traditional role as a supplier of surplus labour to industrial or monopoly capital.

Until the mid-1990s the dominant strategy of development economists at the World Bank and other agencies in the UN system was to encourage the masses of dispossessed or 'rural landless workers'—the 'rural poor' in the lexicon of World Bank economists—to abandon agriculture and their rural communities and to take the development pathway out of rural poverty, namely migration and labour (World Bank, 2008). However, by the mid-1990s, the evident absence of an industrialisation process and a functioning labour market—and the inability of the urban economy to absorb this excess supply of surplus agricultural labour—this development strategy was turned around in the direction of slowing down the regular outflow of rural migrant labour.

At issue in this new strategy was the problem of reducing the pressures on both governments and the private sector to absorb the excess supply of surplus rural labour, and also what sociologists at the time described as 'the new rural-ity', namely the response of the rural poor to the forces of social change and capitalist development in the form of a strategy of diversifying their sources of household income (Kay, 2008). Lula's new social policy of conditional cash transfers to the poor played into this strategy.

However, the expansion of both market-seeking and resource-seeking extractive capital in the agricultural sector, and the rapid growth of both agroextraction and agribusiness within the circuits and supply chains of monopoly capital, changed conditions regarding the international and regional political economy of agriculture. As noted by UNCTAD in its 2009 report on world investments—with reference to these changed conditions—'[a]fter a long period of decline in ... [the] participation [of multinational corporations] in agricultural production, a resurgence may ... be under way' (UNCTAD, 2009: 110).

As for the consequences of this resurgence, by a number of accounts they include:

1. the expansion and rapid advance of capital on the extractive frontier;
2. the emergence of new modalities for the expansion of capital into the agricultural sector, including landgrabbing, agroextraction, investment by private equity funds, the formation of wholly owned affiliates, the institution of joint ventures and management contracts, as well as the replacement of foreign direct investments with contract farming;
3. a process of cross-border mergers and acquisitions, leading to vertical integration as well as the concentration of capital in both agriculture and associated industries such as food processing (Rastoin, 2008);
4. a major rise of investments in agriculture and related activities, particularly food processing, linked to the inflow of resource-seeking or extractive capital, or agroextraction (UNCTAD, 2009: 113);
5. a technological restructuring of agricultural production, particularly as regards the dynamics of R&D and intellectual property rights and the patenting of technological innovations; and
6. control of the new means of production, based on use of genetically modified crops, agrochemicals and new sowing techniques has empowered multinational chemical and trading companies and other agribusinesses, and their vertical integration along the production chain are generating a commanding production structure (Turzi, 2007).

7. companies in the agroextractive sector have used their scientific and technological superiority to advance the sale of their agrochemical products, integrating with traders and processors and leveraging scale advantages to establish dominant buying positions by drawing on their financial strength (Turzi, 2011);
8. national borders on the extractive frontier are losing ground to a corporate-driven model of territorial organisation, giving rise to new geopolitical fault lines and, in the case of Argentina, Bolivia, Brazil, Uruguay and Paraguay, the formation of their combined geoeconomic space as a single unified Soybean Republic (Turzi, 2011); and
9. the expansion of corporate capital into the agricultural sector is reducing the land available for food production, increasing pressures on small-scale scale peasant production and family farming, including an enclosure of the commons,[12] with a consequent expulsion of poor peasants from agriculture and their rural communities on the extractive frontier.

In addition to these developments, renewal of a stalled rural exodus has fuelled the growth of a global workforce and the formation of an industrial reserve army, and the emergence of new dynamic forces of resistance and alternative development (Zibechi, 2007, 2015).

The dynamics of the resistance: the Zapatista initiative

At the end of the twentieth century, in conditions of momentous change in both the global economy and domestic politics (a reconfiguration of economic power with the ascension of China, a seatide of regime change leading to a policy of 'inclusionary state activism') Latin America became fertile ground for the construction of alternative forms and models of development, and for some academics and activists a new dawning of anti-systemic movements at the global level. Among the main characteristics of these movements,[13] which can be traced back to the Zapatista uprising on 1 January 1994,[14] are a concern for territorial rights and integrity, radical autonomy (material and political sovereignty), direct or participatory democracy, the reaffirmation of traditional culture and identity, the creation of their own education and health systems, the education and formation of their own intellectuals, gender equality, collective and horizontal organisation of work and the drive for an alternative form of development (or an alternative to development) based on relations of social solidarity and harmony with nature (Acosta, 2012; Gudynas, 2013ab; Zibechi, 2007, 2015).

The Zapatista movement, formed in the mountains of the southeast of Mexico in conditions of the turn of many governments in the region towards free market capitalism, has played a leading role in this new period of anti-systemic resistance and rebellion. In fact, the Zapatistas have radically redefined the traditional concept of resistance (passive and reactive), changing 'the resistance struggle into a transformative struggle' capable of building anew a society free of exploitation, deprivation, oppression and repression in the reclaimed geographic space under its control. But this not only requires the creation of islands or local spaces of popular resistance, but rather archipelagos (see the Sixth Declaration of the Lacandon Jungle) that challenge the capitalist system with an emancipatory vision and a liberating and revolutionary praxis.

To transcend or move beyond capitalism—Marx cautioned us in *Capital* (Marx, 1975)—not only implies the transformation of the existing social relations of production, ending all kinds of exploitation of 'man by man'; it also implies the need to create a new mode of production in accordance with new social relations. Just as capitalism in its early stages inherited a technical mode of production from feudalism and transformed it according to its own norms and logic, moving from humanity's pre-history—in reference to all forms of social organisation divided into classes—to history, i.e. towards a society without classes, necessarily requires moving from the capitalist technical mode of production to one that transcends it. This need becomes even more imperative in the current phase of capitalist development, characterised by the dominance of monopoly capital, which, in its insatiable pursuit of profit and the appropriation of the wealth of nations turns the progressive character that Marx attributed to the capitalist development of the forces of production on its head.

From this emancipatory and revolutionary perspective, Zapatismo, like other antisystemic social movements that are oriented towards an alternative future, an alternative to 'development' as we have come to know it, i.e. as capitalist development,[15] proposes to foster development of the productive forces in a way that privileges their use value and that is based on the fundamental principles of social solidarity and in harmony with nature. As the Zapatistas see it, education is a fundamental part of this process of constructing a social and solidarity economy,[16] imbuing it with the 'most realistic and true curriculum, that conveys what the people truly need for their liberation' and an eye toward 'fostering and empowering scientific consciousness and critical thinking, as intellectual weapons of the resistance and the struggle of ... communities in search of a new world beyond capitalism, a world that 'encompasses many worlds' (Aguirre Rojas, 2008: 189).

In this way, the Zapatista rebellion can be seen—or is seen by some (e.g. Burbach, 1994)—'as the first postmodern movement in history'. As Villoro (2016: 18), a Mexican chronicler of the widespread albeit largely subterranean popular resistance to capitalism in its current form, puts it:

> Zapatismo is contemporary in the way in which it has raised a social opposition to that which has lasted far too long. It does not seek to roll back the wheel of the days travelled toward some lost arcadia, that nostalgic moment of creation, nor derail the train of progress. It seeks something more concrete and ambitious: a new age.

In this connection, with a view not so much to mobilise the forces of resistance against capitalism and extractivism but to advance an effective knowledge-based dialogue with representatives of the 'hard sciences', the Zapatistas in

December 2016 organised a national 'encounter' in San Cristóbal de las Casas, Chiapas. In the context of this encounter with opposing viewpoints—'The Zapatistas and the *ConCiencias* for Humanity'[17]—spokesperson Subcomandante Insurgente Galeano made the following comment:

> … if the children that 25–30 years ago were born during the preparation for the uprising and those that were born 15–20 years ago were born in resistance and rebellion; those born in the last 10–15 years were born in a process of consolidated autonomy, with new characteristics, among which is the need for Science.
>
> (Subcomandante Insurgente Galeano, 2016)

This comment reveals the deep meaning of the Zapatista initiative: to establish a bridge between a world in resistance where non-capitalist social relations have been incubated, with those who personify the advances achieved by knowledge under capitalist modernity in hopes of opening routes toward an alternative path of the development of knowledge for transformative change. And although this is only a first tentative step toward transforming the technical mode of capitalist production, and reorienting toward an *alternative modernity*, it is, nevertheless, an effort with enormous potential to advance emerging anti-systemic social movements seeking a world beyond capitalism and extractivism, reaffirming for them the strategic as well as symbolic importance of Zapatismo.

Conclusion

The installation in the 1980s of what was then a 'new world order' ushered in and brought about a new phase in the capitalist development of the forces of production described by David Harvey as a 'brief history of neoliberalism'. As in all such transitions this brief 30-year interlude in the evolution of capitalism resulted in a major restructuring of the system, releasing and giving rise to dynamic forces of change at the level of both production and politics. Systemwide, these forces of change included: (i) an expansion of productive capital in the form of foreign direct investment freed from regulatory constraint; (ii) globalisation in the form of national economies being integrated into the world capitalist system under the new rules of engagement; (iii) the deregulation of markets and the liberalisation of both international trade and the flow of productive capital;[18] (iv) a shift in the sectoral distribution of productive capital flows, marked by a relatively greater expansion of 'extractive' or 'resource-seeking' investment capital in the search of opportunities for superprofits[19] provided by the market demand for natural resources and primary commodities; (v) the financialisation[20] of the economy, leading to an expansion of capital markets relative to product markets and the hegemony of financial capital, as well as a growing disconnect between the economy based on capital markets and the real economy based on production, and a steady increase in the systemic propensity to towards crisis; and (vi) increased propensity towards the concentration and centralisation of capital, leading to growth of monopoly power over product markets as well as the hegemony of financial capital.

As for the Latin American periphery of the system where the neoliberal policy agenda was implemented more forcefully than elsewhere, these forces of change took form as (i) a dramatic increase in the flow of extractive, or resource-seeking, capital, and associated 'developments' that include a turn of some governments (predominantly in South America) towards an extractivist strategy of national development, a strategy that combines a 'post-neoliberal form of 'inclusionary state activism' with a strategy of primary commodity exports (Veltmeyer, 2013); (ii) the formation of a large rural semiproletariat of landless or near-landless 'peasants' or rural workers, many of whom are compelled to take the 'development pathway' out of rural poverty, namely labour and migration (Delgado Wise and Veltmeyer, 2016); an expansion of agroextraction as a strategy deployed by Capital under conditions of 'large-scale foreign investments in land', the monopoly power of corporate agribusiness, a renewed dependency (the 'new dependency') of the state and local governments on FDI, with an associated coincidence of economic interests (superprofits for Capital, resource rents and windfall revenues for the state);[21] (iii) widespread implementation of a neoliberal policy regime based on a policy of privatisation and actions designed or with the effect of restricting access to the 'global commons' as well as means of production and a livelihood based on agriculture; and (iv) widespread rejection in the popular sector of the neoliberal policy agenda, as well as active resistance in the form of anti-systemic social movements to the advances of both corporate or monopoly capital and extractive capital.

These developments have been widely studied and are part of an ongoing debate. However, although they necessitate closer study this chapter has a more limited concern with two particular issues of agrarian political economy. One is the role of technological innovation in the capitalist development process, an exploration of the restructuration dynamics associated with what we describe as the 'imperial system of innovation'. This concept and theme are characterised by an absence in contemporary studies of imperialism, hence our aim to highlight and draw attention to them and to explain the associated dynamics. The second concern of the chapter is to advance the concept of agroextraction as a new way of addressing the agrarian question today. Our conclusion is that both the concept of an imperial innovation system and the concept of agroextractivism are keys to an understanding of the contemporary dynamics of capitalism in the Latin American context.

Notes

1 Within a Marxist framework imperialism is generally viewed either as Lenin did, as a phase in the evolution of capitalism, or as Petras and Veltmeyer (2014) do, as the exercise of state power in support of capital, an institutional mechanism to secure the advance and hegemony of capital. But in this chapter 'imperialism' is conceived as an interconnected set of mechanisms that are designed and work to advance the

accumulation process and to secure the hegemony of capital over the whole system. In this context both state power and economic power, i.e. the state system and the multinational corporations that dominate the global economy, are viewed as agencies of imperialism.

2 Extractivism, as the extraction of natural resource wealth and the export of this wealth in primary commodity form, has been extensively studied in recent years with reference to and in the context of two main sectors—the production of fossil fuels for energy (oil and gas) and industrial minerals and metals. However, extractive capital also operates in the agricultural sector—what we might term 'agroextraction' or agro-extractivism (see Chapter 2). On the economic and policy dynamics of agroextraction see Petras and Veltmeyer (2014: Chapter 3). The focus and concern of this chapter is with these dynamics, which are not necessarily the same as extractivisms in other sectors.

3 We focus on Silicon Valley because it is where the largest investment in risk capital in the world is made. In addition, the US has the world's largest patent registry, concentrating most of the world patents as well as those that are arguably the most strategically important regarding capitalist development. Six of the ten most important innovative companies in the world are US-based, as are 16 of the top 25 (www.forbes.com/innovative-companies/list/#tab:rank).

4 'Human capital' in this context refers to the accumulation of scientific knowledge or 'social technology' (Patel, 1993) when used as a productive resource to expand the forces of production and generate what Adam Smith (and Marx, for that matter) termed the 'wealth of nations'. In this conception 'human capital' (the 'general intellect' as Marx conceived of it) is one of four basic forms of wealth-generating capital, the others being 'financial' (what Marx viewed as the money form of capital), 'natural' (the endowment of nature) and 'manufactured' (infrastructure, physical technology, industrial plant and equipment, etc.). On the 'development' dimensions of these different forms of 'capital' see UNU-IHDP and UNEP (2012).

5 Until recently, development economists always analysed the wealth of nations, and the level of economic development, in terms not of wealth but the total income generated in the production process (annual increments in the GDP). But in 2012 a consortium of UN agencies published the first real study of the 'wealth of nations'—wealth, or capital, measured along four dimensions: *financial*; *physical*; *natural* (capital embodied in sub-soil resources such as minerals and metals, fossil fuels and other sources of energy, agro-food/forest products, etc.); and *human* (capital in the form of knowledge and skills). In the comparative analysis of the wealth of nations vis-à-vis the structure of capital reported on in this study it is human capital, knowledge as a productive resource, that has the pride of place—the determinant factor in a society's overall level of economic development within a 'modern knowledge-based' economy (UNU-IHDP and UNEP, 2012).

6 A system of innovation is a 'set of actors, organisations and institutions that interact in the generation, diffusion and use of new and economically useful knowledge in production processes' (Fischer, 2001, cited in Garrido, Martínez, Rendón and Granados, 2016: 3147). In the classical view of the configuration of the system of national innovation devised by the economist John Kenneth Galbraith and developed by the scientist Jorge Sábato, 'there is a series of interactions between the productive sphere, the scientific technological infrastructure and the state that generates a virtuous circle that allows to put science and technology at the service of economic development' (Arocena and Sutz, 2002). The key to this model is the existence of three interrelated vertices (the state as designer and executor of policies, scientific-technological infrastructure as a supplier of innovation and productive sphere as a source of demand for innovation).

7 As for the ETC group '[t]he Industrial Food Chain uses at least 75% of the world's agricultural resources and is a major source of GHG emissions, but provides food to

less than 30% of the world's people' (ETC Group, 2015). Also, '[t]he Chain relies on the $41 billion commercial seed market—55% controlled by three companies (Monsanto, DuPont and Syngenta). Industrial farmers are dependent on GM-targeted pesticides bought from three companies (Syngenta, BASF and Bayer) that control 51% of global sales worth $63 billion' (for 2014 sales figures see ETC Group, 2015). There have been more than 200 takeovers of smaller seed companies since the introduction of GM seeds 20 years ago (*The Economist*, 2015, Electronic edn; see also Howard, 2015: 4). If the unprecedented mega-mergers currently being negotiated are successful, the three surviving giants may monopolise 60% of commercial seeds and 71% of pesticides (IPES-Food, 2017; McDougall, 2015). This will give them still greater control over the combined market for herbicide-tolerant GM plant varieties."

8 On this dynamic—the sectoral distribution of capital inflows in the form of FDI, and pronounced trend (in the 1990s and into the new millennium) towards the inflow of 'resource-seeking' or extractive capita—see Veltmeyer (2013) and Veltmeyer and Petras (2014).

9 Other major players in the expansion of agribusiness into the complex of soyabean production in Latin America include El Tejar, one of several large Argentine agribusiness companies that have moved into Brazil to take advantage of its productive capacity. Other large agroextraction corporations that have moved into the new and expanding frontier of agroextraction include Los Grobo, Cresud, MSU, ADM, Bunge, Dreyfus, Toepfer, NOBLE and China's state corporation COFCO (Van Gelder and Dros, 2002).

10 On this trend towards the (re)primarisation of exports see Cypher (2010).

11 On this dynamic and the associated debates see, inter alia, Boltvinic and Mann (2012, 2016).

12 In considering the 'global commons' a distinction needs to be made between 'land', the struggle for which dominated the rural political landscape throughout the twentieth century and which, according to Walter Barraza, the *camache* (chief) of the Tonokote people of the Santiago del Estero province, Argentina, 'relates to private property' as a 'capitalist concept'), and 'territory', which 'includes … people who live in that place … [with an] obligation to take care of its nature'. He adds that 'we native peoples live in harmony with our animal brothers, plants, water. We are part of the territory, which provides us with everything we need. Cutting forests down is like cutting a limb. They are coming for natural resources, while we live in harmony with those resources' (Pedrosa, 2017).

13 For an analysis of the social and political dynamics of these social movements in the Latin American context see Petras and Veltmeyer (2013). As Petras and Veltmeyer see it, it is the dynamics and activism of these movements, formed by rural landless workers, semiproletarianised 'peasant' farmers and indigenous communities in the countryside on the frontier of extractive capital, to which the widespread rejection of neoliberalism and the neoliberal policy agenda in the region, and the subsequent emergence of a 'progressive cycle' in Latin American politics, can be directly attributed.

14 The EZLN (Zapatista Army of National Liberation) is but one of a number of peasant and indigenous movements formed across Latin America in the 1990s in resistance to the neoliberal policy agenda. On this see Petras and Veltmeyer (2013). However, the Zapatista movement represent the cutting edge of these anti-systemic (anti-neoliberal, anti-capitalist) social movements, the 'first postmodern [peasant] rebellion and social movement' in the history of capitalism (Burbach, 1994).

15 On these other social movements in the Latin American context, particularly as relates to the indigenous post-development notion of *vivir bien* (to live well in social solidarity and harmony with nature) see, inter alia, Acosta (2012), Gudynas (2013ab, 2017), Farah and Vasapollo (2011), and Zibechi (2007, 2015).

16 On the Latin American experience with diverse experiments in the construction of a social and solidarity economy see, inter alia, Barkin and Sánchez (2017), and Vieta (2014).

17 *ConCiencias*—literally, 'WithScience' and a play on the double-meaning of *'conciencia'* (conscious awareness, conscience) in Spanish.

18 Deregulation and the liberalisation of trade and capital flows, as well as privatisation and globalisation, are key features of the 'structural reforms' mandated by the Washington Consensus on the virtues of free market capitalism. On the policy dynamics of this 'structural adjustment program see, inter alia, Petras and Veltmeyer (2001).

19 Superprofits in this context refers to the windfall returns provided by the extraction and the exportation of natural resources in primary commodity form—the appropriation of resource and technology rents as well as surplus value plus resource and technology rents. In some extractive sectors rates of return of 25 to 40 per cent, even 60 per cent, on invested capital are not uncommon (ECLAC, 2012: 71). ECLAC attributes the extraordinary increase in the profits of transnational corporations in Latin America since 2003 to 'a sharp rise in the profitability of (resource-seeking) FDI in the region'. Data on FDI disaggregated by sector shows that investments in the mining and hydrocarbon sectors, particularly in Peru, Chile and Colombia with declared profit rates of 25 per cent. By some accounts (see Blas, 2013) the big commodity trading houses in the agricultural sector enjoyed returns in excess of 50–60 per cent in the mid-2000s and even in the context of a 'global financial crisis' and a downturn in some commodity prices they are still averaging 20–30 per cent, not bad by any business standard.

20 Financialisation is a term sometimes used to describe the development of financial capitalism during the period from 1980 until 2010, in which debt-to-equity ratios increased and financial services accounted for an increasing share of national income relative to other sectors. More generally, it refers to a process whereby financial markets, financial institutions and financiers or financial capitalists gain greater influence over economic policy and economic outcomes.

21 The central focus of this chapter is on what we describe as agroextraction. In other extractive sectors, such as mining for minerals/metals and drilling for oil and gas, the development and political dynamics are not necessarily the same. For example, rather than having to invest in the purchase of land ('landgrabbing', in the discourse of critical agrarian studies) the agents of Capital are generally able to lever the dependence of the state on FDI into concessions and long-term (30-year plus) leases to explore and mine/drill.

References

Acosta, A. (2012). *Buen Vivir. Sumak kawsay. Una oportunidad para imaginar otros mundos*. Quito: AbyaYala.

Aguirre Rojas, C. (2008). *Mandar Obedeciendo. Las lecciones políticas del neozapatismo mexicano*, Mexico: Contrahistorias. La otra mirada de Clío.

Amin, S. (2013). *The Implosion of Capitalism*. London: Pluto Press.

Aroceno, R. and J. Sutz (2002). "Looking at National System of Innovation from the South," *Industry and Innovation*, 7(1): 55–75.

Arocena, R. and J. Sutz. (2005). "Innovation Systems and Developing Countries," *DRUID Working Paper*, No. 02–05. Danish Research Unit for Industrial Dynamics.

Barkin, D., M. Fuente and Rosas, M. (2009). "Tradición e innovación. Aportaciones campesinas en la orientación de la innovación tecnológica para forjar sustentabilidad," *Trayectorias*, 11(29): 39–54.

Barkin, D. and A. Sánchez. (2017). "The22Collective Revolutionary Subject: New Forms of Social Transformation," unedited paper for 'Revolutions: A Conference', Winnipeg, September.

Battelle. (2014). *Global R&D Funding Forecast*. Battelle-R&D, 2013, Accessed on 28 February 2017 at www.battelle.org/docs/tpp/2014_global_rd_funding_forecast.pdf.

Blas, J. (2013). "Commodity Traders Reap $250bn Harvest," *Financial Times*, 14 April.

Boltvinik, J. and S. Archer Mann (Eds) (2016). *Peasant Poverty and Persistence in the Twenty-first Century: Theories, Debates, Realities, and Policies*. London, England: Zed Books.

Borras, S.M. Jr, and J.C. Franco. (2012). "Global Land Grabbing and Trajectories of Agrarian Change: A Preliminary Analysis," *Journal of Agrarian Change* 12(1): 34–59.

Burbach, R. (1994). "Roots of the Postmodern Rebellion in Chiapas," *New Left Review*, 1(205).

Chesbrough, H. (2008). "Open Innovation: A New Paradigm for Understanding Industrial Innovation," pp. 1–14 in H. Chesbrough, W. Vanhaverbeke and J. West (eds), *Open Innovation: Researching a New Paradigm*. Oxford: Oxford University Press.

Cypher, J. (2010). "South America's Primary Commodities Boom: Development Opportunity or Path Dependent Revision?" *Canadian Journal of Development Studies*, 30(3–4): 565–638.

De Castro, F., B. Hogenboom and M. Baud (eds) (2016). *Environmental Governance in Latin America: Conflicts,* Projects *and Possibilities*. London: Palgrave Macmillan.

Delgado Wise, R. (2015). "Unraveling Mexican Highly-Skilled Migration in the Context of Neoliberal Globalization," pp. 201–218 in S. Castles, M. Arias Cubas and D. Ozkul (eds), *Social Transformation and Migration: National and Local Experiences in South Korea, Turkey, Mexico and Australia*. London: Palgrave MacMillan.

Delgado Wise, R. and M. Chávez Elorza (2016). "Patentad, patentad: apuntes sobre la apropiación del trabajo científico por las grandes corporaciones multinacionales," *Observatorio del Desarrollo*, 4(15): 22–30.

ECLAC—Economic Commission for Latin America and the Caribbean. (2012). *Foreign Direct Investment in Latin America and the Caribbean 2012*. Santiago: UN.

ETC Group. (2015). "Breaking Bad: Big Ag Mega-Mergers in Play, Dow + DuPont in the Pocket? Next: Demonsanto?" *Communiqué* 115, December. www.etcgroup.org/files/files/etc-whowillfeedus-english-webshare.pdf.

Ezquerro-Cañete, A. (2016). "Poisoned, Dispossessed and Excluded: A Critique of the Neoliberal Soy Regime in Paraguay," *Journal of Agrarian Change*, 16(4): 702–710.

FAO—Food and Agricultural Organization of the United Nations (2011). *Land Tenure and International Investments in Agriculture*. Rome: FAO.

Farah, I. and L. Vasapollo (eds) (2011). *Vivir bien: Paradigma no capitalista?* La Paz: CIDES-UMSA.

Foladori, G. (2014). "Ciencia ficticia," *Estudios Críticos del Desarrollo*, IV (7): 41–66.

Garrido Ruiano, M.F., J.C. Martinez Medrano, R. Rendón Medel and R.E. Granados Carvajal. (2016). "Los sistemas de innovación y su impacto en el desarrollo territorial" (Innovations Systems and their Impact on Regional Development), *Revista Mexicana de Ciencias Agrícolas*, No. 15, 30 June–13 August.

Gudynas, E. (2013a). "Postextractivismo y alternativas al desarrollo desde la sociedad civil," pp. 189–224 in *Alternativas al capitalismo. Colonialismo del Siglo XXI*. Quito: Ediciones Abya Yala.

Gudynas, E. (2013b). "Debates on Development and its Alternatives in Latin America: a Brief Heterodox Guide," in M. Lang, L. Fernando and N. Buxton (eds), *Beyond Development: Alternative Visions from Latin America*. Amsterdam: Transnational institute.

Gudynas, E. (2017). "Postdevelopment as Critique and Alternative," in H. Veltmeyer and P. Bowles (eds) *The Essential Critical Development Studies Guide*. London: Routledge.

Gutiérrez Escobar, L. and E. Fitting (2016). "Red de Semillas Libres: crítica a la biohegemonía en Colombia." *Estudios Críticos del Desarrollo*, VI (11): 85–106.

Harvey, D. (2005). *A Brief History of Neoliberalism*. Oxford: Oxford University Press.

Harvey, D. (2014). *Diecisiete Contradicciones y el Fin del Capitalismo*. Quito: IAEN-Instituto de Altos Estudios Nacionales del Ecuador.

Howard, P. (2015). "Intellectual Property and Consolidation in the Seed Industry." *Crop Science*, Vol. 55, November–December.

IPES-Food. (2017). "Too Big to Feed: Concentration in the Agri-food Industry." International Panel of Experts on Sustainable Food Systems, Thematic Report 3. http://businessdocbox.com/Agriculture/68318041-Who-will-feed-us-the-industrial-food-chain-vs-the-peasant-food-web-3-rd-edition.html.

Kay, C. (2008). "Reflections on Latin American Rural Studies in the Neoliberal Globalization Period: A New Rurality?" *Development and Change*, 39(6): 915–943.

Lapegna, P. and G. Otero. (2016). "Cultivos transgénicos en América Latina: expropiación, valor negativo y Estado," *Estudios Críticos del Desarrollo*, VI(11): 19–44.

Leguizamón, A. (2016). "Disappearing Nature? Agribusiness, Biotechnology and Distance in Argentine Soybean Production," *The Journal of Peasant Studies*, 43(2): 1–18.

Marx, K. (1975 [1866]). *El Capital*, Tomo I, vol. 2, Mexico: Siglo XXI.

Marx, K. (1977 [1859]). *A Contribution to the Critique of Political Economy*. Moscow: Progress Publishers.

Marx, K. (1981 [1863–1883]). *Capital. A Critique of Political Economy*, London: Penguin books.

McDougall, P. (2015). "Top 20 Global Agrochem Firms: Growth Slowing Down." news agropages.com. 30 October.

McKay, B. and G. Colque (2016). "Bolivia's Soy Complex: The Development of 'Productive Exclusion'," *Journal of Peasant Studies*, 43(2): 583–610.

McKinsey Global Institute (2016). "The US Economy: An Agenda for Inclusive Growth," *Briefing Paper*, November. See also: http://economipedia.com/ranking/empresas-mas-grandes-del-mundo-2015.html.

Messitte, P. (2012). "Desarrollo del derecho de patentes estadounidense en el siglo XXI. Implicaciones para la industria farmacéutica," pp. 179–200 in A. Oropeza and V.M. Guízar López (eds), *Los retos de la industria farmacéutica en el siglo XXI. Una visión comparada sobre su régimen de propiedad intelectual*, UNAM-Cofep.

Miguelez, E. and C. Fink. (2012). "Measuring the International Mobility of Inventors: A New Database," *WIPO Economic Research Working Paper*, No. 8e, WIPO. Available in www.wipo.int/pct/en/pct_contracting_states.html.

Míguez, P. (2013). "Del General Intellect a las tesis del "capitalismo cognitivo": aportes para el estudio del capitalismo del siglo XXI", *Bajo el Volcán*, 13(21): 27–57.

Motta, R. (2016). "Capitalismo global y Estado nacional en las luchas de los cultivos transgénicos en Brasil," *Estudios Críticos del Desarrollo*, VI(11): 65–84.

PAN—Pesticide Action Network (2011). *Persistent Poisons*. www.panna.org/category/issues/persistent-poisons?page=1

Patel, Surendra. (1993). *Technological Transformation in the Third World*. Helsinki: World Institute for Development Economics Research, Vol. IV.

Pedrosa, M. (2017). "Argentina: Native Communities Face Eviction, Death if Protective Law Is Not Renewed by Congress," *Tiempo Argentino/Resumen Latinoamericano/*8 September.

Petras, J. and H. Veltmeyer. (2001). *Globalization Unmasked*. London: Zed Books.

Petras, J. and H. Veltmeyer. (2013). *Social Movements in Latin America: Neoliberalism and Popular Resistance*. Basingstoke UK: Palgrave Macmillan.

Petras, J. and H. Veltmeyer. (2014). *Extractivist Imperialism in the Americas*. Leiden: Brill Books.

Porto Goncalves, C.W. and E. Leff. (2015). "Political Ecology in Latin America: The Social Re-Appropriation of Nature, the Reinvention of Territories and the Construction of an Environmental Rationality," *Desenvolvimento e Meio Amiente*, 35: 65–88. Available at: http://revistas.ufpr.br/made/article/viewFile/43543/27087.

Rastoin, J-L. (2008). "Les multinationales dans le système alimentaire," *Projet Revue de Ceras*, 307: 61–69.

Rodriguez, F. (2008). "El sistema de patentes e el desarrollo tecnológico: algunas consideraciones en el marco d ela libre competencia," *Propiedad Intelectual*, 7(11): 87–109.

Rosset, P. (2011). "Food Sovereignty and Alternative Paradigms to Confront Land Grabbing and the Food and Climate Crises," *Development*, 54(1): 21–30.

Saxenian, A.L. (2002). *Local and Global Networks of Immigrant Professionals in Silicon Valley*. San Francisco, CA: Public Policy Institute of California.

Saxenian, A.L. (2006). *The New Argonauts: Regional Advantage in a Global Economy*. Boston, MA: Harvard University Press.

Schoneveld, G. (2010). "Potential Land Use Competition from First-Generation Biofuel Expansion in Developing Countries," *Occasional paper 58*. CIFOR. Bogor, Indonesia.

Subcomandante Insurgente Galeano. (2016). "Las Artes y las Ciencias en la historia del (neo) Zapatismo," *Enlace Zapatista*, consulted 28 February 2017 at http://enlacezapatista. ezln.org.mx/2016/12/28/las-artes-y-las-ciencias-en-la-historia-del-neo-zapatismo/.

The Economist. (2015). "Agricultural suppliers—Controversial hybrids." 27 August.

Turzi, M. (2007). *The Political Economy of Agricultural Booms: Managing Soybean Production in Argentina, Brazil and Paraguay*. Cham, Switzerland: Palgrave Macmillan/ Springer International.

Turzi, M. (2011). "The Soybean Republic," *Yale Journal of International Affairs*, Spring–summer: 59–68.

UNCTAD. (2006). "Tracking the trend towards market concentration: the case of the agricultural input industry," UNCTAD Secretariat. www.panna.org/sites/default/files/ UNCTAD_CorpConcenAg%20(2005).pdf.

UNCTAD. (2009). *World Investment Report. Transnational Corporations, Agricultural Production and Development*. New York and Geneva: United Nations.

UNDP (2007/8). *Human Development Report: Fighting Climate Change. Human Solidarity in a Divided World*. New York: UNDP.

UNDP (2009). *Human Development Report 2009: Overcoming Barriers: Human Mobility and Development*. New York: UNDP.

UNU-IHDP and UNEP. (2012). *Inclusive Wealth Report 2012. Measuring Progress toward Sustainability*. Cambridge: Cambridge University Press.

Van Gelder, J.W. and J.M. Dros. (2002). *Corporate Actors in the South American Soy Production Chain*. Bern, Switzerland: Worldwide Fund for Nature (WFN).

Veltmeyer, H. (2013). "The Political Economy of Natural Resource Extraction: A New Model or Extractive Imperialism?" *Canadian Journal of Development Studies*, 34(1), March: 79–95.

Veltmeyer, H. and J. Petras. (2014). *The New Extractivism: A Model for Latin America?* London: Zed Books.

Vieta, M. (ed.) (2014). *Social and Solidarity Economy: Towards Inclusive and Sustainable Development*. Geneva: ITC-ILO.

Villoro, J. (2016). "La duración de la impaciencia," pp. 15–26 in Sexta Comisión. *El Pensamiento Crítico Frente a la Hidra Capitalista II*. Mexico: EZLN.

World Bank (2008). *World Development Report 2008: Agriculture for Development*. New York: Oxford University Press.

Zibechi, R. (2007). *Autonomías y emancipaciones. América Latina en movimiento*. Lima: Programa Democracia y Transformación Global.

Zibechi, R. (2015). *Descolonializar el Pensamiento Crítico y las Rebeldías. Autonomías y Emancipaciones en la era del progresismo*. Mexico: Bajo Tierra Ediciones.

4 Social movements and the state in the post-neoliberal era

Gerardo Otero, Efe Can Gürcan and Horacio Mackinlay

The purpose of this chapter is to critically engage the Latin American literature on the politics of development regarding two main strands of political practice since the neoliberal turn in the 1980s, but especially after the 1994 Zapatista insurrection. These two main strands and associated schools of thought are the autonomists or the 'social left' focused on civil society; and the symbiotic or 'political left' concerned with and focused on electoral politics. Our concern is with the case of Mexico, where the left-leaning MORENA (National Regeneration Movement) party, with Andrés Manuel López Obrador (AMLO) as its presidential candidate, won the elections by a landslide in 2018.

Politically, a major feature of the neoliberal era is that most countries returned to or initiated a liberal democratic regime after a hiatus of authoritarian or military governments. After the seeming defeat of the revolutionary strategy of direct assault on the state, the ruptural route, the question became whether progressive forces would focus on gaining state power via elections, the symbiotic route; or on trying to influence state policy via social movement mobilisation from the bottom-up, i.e. the autonomist, or interstitial route. We will argue that social movements that supported electoral transitions and governments became demobilised or coopted by emerging social-assistance policies of the state, while autonomist movements that refused to engage with the state became mostly marginalised. Both strategies have mostly failed their popular constituencies. The way forward for progressive social movements is to both engage with the state while staying mobilised in order for movements to retain their independence from the state and autonomy from other organisations, namely political parties. This is, in fact, the challenge for MORENA and sympathiser social movements in Mexico: how can they support each other while advancing in a popular-democratic agenda of sustainable development?

In the chapter we advance the argument that, at least since the 1980s, the social movements that supported governments and transformations by the electoral route—what theorists have termed the 'parliamentary road' to state power'—ended up being coopted by the patron–client policies and social assistance policies that characterised neoliberalism, while autonomist movements that refused to engage the state remained marginalised. Both strategies therefore failed their social constituencies. We thus propose that the only potentially viable alternative is that social movements adopt a double strategy of engaging the state but remaining firmly rooted in mobilised organisations within civil society. In this way, movements will be able to retain their independence from the state and their autonomy from other organisations, namely political parties. This is, in fact, the fundamental challenge for MORENA: to establish a mutual support with social movements so as to implement and advance a post-neoliberal development agenda with a popular-democratic character.

We first offer a brief overview of how the strategies for transformation have panned out in Latin America. Then we zoom into Mexico's case, followed by an outline of the theory of political–cultural class formation, whose encompassing framework allows for an in-depth examination of the culture, leadership and state-related dynamics of symbiotic and autonomist mobilisation in consideration of their social-class background. Finally, we offer some conclusions on MORENA's main challenges as a governing party, and in doing so we assume that MORENA bears the main responsibility for both governing and strengthening social movements ability to mobilise and continue to exert pressure from below. This is the only way in which progressive social forces can move forward in deepening democracy in the midst of capitalism.

Latin America's 'left turn'

After the electoral triumph of Hugo Chávez in Venezuela in 1998, a succession of other self-defined leftist political forces won state power, to the point that well over 60 per cent of the Latin American population were ruled by at least nominally leftist governments. Economically, these governments rode a boom in the export of primary commodities until 2014, with varying degrees of success or failure in attaining development goals, such as reducing poverty and inequality (Veltmeyer and Petras 2014), although they did not succeed in diversifying the economy. If the Zapatista movement emphasised political action inside civil society while shunning state intervention, in the Andean region the main mantra became a change in development focus from economic growth to *buen vivir* or living well. Brazil and Argentina followed their own version of development (Wylde, 2016), in which social-movement influence translated into some redistributive policies by the state. The progressive literature tends to interpret the variety of experiences since the 1990s either in an anti-statist strand, à la Zapatistas; or in a statist, top-down strand that argues that only the state is capable of addressing societal change.

Anti-statist autonomism

In the literature, the anti-statist strand is represented by the likes of John Holloway and Raúl Zibechi. These scholars portray social movements as desirably dispersed anti-state forces that need to avoid state contact and cooptation (Gürcan and Otero, 2013). Holloway's *Change the World Without Taking Power* (2010) argues that the state is by definition unable to instigate radical social change, and that the task of creating a different world needs to be carried out without the state's involvement. More precisely, he views the state as 'a bulwark against change' and 'a rigidified or fetishised form of social relations', i.e. a social institution 'in the form of something external to social relations' (Holloway 2010: 72, 92). Furthermore, Holloway's denial of class analysis leads him to assert that the revolutionary subject is not 'definable' (or, more precisely, it is inherently anti-definitional). The struggle thus needs to be broadly formulated within the context of 'anti-power', equated to the fight for human dignity, the unity of the oppressed regardless of its class background and the disarticulation of fetishism.

Similarly, Zibechi in *Dispersing Power* (2010) aims to demonstrate that bottom-up (or non-state) organising resides at the heart of social emancipation. Drawing on the experience of urban settlements of the Aymara in El Alto, Zibechi devotes his first three chapters to an elaboration of the role of 'community' conceived as a social machine that provides social cohesion for collective action. He describes the ways in which urban Aymara communities rely on affinity-based relationships and self-managing activities by preserving and adapting their culture.

In Chapter 4 Zibechi establishes a discrepancy between state and anti-state powers, between those who want to homogenise and those who strive to disperse. Based on the experience of the Law of Popular Participation (LPP, approved in 1994), which established legal requirements for the institutionalisation of neighbourhood councils in Bolivia, Zibechi argues that state regulation has a negative impact on grassroots organising so that it establishes a superficial separation between the representatives and local residents. Zibechi goes on to assert that the *Conciencia de Patria* (Conscience or Awareness of the Motherland, CONDEPA), once a popular-democratic political party that appropriated the Aymara cultural legacy and achieved major electoral success, was transformed into a de-ideologised and clientelist movement co-opted by the state apparatus.

In Chapter 5 Zibechi discusses the emergence of community justice in El Alto in opposition to corrupt state institutions. Based on a model of 'self-organised pluricultural society' that ensures the autonomy over local resources, the sixth chapter offers a more detailed investigation of how community power can assume an alternative function to that of the state. Here Zibechi makes a case for spontaneous, leaderless mobilisation. He maintains that the real success of the water and gas wars in the Bolivia of 2000 and 2003 lies in the absence of the traditional division between the leaders and the led thanks to rural community (*ayllus*) organising and urban communities and local neighbourhood committees (Zibechi, 2010: 2). He points to the ways in which the uprisings in Cochabamba in early 2000 and in the highlands and the Aymara city of El Alto, followed by road blockades in 2000, 2003, and 2005, contributed to the delegitimisation and fragmentation of state authority (Zibechi, 2010: 12). Zibechi thus brings to the forefront the crucial importance of grassroots organising conceived as an act of self-education, self-activity, and self-organisation (Zibechi, 2010: 3–4). He goes on to argue that the success of social mobilisation depends on the strategy of 'communalising', understood as 'a process in which social bonds take on a communitarian character, thus strengthening reciprocity' (Zibechi, 2010: 20). Relying on the principle of the collective management of resources, this strategy emerges out of the rise of a community consciousness and neighbourhood cohesion as a form of survival. These forms of cohesion prevent the separation of the leaders and the led as well as that 'between economy and politics or between society and state' (Zibechi, 2010: 16–19, 27). According to Zibechi, there are three key features of the communalising strategy: 'collective decision-making at each step, the rotation of leaders and tasks, and the outpouring from below. (Zibechi, 2010: 43).

Overall, both Holloway and Zibechi have the merit of making a strong case for the fact that what matters for social emancipation or empowerment is not atomised individual subjects, but rather collectivities that struggle for autonomy. Cooptation is a major hindrance to social emancipation. However, the major weakness of their arguments lies in their civil-society centric and class-blind approach that romanticises all 'anti-state' practices and community organising, and their concomitant essentialist and demonising conception of the state and leadership, which are assumed to be always and with no exception an instrument of capital. Especially outside the Bolivian context, communities tend to be complex and contradictory organisms that are divided along class lines (Veltmeyer, 2001a: 59; 2001b: 29; Veltmeyer, 2018).

Postneoliberalism and the symbiotic approach

The symbiotic approach to social movement analysis is represented by the postneoliberal school (e.g. Rucket, McDonald and Proulx, 2017). Postneoliberalism is a set of public policies that have been adopted by leftist governments elected in the twenty-first century in Latin America, including those of Argentina, Bolivia, Brazil, Chile, Ecuador, El Salvador, Nicaragua and Uruguay, with a goal of transcending the neoliberal Washington Consensus (Wylde, 2016). Far from simply wanting to return to the state interventionism of the era of import substitution industrialisation (1930s to 1980s), postneoliberalism consists of a new type of policy based on local traditions and communities, responding to them with the intent to forge a new state-society pact (Grugel and Riggirozzi, 2012: 3).

This formulation sounds very much like the convergence or fusion of both a symbiotic and an interstitial strategy of transformation. But postneoliberalism has been implemented in a wide variation in Latin American political practice. Some radical (ruptural) observers called the emergence of the left in the region the 'pink tide', instead of the red revolution that they would have preferred. To them, the pink tide has resulted in mild policies that became a new form to enable extractivism, or development based on the extraction and export of raw materials, through social assistance policies that ultimately reaffirmed an imperialism of the twenty-first century (e.g. Veltmeyer and Petras, 2014; Webber, 2017). The postneoliberalism school proposes a more nuanced approach about the Latin American left. Rossi (2015), for instance, argues that including progressive movements in the networks of political formation and welfare cannot be reduced to simple examples of populist cooptation. Those inclusive projects actually correspond to the struggle for recognition and reincorporation to society. Previously, progressive movements had been excluded by neoliberal governments. The post-neoliberal policy context promotes their mobilisation as recognised and legitimate actors, with legitimate demands for access to jobs, water, health, vocational training and education. Some movements, therefore, have been turned into social transformation agents rather than simply subjects coopted by the state apparatus (Rossi, 2015).

Toward a popular-democratic synthesis

In this chapter, we argue that what is needed is a synthesis of both interstitial and symbiotic positions without abandoning class analysis, and by assigning the necessary analytical value to leadership types and their relations with constituencies, without excluding the possibility that eventually there may be a historical juncture in which a ruptural strategy could become viable. At the start of the twenty-first century, however, we consider that the ruptural strategy has been defeated around the world or has always produced authoritarian results, even when some significant human-development achievements were attained in the Cuban case, for example. We now have sufficient evidence from the leftist governments in Latin America to assess the extent to which they distanced themselves from their social constituencies, so that their initial progressive goals were not attained. But we also have sufficient evidence to suggest that some centre-left governments did, in fact, achieve significant development goals. The evidence also suggests that, while some significant redistributive measures were attained on the basis of oil rent in Venezuela, or the rent derived from other raw material exports like soybeans from Argentina, these achievements were attained only in the short term and were short lived: once the commodities boom dissipated, these countries started to have serious problems because they had not produced the development goals that they had sought.

Compared with these experiences, Andrés Manuel López Obrador's administration in Mexico starts with a gloomy international perspective, with a world economy dominated by declining rates of growth. But it also has the advantage of being able to take into account the Latin American experience to avoid its pitfalls. Doing so will require a great balancing act between a series of challenges, including the following: maintaining macroeconomic equilibria and favourable capital-investment conditions; while limiting the excesses and flagrant privileges that have favoured the powerful groups; allowing and promoting the collective empowerment of popular, workers and middle-class groups that have been abandoned by the neoliberal project. The latter would have to be included as the new leading groups in the new popular-democratic development paradigm. To conclude, what is needed is to promote the mechanisms for accountability by government and leaderships at all organisational levels, so that government action reflects the desires and aspirations of popular masses.

MORENA's historical victory

In Mexico's 2018 elections, left-of-centre Andrés Manuel López Obrador (AMLO), third-time presidential candidate since 2006, was finally allowed to win with over 30.1 million votes (53.2 per cent) and over 63.4 per cent of citizenship participation (INE, 2018). AMLO may have won in 2006, but widespread irregularities led to an official razor-thin margin favouring his opponent by 0.6 per cent (Bruhn and Greene, 2007; Rubio and Davidow, 2006). In the 2018 vote for the presidency, MORENA won all of Mexico's 32 states except for one, and MORENA also commanded a majority in both chambers of congress as of 1 September 2018. AMLO's presidency started on 1 December.

Besides AMLO's remarkable win, what is most exciting to us is that food sovereignty was a central issue that defined MORENA's electoral campaign. MORENA's emphasis on this issue played an important role in gaining the electorate's favour. If implemented, the food-sovereignty policy would reverse the free-trade orientation that has prevailed in Mexico since 1986, against the established neoliberal wisdom that food security can be achieved via trade (Otero, et al., 2013). MORENA's expectation is that by supporting smallholder peasants to supply domestic food production outmigration will be stemmed. Rather than being forced to migrate (Bartra, 2004; Hellman, 2008; Otero, 2011), rural people will be able to stay in their places, with their families and communities, while making a decent living (López Obrador, 2017: 181–204) and supplying enough food for the urban population.

Since the French Revolution, there have been three strategies for socioeconomic and political–cultural transformation (Wright, 2010: 273–374): a rupture or a direct assault on the state; interstitial, working autonomously in the margins of society; and symbiotic in which both ruling and dominated parties cooperate in a positive-sum game. Mexico's three earlier transformations—independence from Spain in 1821, the liberal-reform constitution of 1857, and the revolutionary process of 1910–1920, yielding the world's major agrarian reform legislation at the time (Wolf, 1969; Otero, 1999, 2004b)—all involved violence. In the fourth transformation, however, subordinate groups hope to move state policy in their favour, even if it is within the bounds of electoral politics, i.e. within the same regime. At least this is MORENA's promise: through elections, it seeks to achieve 'the fourth revolution', or transformation, of Mexico.

This transformation will be guided by the dictum: '*por el bien de todos, primero los pobres*' or 'for everyone's good, the poor come first'. As AMLO put it in one of his books, 'We want modernity, but forged from below with everyone and for everyone' (López Obrador, 2017: 178). Given that the poorest of the poor reside in Mexico's countryside, this discussion will focus on MORENA's food-sovereignty program, the extent to which the electoral platform becomes policy, and the relations between peasants and the state. The new government wants to transcend the way the state has engaged with peasants since the late 1980s: as *objects* of public assistance. Instead, AMLO wants peasants to become *subjects* of their own development.

Let us briefly illustrate the failure of neoliberal clientelism and social assistentialism. In 2003, after the vigorous peasant mobilisation called 'El campo no aguanta más' (the countryside can bear no more), once the mobilisation declined, the state reneged on the structural reforms that had been agreed on in the National Agreement for the Countryside. These included the revision of the NAFTA chapter on agriculture, the Agrarian Law, and the codification of agrarian procedures. In exchange, the state offered several productive projects and funding for administrative programs on a short scale, so as to make organisations that had mobilised happy (Bartra and Otero, 2009). Eventually, funding for these initiatives got stagnated due both to the workings of the state and the organisations' dynamics, which generated their division and multiplication that neutralised their negotiation ability (Carton de Grammont and Mackinlay 2006).

As for social expenditures, for 2017 the Mexican government spent a mere 9.3 per cent of its budget, which represents slightly more than a third of the Latin American and Caribbean regional average expenditure of 24.6 per cent (OECD, 2017: 1). During the neoliberal era, the greatest part of social expenditures for the countryside was channelled through several poverty-alleviation programs that never had any intention of influencing the productive sphere (except partially Pronasol during the Salinas de Gortari administration [1988–1994]). Their goal was to address people in conditions of 'moderate' or 'extreme' poverty–mostly in the realms of food, health, housing and education. Beyond the countryside, although it's included too, the National Council for the Assessment of Social Policy (Coneval) states that over 50 per cent of Mexican youth earn wages between one and three minimum salaries; but this amount is insufficient to cover food, transportation and education needs. Furthermore, 59 per cent of the labour force in Mexico works in the informal sector with no benefits (ADNPolítico, 2018). Hence the importance of discussing the extent to which MORENA's new government will be able to regenerate the peasantry, both for its own good and to achieve food and labour sovereignty.

The new state–peasants relation will be founded on considering peasants as economic *subjects*. Appropriate public policies will enable them to provide Mexico with food self-sufficiency (ANEC 2018). Mexico's food-import dependency became dramatically exposed during and after the world food-price crisis in 2007–2008, with further price spikes until 2011 (McMichael, 2009; Otero, 2011; Otero, et al., 2013). Achieving the fundamental change from food-export orientation to food sovereignty could also reverse Mexico's loss of labour sovereignty, defined as a country's ability to offer gainful employment to the majority of its workforce (Bartra, 2004; Otero, 2011). On a global scale, food sovereignty is the major program pursued by the peasant movement through its transnational organisation, Vía Campesina (Desmarais, 2007; Wittman, 2009; Edelman, 2014; McMichael, 2013). The question will be the extent to which the new government brings along food and labour sovereignty in the agroecological, sustainable way demanded by the peasant movement. Implementing this program will require a peasantry that is formed politically to struggle for its own interests.

The peasantry and political-cultural class formation

The theory of political-cultural formation is equipped with strong theoretical devices to make sense of Mexico's future symbiotic and interstitial transformations, which allow for a comprehensive framework grounded in class analysis. As can be induced from María Inclán's (2018) literature review on Latin America's social movements, the extant literature is heavily dominated by state-centric perspectives focused on political opportunities and regime change at the expense of class analysis and other bottom-up dynamics related to leadership and autonomous organising. The theory of political-cultural formation fills an important niche in the corpus of thought on Latin America's social movements and responds to the challenges of the MORENA era, as described in previous sections.

The political–cultural formation of the peasantry includes (a) its regional cultures, (b) how its organisations engage with the state and (c) the mechanisms (if any) to keep their leadership accountable. The peasantry has always been at the forefront of class struggles and taken the lead in strengthening Mexico's civil society, as exemplified in neo-Zapatista's case with a worldwide impact. The 1994 neo-Zapatista uprising in Chiapas initially pursued a ruptural transformation in the Leninist mould (Rubin, 2002). It led the way in protesting the ravages of neoliberalism in Latin America (Harvey, 1998; Gilbreth and Otero, 2001), just when Jorge G. Castañeda (1993) had proclaimed the end of armed insurrection in the region. After 12 days of armed struggle, though, and massive protests throughout Mexico demanding a peaceful solution to the conflict, the Zapatista National Liberation Army (EZLN) agreed to a ceasefire with the government. But after frustrating on-off negotiations, the EZLN refused to engage the state further after 1996. The Zapatistas focused on an interstitial, autonomist strategy, trying to organise the subordinate groups and classes in civil society against the state (EZLN, 2005). In so doing, they boycotted the 2006 electoral process in which AMLO most likely won but supposedly lost in that contested and doubted vote. This was a highly questioned election in which officially Felipe Calderon was the winner by a mere 0.6 per cent of the vote. (Bruhn and Greene, 2007; Otero, 2008; Rubio and Davidow, 2006).

Conversely, from a Latin American regional perspective, Mexico might have been too late in joining its 'left turn' (Castañeda, 2006) in its symbiotic transformation strategy: the rise of left-of-centre governments that proliferated since the triumph of Hugo Chávez in Venezuela in 1998 (Inclán, 2018; Ellner, 2008, 2014; Gürcan, 2013; Hunt, 2016; Panizza, 2005; Cameron and Hershberg, 2010; Ruckert, McDonald and Proulx, 2017). This left turn came to encompass over 60 per cent of Latin America's population, but declined after the end of the commodities boom in 2014 since it failed to build a self-sustained alternative of development while, in some cases, allowing immense corruption to deepen. Thus, after the Zapatista insurrection in Mexico, the left was divided between an interstitial, autonomist 'social left', focused on civil society, and a symbiotic 'political left', focused on electoral processes (Otero, 2008). But these strands converged by 2012: MORENA became a social-movement party (Bolívar Mesa,

2017; Espinosa Toledo and Navarrete Vela, 2016) by unifying several social movements and elements of leftist political parties. Only six years later, MORENA won the 2018 elections.

Other questions that can be raised for the new government are: to what extent can the state transcend the assistentialist social policies to promote production toward a sustainable economic development, and how far will peasants have to nudge the state so that it intervenes in favour of their social reproduction and become the subjects of such policies? The role of MORENA as an intermediary between the state and social movements will be critical. It must avoid leaning too much in either direction to keep a healthy balance that is capable of moving sustainable development forward. MORENA's affiliated social movements have the potential of becoming a 'class-for-itself' in the Marxist sense.

Karl Marx briefly referred to the conversion from a class-in-itself into a class-for-itself. Class-*in*-itself refers to the objective existence of social groupings that have a common relation to the means of production (e.g. owners of capital or sellers of labour power). Class-*for*-itself presupposes not only its objective existence but also a subjective awareness of such existence, an identification of its class interests and, most decisively, the construction of an organisation to struggle for those interests (Marx, 1978: 608). As Pierre Bourdieu put it:

> Classes in Marx's sense have to be made through a political work that has all the more chance of succeeding when it is armed with a theory that is well-founded in reality, thus more capable of exerting a theory effect—*theorein*, in Greek, means to see—that is, of imposing a vision of divisions.
>
> (1989: 17)

MORENA, therefore, needs to gain clarity over the theoretical construction of class divisions in Mexico, so as to enlighten the road ahead: not to deepen such divisions but, on the contrary, in the higher limit, to contribute to eliminate them by transcending class society.

How do culture, state intervention and leadership contribute to political–cultural class formation? At a minimum, the collective empowerment or political–cultural formation of subordinate classes means pushing the state to intervene in favour of their social reproduction; at a maximum, it entails broad societal transformation in a democratic, ecosocialist direction, enhancing the conditions to limit the excessive privileges of the wealthiest and permitting human flourishing in harmony with the earth. In particular, we want to understand the conditions under which organised men and women can make their own history, following Marx's well-known dictum that: 'Men make their own history, but do make it just as they please; they do not make it under circumstances chosen by themselves, but under circumstances directly found, given and transmitted from the past' (Marx, 1978 [1852]: 595). This dictum alludes to the relation between collective will and structural determination or, as is usually put succinctly in the social sciences, the agency-structure conundrum (Archer, 1995; Carlsnaes, 1992; Morselli, 2014): what can be chosen and what is already determined.

Max Weber distinguished among three levels of social action that have a rough parallel to Marx's concepts referred to above: at the individual level, Weber's 'class situation' is similar to class-*in*-itself. 'Communal action' in Weber is partially similar to Marx's class-*for*-itself: 'it is oriented to the feeling of the actors that they belong together' (Weber, 1978: 183). 'Societal action', on the other hand, supplements class-for-itself in that it 'is oriented to a rationally motivated adjustment of interests'. But here's the conundrum for Weber: 'The rise of societal or even of communal action from a common class situation is by no means a universal phenomenon' (1978: 183).

Studying the historical occurrences of 'class action' or 'mass action', Weber observes: 'The degree to which "communal action" and possibly "societal action," emerges from the "mass actions" of the members of a class is linked to general cultural conditions, especially to those of an intellectual sort' (1978: 184). Weber's sociology was the main classical source of contemporary social movement theories of resource mobilisation and political opportunities (e.g. McAdam, 1999; McAdam et al., 1996) and anticipated that the 'modern proletariat', in particular, would not accept the structure of a concrete economic order as an 'absolutely given fact', as may have been common in antiquity, dominated by fatalism. For Weber, the modern proletariat was likely to protest 'in the form of rational association' (1978: 184). Yet, there is no direct determination by class situation of communal or societal action. Similarly, class-*in*-itself does not directly and spontaneously derive into class-*for*-itself. It is thus necessary to study what mediations take place for the transformation of one into the other. And, historically, we need to understand why the peasantry has come to play the important role that it has had since the early twentieth century: can it actually lead through electoral means a substantial transformation, even if it is one of a symbiotic type; or is it condemned to play a role subordinate to the bourgeoisie?

Erik Olin Wright (2010) defined emancipatory social science as an intellectual enterprise concerned with identifying obstacles, possibilities and dilemmas of social transformation. Heavily inspired by Marx's sociology, Wright's chief contribution regards the structural conditions for emancipatory transformation but remains short on the subjective, organisational, conditions. His *Envisioning Real Utopias* (2010) offers an excellent starting point by making three main contributions: (1) a critique of capitalism; (2) a theory of alternatives which Wright labels the 'socialist compass'; and (3) a 'theory of transformation that tells us how to get from here to there—how to make alternatives achievable' (2010: 26). For Wright, a theory of transformation involves four central components: (a) a theory of social reproduction, or how those in dominant positions—economic and political—resist change; (b) a theory of the gaps and contradictions within the process of reproduction, so that those interested in change can work in the interstices of society, as well as in its dominant institutions, to promote change; (c) a theory of the underlying dynamics and trajectory of unintended social change, as this also needs to be grappled with and is the most challenging aspect to generate knowledge about; and, finally, (d) a theory of collective actors, strategies and struggles.

Here we briefly outline a theory of collective actors, strategies and struggles: how have peasant organisations become politically formed to promote food sovereignty and popular-democratic transformation? Following Gramsci (1971), we will discuss the cultural and ideological conditions for the construction of a popular-democratic alternative to bourgeois hegemony. We propose three mediating determinants between class-structural processes and political outcomes: regional cultures, state intervention, and leadership types and modes of grass-roots participation. Regional cultures point to the particularity and specificity of cultural configurations in local movement dynamics and geography, or the socio-territorial and autonomy aspect of movement organisations (Bartra and Otero 2005, 2009; Vergara-Camus, 2014; Zibechi, 2010; Dinerstein. 2015). From a variety of regional cultures, the struggle for autonomy allows movements to imagine the kind of society they want for themselves (Otero, 1989; Dinerstein, 2015), as with the food-sovereignty program. 'The politics of autonomy', says Dinerstein, 'confronts value with hope' (2015: 204) in prefiguring future society.

We derived the state-intervention factor from a critical reading of the political-opportunity structure perspective in social movement theories (McAdam, 1999), replacing its top-down state-centrism, which asks how the state impacts social mobilisation. From this perspective, it would seem like social movements simply respond to the context provided by the state, whether more or less permissive, but without having their own dynamics. In her literature review essay on these theories, María Inclán (2018) reveals that the political-opportunity structures perspective is the most popular. In Latin America, scholars have prioritised the study of regime change, such as 'transitions to democracy', as the chief source of social mobilisation. In contrast with this perspective, we combine what we call the 'bottom-up linkages approach' or BULA—about the ways in which peasant organisations can nudge state policies in favour of their social reproduction—with an approach that looks into how MORENA, having gained access to exercising state power, might affect mobilisations from above.

State intervention, in this theory, mediates the political outcomes in that such intervention has the possibility of shaping the character of resulting organisations for struggle in three ways, from the movements' point of view: (1) a favourable policy for the social reproduction of those mobilised that results in their cooptation, (2) a negative or repressive policy, or (3) a favourable policy after which the movements can remain independent from the state and continue fighting for their long-term interests and imagining a better society beyond immediate concessions. As a mediating determinant, state intervention is not simply a causal relation in which one entity causes the other. Rather, it is a causal *relation* in which the public policy that the state designs and implements emerges as a function of how the state is related to the social movement. Evidently, however, the state is the dominant factor in this relation. And yet, the state is not all-powerful; it at least responds to the force of mobilised organisations to some extent. Given this bidirectionality relation, Pablo Lapegna (2017), rather than 'cooptation', has preferred to use the concept of 'dual pressure', from the bottom-up and the top-down, in referring to social movements. For us, however, the central question regarding this mediation concerns its political result from the movements' point of view: bourgeois-hegemonic, oppositional, or popular-democratic. Only the latter result could be properly regarded as leading toward the formation of a class-for-itself.

Finally, the political–cultural formation of subordinate classes depends on the extent to which their leaderships can maintain an organisational dynamism and inclusive demands. These become materialised by encouraging the democratic participation of their constituencies, alliances with kindred groups and account-ability (Fox, 1992, 2007), and maintaining their independence from the state and their autonomy from other organisations (Otero, 2004a). Of course, political–cultural class formation is not something that can be achieved once and for all. Rather, it is a fluid and contingent process, especially with regard to its character. The durability (or not) of the popular-democratic character of organisations depends to a great extent on leadership types, which should be confused with personality traits or the psychology of the leaders only.

Food sovereignty: a major challenge to MORENA, 2018–2024

After more than 25 years since the 1992 agrarian reform legislation that enabled the privatisation of social ownership (*ejido* and communal land) (Mackinlay 1994; Pérez Castañeda 2002; Pérez Castañeda and Mackinlay, 2015; Otero 1999), there is consensus that it would be hard to revert this situation to the status quo ante. Since that counter-reform was legislated, practically the totality of individual and communal land surfaces has become certified as private ownership (Robles Berlanga, 2009). Those situations that have yet to be regular-ised (1,716 *ejidos* and communities that represent 5.3 per cent of the total and about 3 per cent of the land surface) have to do with a variety of causes. Most of them are due to imperfections in juridical or administrative activity of agrarian institutions (one third); others are due to the refusal of agrarian communities to accept governmental programs that have executed the 1992 reforms (PROCEDE for *ejidos*, and PROCECOM for communities); and yet others are due to agrar-ian conflicts about property limits that are hard to resolve; while a minority are due to communities being located in urban areas with irregular settlements (RAN, 2018). On the other hand, this legislation has a number of inconsistencies and lacunae that have become a source of juridical insecurity for *ejidatarios* (holders of *ejido* land) and community members, with regard to issues of inherit-ance, contracts and usufruct, and also for private ownership. These unresolved cases have caused the saturation of agrarian tribunals with pending matters.

The Agrarian Law

MORENA's most immediate challenge is thus to reform the Agrarian Law so as to confer legislation an orientation that strengthens juridical security in land tenure, promotes investment, including that of small local investors, generates a more adequate treatment to big capital and articulates the land property system to rural development planning. In the mid-term, land-tenure regularisation must be finalised throughout the national territory—an issue that could be accomplished before the end of the new administration's six-year term in 2024. This regularisation would have to end all the property limits conflicts and agrarian disputes once and for all, as they have darkened the rural landscape since colonial times.

The *ejido*, as an institution, must be liberated from the dual role that has been assigned to it historically, in making it work both as a productive unit and a unit of territorial management, making its officers responsible for social and public services in their population centres. This overlap in productive and territorial management roles, in fact, displaces people living in the population centres of the *ejido* that are not also *ejidatarios*; they are condemned to a non-citizenship situation in their own communities. What is needed, then, is that community management relies on a different type of representation to that of *ejidos*, so that the latter can focus exclusively on matters of production, while the new organisation can focus on a type of territorial management that is inclusive, democratic and accountable.

Rural development planning

The rural development planning system needs to be thoroughly revised so as to allow participatory involvement in it by civic and peasant organisations with local, regional and national coverage (Pérez Castañeda, 2007a, 2007b). The goal should be to simplify the national rural development planning system in an integral form (in levels, procedures, instruments, criteria, legal framework, etc.), so that local and regional organisations can function properly. The goal should be to strengthen rural economic activity in general within the framework of territorial development and to promote social and environmental action.

There are numerous forms of governance for the several regional peasant organisations that exist, such as Producer Unions (Uniones de Productores), Rural Collective Interest Associations (ARIC), Ejido Unions, Rural Production Societies and many others, so that they raise their demands to get state support for their projects. There are too many planning agencies, however, which is confusing and time-consuming for producers, on one hand. On the other hand, according to the existing legislation that created these agencies (e.g., the Sustainable Rural Development Law, the General Social Development Law, the Water Law, the Forestry Law), the agencies should be better coordinated among them but very few actually are. When they do try to coordinate, these agencies do not have the resources to function and execute their programs (Pérez Castañeda, 2017).

Other measures need to be implemented to revert the huge organisational dispersion that prevails in the rural sector. The Mexican government has historically neglected both the productive economic organisation and the trade support organisation, so that the former has become dismantled—and dispersed—while the latter is obsolete. For instance, there are numerous Producer Unions in specific crop commodity systems like sugar, maize, beans, wheat, etc., that are promoted by different peasant organisations, many of which function in a patron–client relation. At most, there should be two such trade unions to facilitate interaction with development agencies to channel resources and directives. This organisational situation sharply contrasts with that of capitalist, entrepreneurial farmers, prior to the neoliberal turn. For these, in some crop commodity systems they constituted efficient trade organisations that provided a number of efficient services to their members. In contrast, those in the 'social sector', i.e. *ejidatarios* and *comuneros*, were rarely able to work efficiently due to the sharp organisational dispersion. The latter, in turn, resulted from the official disdain toward the social sector (Mackinlay, 2004).

During the neoliberal era, working from the premise of letting individual or organised producers do their own thing, letting them deal with market forces with their own resources and at their own risk, their organisational deficiencies became enhanced. This is why it is indispensable to reconstruct the organisational network for production at all levels and to update and strengthen the trade structures so that they can work as the struts to agrarian and forestry development. One positive situation that needs to be highlighted is that the agrarian legislation reforms reduced the differences between the social and the private sectors in that the similar rules of the game were set up for both. This homogenisation, in tandem with trade liberalisation that affected both sectors deeply, determined that the formerly rigid separation of both sectors by land-tenure type and political orientation has almost diluted.

As of 2018, the dividing line in Mexico's countryside is between large national and international agribusiness corporations linked with the national market, imports and exports, on one hand; and the small and medium producers and their associations, on the other—some of them also oriented toward the export market, but subject to intermediaries or unfavourable negotiating conditions, given the absence of legal and marketing advising as well as infrastructure. The majority of small and medium producers are focused on the domestic market (Mackinlay 2008a).

Farmworkers

According to the 2017 National Agricultural and Livestock Survey conducted by Mexico's National Institute of Statistics, Geography and Informatics, INEGI, there are 11.8 million farmworkers in the sector in (89 per cent male and 11 per cent female), with an average of between 23.5 and 31.3 hired days per year who make an average pay of $167 pesos per day. According to an analysis by the National Council for the Prevention of Discrimination only 35 per cent have a contract and 7 per cent have benefits; and have an average schooling of 5.9 years (incomplete elementary school) (Mariano Ruiz Funes, 2018).

Since capitalist agriculture has existed in Mexico, farmworkers have never been allowed to organise in unions, regardless of what party has been in power

(Lara 1996). Therefore, MORENA's government should favour—instead of blocking as has always been the case—farmworker's unionisation. The government should carry out a particularly sharp vigilance in those regions in which farm work predominates; i.e. in the fruit and horticulture export emporia of the Bajío region (states of Guanajuato and Querétaro) and the northwestern region. The goals should be both to enforce employer compliance with labour law regarding fair wages and fair and dignified worker treatment, and to eradicate child labour in the countryside (Lara 1998). Measures should be taken to supervise intermediaries and labour contractors and people that transport farmworkers to different parts of the country (Sánchez Saldaña 2006). The social security legislation should be improved and better enforced, given that in 1997 and 2005 the law was reformed to grant farmworkers full rights (labour risk security, illness and maternity, disability and life, retirement, unemployment in old age, child care services and other benefits), comparable to wage workers in other sectors of the economy. The law's concrete procedures, however, do not favour homologation of rights. Furthermore, employers have systematically refused to implement them. Paradoxically, this situation, in fact, leaves farmworkers less protected with the law than before its existence—so they have less access to medical attention and work accident insurance in the clinics of the Mexican Social Insurance Institute (IMSS) (Mackinlay 2008b: 137–142).

Mining, Aeolic, geothermic and other megaprojects

In contrast to other progressive governments in Latin America, AMLO and MORENA's administration should take a much more pro-active attitude in defence of the environment and agrarian communities affected by resource extraction in their territories. It is very encouraging that the new government announced that it will forbid the extractive method of hydraulic fracturing or fracking, but there are pre-existing contracts in other areas that are firmly established. New mechanisms need to be created to enable *ejidos* and communities to at least engage and negotiate with large multinational firms in less disadvantageous conditions, and to substantially expand their participation in profit sharing. A substantial part of these profits should be paid in the form of taxes so that the state may expand its fiscal resources for other redistributive measures. In cases of stern opposition and discontent by communities, the government should issue measures to revert existing unfair contracts so as to bring them in line with the new rule of law.

Mexico's political constitution was reformed in 2013 to give private firms access to underground resources (gas and oil) and the generation of (electrical and geothermic) energy. Stemming from this fact, several secondary laws were issued which debilitated the defences that agrarian communities used to have, favouring the penetration of large corporations in the sector. The former have been exposed to the interests of the latter (Pérez Castañeda, 2014). The new government will need to implement reforms to the agrarian laws that enable the legal functioning and capabilities of *ejidos* and communities so as to revert this threat and, to the extent possible, turn it into a development opportunity for them.

Conclusions

Thus far we have outlined the profile of progressive movements in Latin America, the social left focused on civil society and the political left focused on the electoral process. We saw how the former governments of the left in the region came to govern over 60 per cent of the population and managed to reduce poverty in several countries, and to apply social programs to a broad sector of the population. But these experiences were relatively ephemeral, given that their viability became extinct once the commodity boom in the world economy was over in 2014 and because, in some cases, the governments deepened corruption. A majority of these leftist regimes, even those like Bolivia, which promoted strong social movements, became installed inside the state apparatus to implement their policies from the top down. The most common occurrence was that they demobilised the social movements and assumed a state logic of electoral power maintenance, even at the expense of some of the principles they once espoused.

In this chapter we proposed that in the case of Mexico its new government has the advantage that MORENA gained electoral power in 2018. With that Latin American experience as its background, MORENA has the possibility of learning from that history and avoiding its pitfalls. In particular, we have proposed the theory of political–cultural formation of subordinate classes. The dynamics of class formation toward a popular-democratic society must be based both from the bottom up and from the top down, from social movements rooted in civil society and from the institutions of the state. We elaborated the principal components of the theory with regard to the organisational aspects of subordinate classes. We proposed that, as a party, MORENA has the main responsibility to contribute to the strengthening of social movements, and to encourage their capacities for mobilisation and to exert pressure from below in their engagement with the state in promoting the popular-democratic alternative. This bottom-up and top-down combination is the only alternative we can see to deepen the popular-democratic project within capitalism with a view to transcend it in the future.

References

ADNPolítico (2018). "Más de 50% de los jóvenes que trabajan gana un sueldo insuficiente [More than 50% of youths gain an insufficient salary]," *ADNPolítico*, 12 August. Available at: https://adnpolitico.com/mexico/2018/08/12/mas-de-50-de-los-jovenes-que-trabajan-gana-un-sueldo-insuficiente.

ANEC—Asociación Nacional de Empresas Comercizadoras de Productos del Campo, National Association of Campesino Commercial Enterprises (2018). "Necesitamos 15 años para construir un campo nuevo [We need 15 years to build a new countryside]." (Interview with Víctor Suarez, future undersecretary of agriculture as of 1 December 2018.) ANEC. http://anec.org.mx/15-anos-para-construir-un-nuevo-campo.

Archer, M. (1995). *Realist Social Theory: The Morphogenetic Approach.* Cambridge: Cambridge University Press.

Bartra, A. (2004). "Rebellious Cornfields: Toward Food and Labour Self-sufficiency," pp. 18–36 in G. Otero (ed.), *Mexico in Transition: Neoliberal Globalism, the State, and Civil Society.* London: Zed Books; Nova Scotia: Fernwood Publishing.

Bartra, A. and G. Otero (2005). "Indian Peasant Movements in Mexico: The Struggle for Land, Autonomy and Democracy," pp. 383–410 in S. Moyo and P. Yeros (eds), *Reclaiming the Land: The Resurgence of Rural Movements in Africa, Asia and Latin America.* London and New York: Zed Books.

Bartra, A. and G. Otero (2009). "Contesting Neoliberal Globalism and NAFTA in Rural Mexico: From State Corporatism to the Political-Cultural Formation of the Peasantry," pp. 92–113 in J. Ayres and L. Macdonald (eds), *Contentious Politics in North America: National Protest and Transnational Collaboration Under Continental Integration.* Houndmills, England: Palgrave Macmillan.

Bolívar Mesa, R. (2017). "Liderazgo político: El caso de Andrés Manuel López Obrador en el Movimiento de Regeneración Nacional (MORENA) [Political Leadership: The Case of Morena's Andrés Manuel López Obrador]," *Estudios Políticos.* 42 (September–December): 99–118.

Bourdieu, P. (1989). "Social Space and Symbolic Power," *Sociological Theory,* 7(1): 14–25.

Bruhn, K. and K.F. Greene (2007). "Elite Polarization Meets Mass Modernization in Mexico's 2006 Elections," *Political Science and Politics,* 40(1): 33–38.

Cameron, M. and E. Hershberg (eds) (2010). *Latin America's Left Turns: Politics, Policies, and Trajectories of Change.* Boulder, CO: Lynne Riener.

Carlsnaes, W. (1992). "The Agency-Structure Problem in Foreign Policy Analysis," *International Studies Quarterly* 36(3): 245–270.

Castañeda, J. (1993). *Utopia Unarmed: The Latin American Left after the Cold War.* New York: Knof.

Castañeda, J. (2006). "Latin America's Left Turn," *Foreign Affairs,* 85(3): 28–43.

Desmarais, A. (2007). *La Via Campesina: Globalization and the Power of Peasants.* Halifax: Fernwood Publishing.

Dinerstein, A.C. (2015). *The Politics of Autonomy in Latin America: The Art of Organizing Hope.* London: Palgrave McMillan.

Edelman, M. (2014). "Food Sovereignty: Forgotten Genealogies and Future Regulatory Challenges," *Journal of Peasant Studies,* 41(6): 959–978.

Ellner, S. (2008). *Rethinking Venezuelan Politics: Class, Conflict, and the Chávez Phenomenon.* Boulder CO: Lynne Rienner.

Ellner, S. (ed.) (2014). *Latin America's Radical Left: Challenges and Complexities of Political Power in the Twenty-First Century.* Lanham: Rowman & Littlefield.

Espinosa Toledo, R. and J.P. Navarrete Vela (2016). "MORENA en la reconfiguración de partidos en México [Morena in Mexican Parties Reconfiguration]," *Estudios Políticos.* 37 (January–April): 81–109.

EZLN—Ejercito Zapatista de Liberación Nacional (2005). "Sexta declaración de la Selva Lacandona." Available at: http://enlacezapatista.ezln.org.mx/sdsl-es/ (last accessed: 12 January 2019).

Fox, J. (1992). "Democratic Rural Development: Leadership Accountability in Regional Peasant Organizations." *Development and Change,* 23(2): 1–36.

Fox, J. (2007). *Accountability Politics: Power and Voice in Rural Mexico.* Oxford: Oxford University Press.

Gilbreth, C. and G. Otero (2001). "Democratization in Mexico: The Zapatista uprising and Civil Society," *Latin American Perspectives*, 28(4): 7–29.

Grugel, J. and P. Riggirozzi (2012). "Post-Neoliberalism in Latin America: Rebuilding and Reclaiming the State after Crisis," *Development and Change*, 43(1): 1–21.

Gürcan, E. (2013). "Hugo Chávez's Unwritten Testament: National-democratic Struggle and Contradictions of Socialism," *Dialectical Anthropology*, 37(3–4): 341–356.

Gürcan, E. and G. Otero (2013). "Critical Considerations on Collective Empowerment: Class, Civil Society and the State." Mobilizing Ideas, The Center for the Study of Social Movements at the University of Notre Dame. Available at: https://mobilizingideas. wordpress.com/2013/05/29/critical-considerations-on-collective-empowerment-class-civil-society-and-the-state.

Gramsci, A. (1971). *Selections from the Prison Notebooks*. New York: International Publishers.

Harvey, N. (1998). *The Chiapas Rebellion: The Struggle for Land and Democracy*. Durham, NC: Duke University Press.

Hellman Adler, J. (2008). *The World of Mexican Migrants: The Rock and the Hard Place*. New York: The New Press.

Holloway, J. (2010). *Change the World Without Taking Power: The Meaning of Revolution Today*. London and New York: Pluto Press.

Hunt, S. (2016). "Rethinking the Politics of the Shift Left in Latin America: Towards a Relational Approach." *Bulletin of Latin American Research*, 34(4): 437–451.

Inclán, M. (2018). "Latin America, a Continent in Movement but Where To? A Review of Social Movements' Studies in the Region," *Annual Review of Sociology*, 44(1): 535–551.

INE (Instituto Nacional Electoral, Mexico's National Electoral Institute). (2018). "Cómputos distritales 2018 [2018's District Computations]." INE. Available at: https://computos2018.ine.mx/#/presidencia/nacional/1/1/1/1 (last accessed: 31 August 2018).

Lapegna, P. (2017). "Soybeans and Power: Genetically Modified Crops, Environmental Politics, and Social Movements in Argentina," *Agricultural History*, 91(3): 442–444.

Lara Flores, S.M. (1996). "Mercado de trabajo rural y organización laboral en el campo mexicano [Rural Labor Market and Labor Organizing in the Mexican Countryside", pp. 69–112 in Hubert C. de Grammont (ed.), *Neoliberalismo y organización social en el campo mexicano* [Neoliberalism and Social Organizing in the Mexican Countryside]. Mexico: Editorial Plaza and Valdés.

Lara Flores, S.M. (1998). *Nuevas experiencias productivas y nuevas formas de organización flexible del trabajo en la agricultura Mexicana* [New Productive Experiences and New Forms of Flexible Labor Organization in the Mexican Agriculture]. Mexico: Procuraduría Agraria and Juan Pablos Editor.

López Obrador, Andrés Manuel. 2017. *2018: La salida*. Mexico City: Editorial Planeta Mexicana.

Mackinlay, H. (1994). "Las reformas de 1992 a la legislación agraria: el fin de la reforma agraria y la privatización del ejido [1992 reforms and agrarian legislation; the end of agrarian reform and ejido's privatization]". *Polis* 93, Department of Sociology, UAM-I, Mexico, pp. 99–127.

Mackinlay, H. (2004). "Los empresarios agrícolas y ganaderos y su relación con el Estado mexicano durante la época del Partido Revolucionario Institucional (PRI) [Agricultural and livestock Enterprises and their Relations with the Mexican State in the PRI Era]" *Polis* 04, Vol. Dos, Department of Sociology, UAM-Iztapalapa, Mexico, pp. 113–143.

Mackinlay, H. (2008a). "Pequeños productores y Agronegocios en México: una retrospectiva histórica. Tendencia de expansión y operación de los agronegocios a principios del siglo 21 [Small producers and Aagribusiness in Mexico: a historical retrospective]". pp. 165–193 in B. Mançano Fernandes (ed.), *Campesinato e agronegócio na América Latina: a questão agrária atual* [Peasantry and Agribusiness in Latin America: The Current Agrarian Question], CLACSO (Argentina) and Editora Expressao Popular Ltda. (Brazil).

Mackinlay, H. (2008b). "Jornaleros agrícolas y agroquímicos en la producción de tabaco en Nayarit [Agricultural Laborers and Agrochemicals in Tobacco Production in Nayarit]". *Alteridades*, Department of Anthropology, UAM-Iztapalapa, 18(36): 123–143.

Marx, K. (1978 [1852]). *The Eighteenth Brumaire of Louis Bonaparte*, pp. 594–617 in *The Marx-Engels Reader*. 2nd Edition. Edited by R.C. Tucker. New York: W.W. Norton & Company.

McAdam, D. (1999 [1982]). *Political Process and the Development of Black Insurgency, 1930–1970*, 2nd Edition. Chicago: University of Chicago Press.

McAdam, D., J.D. McCarthy and M.N. Zald (eds) (1996). *Comparative Perspectives on Social Movements: Political Opportunities, Mobilizing Structures, and Cultural Framings*. Cambridge: Cambridge University Press.

McMichael, P. (2009). "A Food Regime Genealogy." *The Journal of Peasant Studies*, 36(1): 139–169.

McMichael, P. (2013). *Food Regimes and Agrarian Questions*. Halifax: Fernwood Press.

Morselli, A. (2014). "The Mutual Interdependence Between Human Action and Social Structure in the Evolution of the Capitalist Economy," *Microeconomics and Macroeconomics*, 2(1): 6–11.

OECD—Organization for Economic Cooperation and Development (2017). "Government at a Glance: Latin America and the Caribbean 2017," Country Fact Sheet. Mexico. OECD. Available at: www.oecd.org/gov/lac-mexico.pdf (last accessed: 31 August 2018).

Otero, G. (1989). "The New Agrarian Movement: Toward Self-Management and Democratic Production," *Latin American Perspectives*, 16(4): 29–59.

Otero, G. (1999). *Farewell to the Peasantry? Political Class Formation in Rural Mexico*. Boulder, CO and Oxford: Westview Press.

Otero, G. (2004a). "Global Economy, Local Politics: Indigenous Struggles, Civil Society and Democracy," *Canadian Journal of Political Science*, 37(2): 325–346.

Otero, G. (ed.) (2004b). *Mexico in Transition: Neoliberal Globalism, The State, and Civil Society*. London: Zed Books; Nova Scotia: Fernwood.

Otero, G. (2008). "Contesting Neoliberal Globalism in Mexico: Challenges for the Political and the Social Left," pp. 163–177 in P. Bowles, R. Broomhill, T. Gutierrez-Haces and S. McBride (eds), *International Trade and Neoliberal Globalism: Towards Re-Peripheralization in Australia, Canada and Mexico*. London: Routledge.

Otero, G. (2011). "Neoliberal Globalization, NAFTA, and Migration: Mexico's Loss of Food and Labor Sovereignty," *Journal of Poverty*, 15(4): 384–402.

Otero, G., G. Pechlaner and E. Gürcan (2013). "The Political Economy of "Food Security" and Trade: Uneven and Combined Dependency," *Rural Sociology* 78(3): 263–289.

Panizza, F. (2005). "Unarmed Utopia Revisited: The Resurgence of the Left-of-Centre Politics in Latin America," *Political Studies*, 53: 716–734.

Pérez Castañeda, J.C. (2002). *El nuevo sistema de propiedad agraria en México*. Mexico: Palabra en Vuelo.

Pérez Castañeda, J.C. (2007a). *La Planeación y el desarrollo rural* [Rural Planning and development]. Chamber of Deputies and Center for Sustainable Rural Development and Food Sovereignty Studies, Cámara de Diputados y Centro de Estudios para el Desarrollo Rural Sustentable y la Soberanía Alimentaria (CEDRSSA).

Pérez Castañeda, J.C. (2007b). *La Propiedad Agraria y el desarrollo rural* [The new System of Agrarian Property in Mexico]. Chamber of Deputies and Center for Sustainable Rural Development and Food Sovereignty Studies, Cámara de Diputados y Centro de Estudios para el Desarrollo Rural Sustentable y la Soberanía Alimentaria (CEDRSSA).

Pérez Castañeda, J.C. (2014). "Tierra, desamortización y ley de hidrocarburos [Land, disentailment and hydrocarbons law]". *Artículos y Ensayos de Sociología Rural*, 9(18), pp. 7–28. Department of Rural Sociology, Universidad Autónoma Chapingo.

Pérez Castañeda, J.C. (2017). "La planeación del desarrollo regional y la Ley de Desarrollo Rural Sustentable" [The Planning of the Regional Development and the Law of Sustainable Rural Development], in *Artículos y Ensayos de Sociología Rural*, 12(24), pp. 35–48, Department of Rural Sociology, Universidad Autónoma Chapingo.

Pérez Castañeda, J.C. and H. Mackinlay (2015). "¿Existe aún la propiedad social agraria en México? [Does Agrarian Social Property Still Exist in Mexico?]" *Polis*, 11(1): 45–82. Department of Sociology, UAM—Iztapalapa.

RAN (Registro Agrario Nacional, National Agrarian Registry) (2018). "Documento de trabajo para la 'Comisión de Agricultura, Ganadería y Desarrollo Rural' de la Cámara de Senadores" ["Working paper for the 'Committee on Agriculture, Livestock and Rural Development' of the Chamber of Senators"], XIV Legislature, November.

Robles Berlanga, H. (2009). *Saldos de las reformas de 1992 al artículo 27 constitucional, México* [Balances of the 1992 Reforms to Constitutional Article 27], Chamber of Deputies and Center for Sustainable Rural Development and Food Sovereignty Studies, Cámara de Diputados y Centro de Estudios para el Desarrollo Rural Sustentable y la Soberanía Alimentaria (CEDRSSA).

Rossie, F. (2018). "Social Movements, the New Social Question and the Popular Sectors in Argentina and Brazil," pp. 78–114 in S. Silva and F. Rossie (eds), *Reshaping the Political Arena in Latin America*. Pittsburgh, PA: University of Pittsburgh Press.

Rubin, J. (2002). "From Che to Marcos: The Changing Grassroots in Latin America," *Dissent*, 49(3): 39–37.

Rubio, L. and J. Davidow (2006). "Mexico's Disputed Election," *Foreign Affairs*, 85(5): 75–85.

Ruckert, A., L. McDonald and K.R. Proulx (2017). "Post-Neoliberalism in Latin America: A Conceptual Review," *Third World Quarterly*, 38(7): 1583–1602.

Ruiz Funes, M. (2018). "Jornaleros agrícolas y distorsiones de mercado [Agricultural Laborers and Market Distortions]," *El Financiero*, 25 October, p. 10.

Sánchez Saldaña, K. (2006). *The Captains of Tenextepango: A Study on Cultural Intermediation*. Mexico: Miguel Ángel Porrúa/Universidad Autónoma de Guerrero.

Veltmeyer, H. (2001a). "Decentralization and Local Development," pp. 46–66 in H. Veltmeyer and E. O'Malley (eds), *Transcending Neoliberalism*. Bloomfield: Kumarian Press.

Veltmeyer, Henry. (2001b). "The quest for another development," pp. 1–34 in H. Veltmeyer and A. O'Malley (eds), *Transcending Neoliberalism*. Bloomfield: Kumarian Press.

Veltmeyer, H. (2018). "Resistance, Class Struggle and Social Movements in Latin America: Contemporary Dynamics," *The Journal of Peasant Studies*, 1–22. https://doi.org/10.1080/03066150.2018.1493458.

Veltmeyer, H. and J. Petras (2014). *The New Extractivism: A Post-Neoliberal Development Model or Imperialism of the 21st Century*. London and New York: Zed Books.

Vergara-Camus, Leandro. (2014). *Land and Freedom: The MST, the Zapatistas and Alternatives to Neoliberalism*. London and New York: Zed Books.

Webber, J. (2017). *The Last Day of Oppression, and the First Day of the Same: The Politics and Economics of the Latin American Left*. Chicago: Haymarket Books.

Weber, Max (1978). *From Max Weber: Essays in Sociology*. Gerth, H.H. and C. Wright Mills (editors and translators). Oxford University Press.

Wittman, H. (2009). "Reworking the Metabolic Rift: La Vía Campesina, Agrarian Citizenship, and Food Sovereignty," *The Journal of Peasant Studies*, 36(4): 805–826.

Wolf, E.R. (1969). *Peasant Wars of the Twentieth Century*. New York: Harper & Row.

Wylde, C. (2016). "Post-Neoliberal Developmental Regimes in Latin America: Argentina under Cristina Fernandez de Kirchner." *New Political Economy*, 21(3): 322–341.

Wright, E.O. (2010). *Envisioning Real Utopias*. London and New York: Verso.

Zibechi, R. (2010). *Dispersing Power: Social Movements as Anti-State Forces*. Oakland: AK Press.

5 The syncopated dance of Mexico's industrial policy

*Juan Carlos Moreno-Brid,
Joaquín Sánchez Gómez and
Stefanie Garry*

Introduction

Since the mid-1980s, the mention of industrial policy in most debates on Mexico's development agenda has been politely brushed off as a relic of ineffective, over-meddling of the state in economic affairs. However, in contrast with this rhetoric, at the level of subnational entities, local authorities have applied a vast gamut of policy tools to attract foreign and domestic investors to boost and create new industrial clusters. There is evidence of success stories that—through the application of modern industrial policies at local levels—have radically transformed the productive matrix of certain regions in Mexico. Indeed, in these cases, such policies have been a crucial in the creation, practically from scratch, of new high-tech export-oriented internationally competitive industrial complexes.

Thus, at the same time that industrial policy faded away from the monitor of the development agenda at the national level, it has been silently and successfully resuscitated at local levels. In this syncopated dance, industrial policy has played second flute to trade policy at the national level. But it has had a leading role, thanks to a concerted action of local authorities, entrepreneurs, academia and civil society in stimulating a number of key activities in specific regions. This article aims to shed light on the contrasts of these antagonistic approaches to industrial policy; the passive ones that have characterised the strategy at the national level and the more active one at the local level. For this matter, we focus on two extremely successful cases of active, targeted industrial policies at the local level that ignited the development of two key industrial clusters: the aeronautical one in Querétaro and the software and computer one in Jalisco.

The chapter is organised as follows. The first section presents an analysis of the evolution of Mexico's industrial policy over the last three decades, tracing the shift from import substitution industrialisation (ISI) towards market fundamentalism. It notes that some targeted exceptions to a largely hands-off industrial policy, enabled the growth, and in some cases, the flourishing of key sectors, with important linkages with the global economy. The following section examines the policies that brought about the surge of the aeronautical cluster in Querétaro. The next one examines Jalisco's strategy to create the most important cluster in Mexico of software and computer activities. The final section presents our conclusions and puts forward some policy recommendation for López Obrador´s industrial development agenda.

Mexico's industrial policy: from import substitution industrialisation (ISI) to market fundamentalism

The rise of market fundamentalism and the demise of ISI (1982–2019)

In the early 1980s, in the aftermath of an acute balance of payments and fiscal crisis, Mexico began a radical shift in its development strategy. Through a series of market reforms, it opened domestic markets to foreign competition, rolled back state intervention in the economy, and set fiscal discipline and low inflation as top priorities for macroeconomic policy. It was argued that the reforms would trigger a boom in private investment that, aided by undistorted market signals, would bring about a structural transformation of the Mexican economy, and push it towards high and persistent export-led growth. From this perspective, manufacturing exports, with comparative advantages based on low labour costs, would become the new, dynamic engine of expansion.

As a sign of the backlash against industrial policy, the surge of manufacturing exports was alleged to have been achieved via the implementation of trade liberalisation and market competition policies, without the help of any subsidies, or special development programs like those applied by the newly industrialising countries in East Asia (NICS). Indeed, a key aspect of Mexico's market reform was the revoking of most of its active industrial policies, including the elimination of subsidies, and the phasing out of sectoral development programs.

As it was put by the Carlos Salinas' government (1988–1994), 'The best industrial policy is not having an industrial policy!' (Moreno-Brid and Ros, 2010). This shift implied that any strengthening of the already existing export-oriented hubs or clusters in Mexico—or the creation of new ones—and any upward movement in global value chains (GVCs) would be driven, if at all, by the response of private investment to the new policy environment. Private investment, so the story went, would blossom *pari-passu* as the crowding-out effects of public investment were retrenched. To put it succinctly, Mexican manufacturers were supposed to become internationally competitive, without any protectionist measures, or support from the government.

This radical wave of market reforms reached its crowning moment in 1993, with the signing of the North America Foreign Trade Agreement (NAFTA) between Canada, the United States, and Mexico. It aimed to create a region of free—in effect, scantly restricted—trade in goods and services, as well as capital flows. Mexico having opened its domestic market since the mid-1980s, NAFTA enabled it to benefit from easier and cheaper long-term access to the US market. Most importantly, being an international treaty, it was aimed to serve as a guarantee that market reforms could not be reversed by any future, say populist, government in Mexico.

NAFTA, coupled with Mexico's membership of the Organisation for Economic Cooperation and Development (OECD), virtually banned the implementation of active industrial policy. It stymied the country's export development programs, as well as the application of trade subsidies. With the agreement in place from 1995 onwards, sub-regional trade in a vast number of goods and services boomed on virtually unrestricted. In some sectors such as agriculture or finance, trade protection measures were lifted gradually, with the promise of elimination over a 10-to-15-year horizon. A very small group of activities, including oil extraction, were to remain fully protected over a much longer period.

The market reforms launched in the mid-1980s were deepened by subsequent administrations. Independently of changes in the political party in power in Mexico, the market friendly 'neoliberal' agenda remained unaltered. The implementation of NAFTA, deregulation, and competition policies continued to rule the roost, overshadowing any other policy tools. Regarding industrialisation, 'horizontal policies' dominated the agenda. These included setting up trade facilitation schemes, cutting red tape, implementing liberal labour reforms, organising trade fairs, establishing microcredit programs, and creating groups for policy dialogue between key agents of the private and public sectors to spur development in certain activities.

A revival of interest in active industrial policy occurred during the administration of Peña Nieto (2012–2018). In fact, the president himself identified it as a legitimate, powerful tool to transform the Mexican economy, boost its productivity, and generate employment. In his campaign he stated:

> [A] new industrial and technological policy should aim to reindustrialise the country, promote exports with higher added value, linked through value chains to bolster the domestic market, fostering higher domestic content in the maquiladora industry ... New sectors will be developed, such as aeronautics, nanotechnology, and simultaneously traditional sectors will be reconverted, such as textiles and footwear.
>
> (Colosio Foundation, 2013)

However, once in office the idea of implementing an active industrial policy did not materialise, save for a few important exceptions. Two of them will be examined in this text. In the *Pacto por México*—the major agreement signed in December 2012 by representatives of the main political parties to carry out additional economic reforms—there are scant references to active industrial policies. Besides stating that Mexico, 'in addition to be a manufacturing power [should] become an economy of knowledge' it does not highlight any policy tools to promote industrial development or such a transition. (*Pacto por México*, 2012).

By considering Mexico as a 'global manufacturing power', the *Pacto* failed to distinguish between the dynamic evolution of Mexico's manufacturing exports in terms of gross sales, and its painfully poor performance in terms of value added, productivity, and as engine of growth for rest of the economy. Moreover, its *National Development Plan 2012–2018* supported the notion that industrial policy can only aim at strengthening Mexico's already existing competitive advantages; not to creating or searching for new ones. In other words, it argued that state's intervention in the economy is justified, if at all, only to correct market failures. The build-up of new industrial hubs, or of new competitive advantages was decidedly out of bounds (Esquivel, 2010; Moreno-Brid and Ros, 2009).[1] In practice, Peña Nieto's agenda on industrial matters took concrete form in policy dialogues between government officers and representatives of business and labour organisations, aimed at identifying key obstacles to development, as well as coordinating actions to remove them. In general, they stayed within the limits of traditional horizontal policies. However, in some selected industries—prominently in the software and aeronautical sectors, and in exporting processing zones—with the support or push from local authorities direct interventions were implemented to build-up or strengthen industrial hubs.

Despite its export success in the last three decades, the overall performance of the manufacturing sector in terms of its pull-factors and linkages with the rest of the domestic economy was disappointing. From 1960 to 1982, the manufacturing's real GDP expanded at an annual average rate of 5.4 per cent. It did serve as an engine of growth for the overall economy, with an estimated multiplier to total GDP that systematically increased and reached a maximum of 1.15. Thereafter, with the opening of the economy it began to lose its capacity to stimulate the rest of the economy. By the end of the 1980s, the multiplier had fallen well below 1.0, and has not recovered since. In addition, the manufacturing industry itself lost momentum. From 1985 to 2012 its annual rate of expansion was 2.9 pe cent. Since then, it expanded at an even slower pace, barely above 2 per cent, on average. With the loss of dynamism, manufacturing's labour productivity also lagged behind. And has failed to create—directly or indirectly—a sufficient number of jobs to adequately absorb surplus labour from the rural areas. This, in turn, has contributed to a premature enlargement of the informal sector (Cordera, 2012; Samaniego, 2008).

A shift to the left

In July 2018, with the collapse of the PRI among voters' preferences, the left-wing party *Movimiento Regeneración Nacional* (MORENA) won the elections, and Andrés Manuel López Obrador was sworn in on 1 December 2018 as president, for the period 2019–2024. Surprisingly, given the constant diatribes against Neoliberalism, his government adopted an extremely orthodox fiscal policy—vowing to register a primary surplus, and to incur no new debt.

Moreover, so far, his administration has also maintained virtually the same 'horizontal' industrial policies as its predecessors. No economic incentives, initiatives or subsidies have been enacted to strengthen existing industrial hubs, or to build new ones. No explicit programs have been launched to search or to create new competitive advantages. One exception is the oil and energy industry, where López Obrador has given a much more prominent role to state-owned enterprises (SOEs), namely, *Petróleos Mexicanos* (Pemex) and the *Comisión Federal de Electricidad* (CFE).

The only application of active development policy so far in this administration has been the reduction of the value-added and income taxes in localities close to the US border. In fact, in its 225 pages, the *National Development Plan 2019–2024* (NDP) does not have a single mention of 'industrial policy'. The word 'manufacturing' appears just four times. Only once is it linked to a policy goal: 'To increase the local content of manufacturing exports from 27% in 2018 to 33% in 2024'. The NDP does mention its intention to 'create webs of local and regional suppliers by developing industrial hubs'. But it does not set any quantitative or qualitative targets to this effect. The only instrument that it specifically mentions to achieve this is public infrastructure. But in 2019 it cut public investment in nearly 20 per cent. As of February 2020, López Obrador′s administration is applying the same policies as previous regimes to stimulate industrial development, namely: competition policy, deregulation, trade liberalisation and facilitation. Its centrepiece is the United States–Mexico–Canada Agreement (USMCA), negotiated as a revision of NAFTA following intense pressure from Trump. It is too early in López Obrador's *Sexenio* to know whether he will remain aligned with the orthodox, conventional approach to industrial policy. Whether he will eventually put in place a modern industrial policy-cum-a-shift to an Entrepreneurial State is an open question, the answer to which may determine the fate of Mexico's quest for development.

Amid this push for market reforms and the vanquishing of active industrial policy, some development programs managed to survive. And a few initiatives at the local level to promote high-tech industries have been launched. The most notorious is the maquiladora program, started in 1965 and, with some changes, until recently still in operation. The automotive industry is a conspicuous example and beneficiary of NAFTA. Two key sectors that were stimulated are the software and aeronautical industries, for which special development programs prevail. In the case of software, *el Programa para el Desarrollo de la Industria de Software* (PROSOFT) was launched in 2002. Another policy initiative to promote industrial development, the Special Export Zones was formally, and very timidly, launched by Peña Nieto in January 2017. This initiative, however, failed to gain sufficient momentum, as well as economic and political support and was cancelled by López Obrador in April 2019.

In the following two sections we analyse key success stories of active industrial policy initiatives in Mexico at the local level: the software compound in Jalisco and the aeronautical cluster in Querétaro. For each case, a taxonomy of the activities that correspond to the industry is presented, as well as an analysis of the key players involved in the industry's operation. Next, stylised facts are presented to contextualise the sector's position in the economy, and highlight its linkages with certain global value chains. Most important, the active policies that were essential for the start-up or scale up of these industrial hubs and clusters in Mexico are further examined; identifying the specific policies and programs at the Federal and at the local level responsible for the success of the industry.

Querétaro: a local industrial policy to link Mexico into the global aerospace value chain

Introduction and global context

The aerospace industry covers all economic activities oriented to the manufacture of materials and products that orbit inside and outside Earth's atmosphere (Carrincazeaux and Frigant, 2007). It includes the design and production of aircraft, helicopters, missiles, satellites, motors and electronic equipment. Unlike the 'extractive industries' the aerospace industry has backward linkages with many other activities in the services sector, as well as with other manufacturing industries, such as electronics, mechanics, refrigeration systems and software, *inter alia*. As two well-known analysts of Mexico's industrial development have stated, 'it is an industry of industries' (Hualde and Carrillo, 2007).

In this industry, different national departments of defence have required the design and manufacture of war aircraft, missiles and other instruments that are manufactured with the collaboration of large companies. Examples include major manufacturers such as Boeing, Lockheed Martin, Bombardier and Airbus. Currently, the commercialisation of products is faster in the commercial aviation industry, as compared the space industry.

In the 1990s, the organisation of OEMs began to undergo a structural transformation, reflecting the accelerating relevance of innovation in electronics and telecommunications for the aerospace industry. Indeed, over the past three decades, innovations in software and electronic systems, as well as in the operation and design of aircraft became as, or even more important than engineering matters exclusively related to the design of machinery and parts (for example the fuselage). This technological shift, not to mention revolution of the industry, forced OEMs to delegate certain, relevant responsibilities to selected suppliers at the global level. These buyer–supplier relationships were organised into a sort of pyramidal structure.

The entire GVC—the production process from draft to final sale and service—was and continues to be led by the OEMs. The technological break, cum organisational restructuring of the aeronautical GVC allowed for and was accompanied by a certain redesign of its international production matrix. This translated into the relocation of some of its manufacturing operations to emerging countries. Such relocation was promoted by the OEMs, actively building-up new industrial hubs to harbour clusters of domestic suppliers and capacity building institutions, such as technological universities and training centres that operate in close collaboration with the OEMs.

Mexico has consolidated an important presence in the global aerospace industry. Currently, there are close to 300 companies, and support entities in the country, most of which have been certified by the National Aerospace and Defense Contractors Accreditation Program (NADCAP), as well as by AS9100. Aerospace sector exports, as shown in Figure 5.1, reached 5.5 billion dollars in 2013. Between 2006 and 2015, exports recorded an average annual growth rate of 15 per cent and reached a value of 7.1 billion dollars in 2016. According to

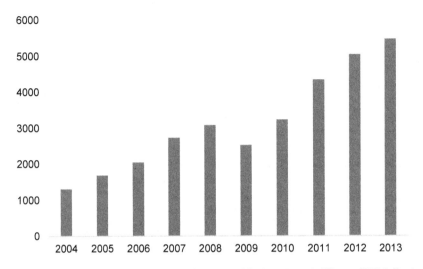

Figure 5.1 Exports of aerospace enterprises located in Querétaro (millions of US dollars).

Source: PROMÉXICO (2015).

Note
This information is the most recently available for the Aerospace Industry exports, according to the set of activities defined in this text. More updated information can be found only for a few activities listed above.

estimates from the 'Strategic Program of the Aerospace Industry 2010–2020', it is expected that the industry's exports will reach 12.3 billion dollars in 2021, with an average annual growth rate of 14%.

The aerospace industry in Mexico: policies and planning for Querétaro's 'take off'

The integration of Mexico into the aerospace GVC took place under a supply scheme at the Tier II and Tier III levels (Sánchez Gómez, 2019). Aerospace activities are operational in 18 Federal entities in Mexico; however, the main industrial district is centred in Querétaro. This process has been fostered through 'the attraction of leading companies, offering fiscal and commercial facilities' with the purpose of taking advantage of the proximity to the United States (Sandoval and Morales, undated). They have managed to generate productive and production linkages with local companies, leading to the formation of agglomeration economies. In this sense, the aerospace industry in Querétaro is composed mostly of supply activities in complementary industries such as chemicals, electrical and telecommunications.

The main products that are manufactured in Mexico by OEMs are harnesses, semi-conductors, components for turbojets, complete structures for the assembly of the fuselage, and recently, aerobatic aircraft that are mostly used by the armed forces. Production occurs with the participation of companies such as Bombardier, Safran, General Electric and Airbus, among others. According to the Ministry of Economy, the aerospace industry has managed to grow by an average of 17 per cent per year, which has allowed the country to position itself as an attractive place for the development of products occupying the lower value-added segments of the aerospace value chain (Morales, Sandoval and Diaz, 2019).

Notably, some of the most important multinational companies in the world operate in Querétaro. These include Bombardier, General Electric, Safran and Honeywell, which have there found favourable conditions to develop production lines and laboratories, as well as engineering and design centres. These enterprises are developing capacities to evolve towards more complex products and production systems.

The impact of Mexico's aerospace industry on value added and employment

The development of the modern aerospace industry in Querétaro is linked to the existence of other industries, such as metalworking, automotive and electronics, which already had developed sufficient human capital stocks in Mexico to support the arrival, and development of new industries linked with the country's existing productive sectors. Table 5.1 displays the industrial classification of activities located in the aerospace hub affiliated to the *Aerocluster de Querétaro*. Map 5.1 below illustrates the distribution of these enterprises within the state of Querétaro.

The main production linkages related to the economic activities comprising the aerospace industry in Querétaro were identified based on the national 2013

Table 5.1 Industrial activities at the aerospace hub in Querétaro

Industry code	Name	Industry code	Name
326290	Other rubber product manufacturing	336410	Aerospace product and parts manufacturing
326192	Manufacture of plastic auto-parts with and without reinforcement	435220	Wholesale of machinery and equipment for the manufacturing industry
331420	Copper rolling, drawing extruding, and alloying	488111	Air traffic control
332710	Machine shops	488112	Airport operations
332810	Coating, engraving, heat treating, and allied activities	541510	Computer systems design and related services
336360	Motor vehicle seating and interior trim manufacturing	611312	Colleges, universities and professional schools
336390	Other motor vehicle parts manufacturing	811312	Commercial and industrial machinery and equipment

Source: North American Industry Classification System (2017).

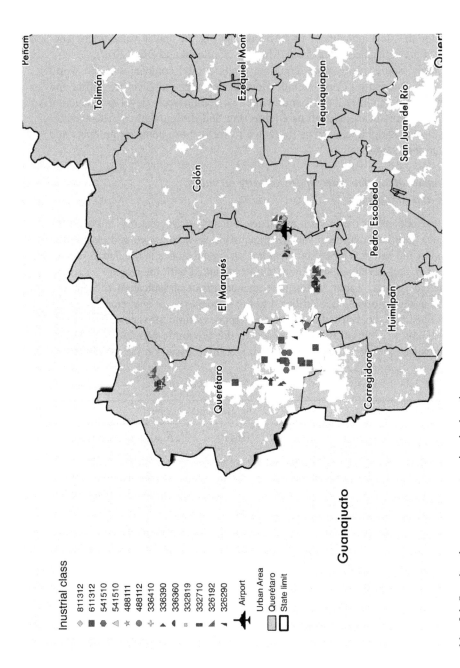

Map 5.1 Querétaro's aerospace enterprises by location.

Source: Authors' own elaboration using DENUE-INEGI (2019).

Input-Output Matrix developed by INEGI (Leontief, 1986). This enabled the authors to assess the impact of each industrial class on the generation of value added and jobs in the rest of the economy.

Figure 5.2 shows the multiplier effect of the industrial activities that comprise the aerospace industry in terms of value added for the total Mexican economy. The highest impact is seen in machinery workshops (332710), where an inflow of an additional million pesos into the sector would generate a total of 1.77 million pesos. In Querétaro, companies such as Protecva, BW Machining and New Motech operate in the machinery workshops industry, and are specialised in the production of laminates, plates for cooling systems and supplies for the electromechanical industry.

According to our results, the main backward linkages in the domestic market are with the ferroalloys and commercial activities industries, as well as with steel complexes, and the production of iron and steel (imports). In contrast, the lowest multiplier effect is on the manufacture of seats and internal mouldings of automotive vehicles (336360), where an additional million pesos in the aerospace sector had a total effect of an additional 500 thousand pesos of value-added production in the industry. In Mexico, companies such as Hawker Beechcraft are responsible for producing complete seats and components and for automotive vehicles.

Figure 5.3 shows the employment multiplier effect of the aerospace industry on other economic activities in Mexico. The highest impact is concentrated in computer systems design and related services (541510), with a multiplier of 3.97 jobs in the overall economy. In contrast, the lowest multiplier effect is in air traffic control (488111), where an additional million pesos in the final demand, creates only one job in the rest of the economy.

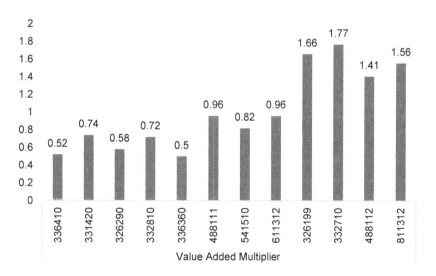

Figure 5.2 Aerospace industry in Mexico: value added multipliers.

Source: Authors' own estimations using the INEGI 2013 Input-Output Matrix.

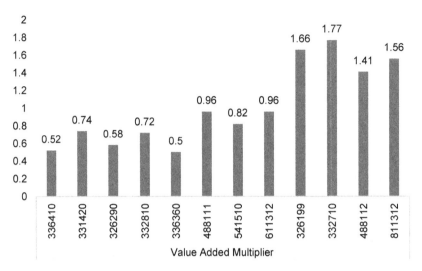

Figure 5.3 Aerospace industry in Mexico: employment multipliers.

Source: Authors' own estimates using INEGI 2013 Input-Output Matrix.

Industrial policy in the aerospace hub: a creative melting pot of the government, academia and enterprises

The first impulse of industrial policy for the aerospace industry in Mexico took place in 2004–2007; laying the foundations for its development. Two notable actors at the Federal level were responsible for launching the original idea, and enacting the relevant program of support to ensure the industry's success. The first was the Ministry of Economy, through the directorates of Foreign Investment, Industry and Technology and Trade. The second one was the Office of the National Strategic Programme for Incubating Technology Companies, also known as the International Accelerator of Technological Companies (TechBA).

The Ministry of Economy began to implement a coordinated series of actions that enabled the development, and eventual flourishing of the aerospace industry in Mexico. Such activities have mainly been centred in Querétaro, where relevant actors have achieved a certain level of integration and coordination between them. In 2005, driven by an initiative of the Director of Safran and Bombardier, the Aerocluster de Querétaro was formally founded. The Aerocluster serves as a melting pot of key industry organisations and actors, linking companies and academics operational in the Querétaro Aerospace hub together with the strategic Federal and local government agencies.

This interaction was made possible the implementation of various industrial policies by the Federal government, as well as by the government of the state of Querétaro. One of them relates to the active fostering of synergies among science, technology and innovation, leading to the establishment of the National

Center for Aeronautical Technologies (CENTA in Spanish). CENTA is specialised in the investigation of light materials for aircrafts, and the development of fatigue and temperature tests. Moreover, CENTA provides space and infrastructure to facilitate the development of entrepreneurs. For example, within its installations, the Hawk 1 and 2 aircraft were developed by HorizonTech.

The success and establishment of the aerospace industry in Mexico is in a way the final result of a long process of economic and institutional development of Querétaro, that made it some time ago a centre of metal-mechanic industries. In the case of Querétaro, the city's airport served as an important connective node, and a pole for attracting industry to the area. Near the airport, an industrial park with sui generis characteristics was established, and the Aeronautical University of Querétaro was founded in 2007.

The university currently offers training programs at the Higher Technical University, with programs in Engineering, as well as Master and Certification Programs for the companies of the Aerocluster de Querétaro. As part of its innovative approach to learning, and to further strengthen industrial linkages, the university pioneered an educational model, in which students learn and work in conditions similar to those of an aeronautical sector production plant. They have implemented an integrated educational program in which there are no classrooms, and which recreates a factory environment where students work with real aircraft. From an early stage in their training, and technical capacity building they are allowed to disarm, arm and repair actual aircraft. Moreover, students, and academics of the university collaborate directly with firms such as Bombardier, Safran and Airbus, among others.

The development of the aerospace hub in Querétaro allowed Mexico to attract investments to produce inputs of high demand into the aerospace GVC, which continue to be linked to higher-value-added manufacturing process abroad. Mexico also produces much-needed components for aircraft service and maintenance. In this sense, Mexico's aerospace industry was able to insert itself into a global supply scheme at Tier II and Tier III levels. Despite this success, further upgrading and value addition in the chain towards the manufacture of commercial aircrafts in Mexico is difficult. The future challenge is therefore how to devise a set of integral industrial policies and programmes that boost scientific and technological development in support of higher value added in Mexico's aerospace hub.

Jalisco: concerted policies to shape the software and computing industry

The software industry in Mexico

The Information Technology (IT) sector includes software development and the outsourcing of business process services. Software itself can be classified into the following dimensions: packaged software, custom software and embedded software. There are also references to in-house software, which is customised software developed internally for specific businesses, or lines of operation. In the case of Mexico, we refer to software as a service, which means not only the adaptation of software packages to the customer's needs, but also its daily operation. It includes then a type of outsourcing of the systems and administrative areas of companies by a computer specialist.

At the beginning of the 2000s, Mexico had high expectations about the potential of the software industry, which was developing and growing at a rapid pace. The expenditure on information and communication technologies (ICTs) was 1.4 per cent of GDP, which placed Mexico in 19th place worldwide. This was, however, way below the 4.3 per cent of GDP spent by OECD countries, and the 5.5 per cent of GDP directed towards ICT development by the United States.

Embedded software refers to sensors, actuators and components that have customised programming inside. This, in essence, refers to software placed inside of relevant technological hardware. It already had begun to appear as a niche market worldwide, and at the national level was beginning to pique the interest of strategic actors, especially in Jalisco, as Francisco Medina, former General Director of COECYTJAL, has stated many times.

One of the most important problems then facing the Mexican software industry was the limited human resources capacities stemming from a lack of specialised training and education. Moreover, inadequate infrastructure, and the absence of a supportive, or enabling legal framework hindered the sector's early development. Lack of models for evaluation, as well as certifications for specific processes were additional barriers. At the enterprise level, lack of access to financing remained an additional challenge.

The economic structure of Jalisco: the relevance of the software industry

The main economic activities in Jalisco are trade (which contributed 22 per cent of total GDP in 2017) followed by manufacturing industries (22 per cent), and real estate services (12.6 per cent). In the case of the software industry, as Table 5.2 below illustrates, it is composed of two main activities: manufacture of computers and peripheral equipment (NAICs code 334110) and electronic processing of information, lodging and other related services (NAICs code 518210).

Map 5.2 shows the geographical distribution of the companies dedicated to these two activities in the municipalities that make up the Metropolitan Area of Guadalajara. In total, total 44 companies are engaged in both activities. Sixteen enterprises are dedicated to the manufacture of computers and peripheral equipment, while 28 enterprises are engaged in electronic information processing.

Table 5.2 Industrial activities in the software industry in Jalisco

Industry code	Name
334110	Computer and peripheral equipment manufacturing
518210	Data processing, hosting, and related services

Source: North American Industry Classification System (2017).

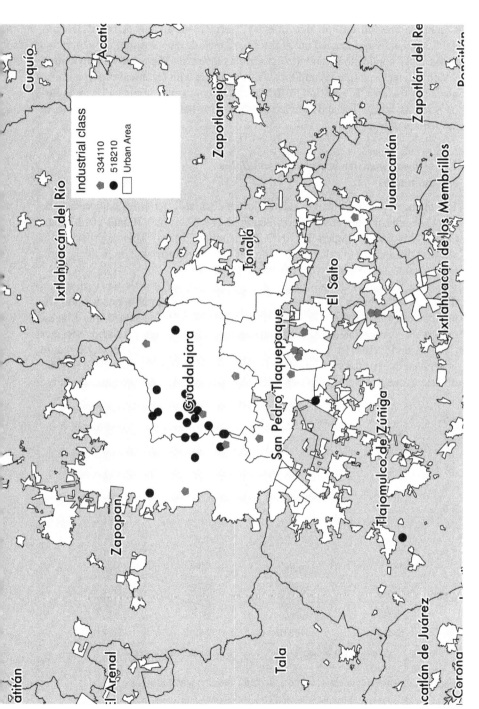

Map 5.2 Software enterprises in the state of Jalisco, by industrial class.

Source: Authors' own elaboration, using DENUE-INEGI (2019).

Among these companies, IBM stands out as a major employer, as it carries out multiple tasks and services in the region. Jalisco is host to the 'Smarter Data Centre', a specialised hub that offers IT services in an 'on demand' scheme. Additional activities carried out at the centre include data hosting, the generation of business applications, and virtualisation processes. The 'Innovation Centre', which connects companies and local entrepreneurs with technical experts, is also hosted in the area. In addition to IBM, leading companies in the software industry such as Jabil, Flex and Hewlett Packard also have significant operations in the federal entity.

The software industry in Jalisco: a multiplier effects analysis

The main production linkages related to the economic activities comprising the software industry in Jalisco were identified based on the national 2013 Input-Output Matrix developed by INEGI (Leontief, 1986). This approach also allowed the authors to calculate the impact of each industrial class in the generation of value added and jobs in the rest of the economy.

Figure 5.4 shows the multiplier effect of the industrial activities comprising the software industry in terms of value added for the total economy and the number of potential jobs to be created. In terms of value added, the highest impact is concentrated in Data Processing, Hosting and Related Services (NAICS code 518210), where an additional million pesos in the sector would generate a total of 0.88 million pesos in the entire economy. In Jalisco, a number of data process, hosting and related services companies are operational. These

Figure 5.4 Software industry: value added and employment multipliers.

Source: Authors' own estimations using INEGI 2013 Input-Output Matrix.

include Advantage IT Solutions, Senden and Nystec. They are specialised in e-commerce operations, hosting, application development, data warehousing and project management.

In contrast, the lowest multiplier effect was observed for Computer and Peripheral Equipment Manufacturing (334110), where an additional million pesos in the sector would have a total effect of only 320 thousand pesos. Within Jalisco, companies such as IBM, ETTO, Sanmina and Seagate, among others, are engaged in this activity.

With regard to the potential of the sector to generate new employment opportunities, the highest impact is concentrated in the same activity as the value-added multiplier, Data Processing, Hosting and Related Services (518210), where an additional million pesos in the sector creates 4.08 job positions in the total economy. In contrast, the lowest multiplier effect is in 34110, where an additional million pesos creates only 0.98 job positions in the rest of the economy.

Industrial policy in Jalisco: the role of PROSOFT in the formation of the industry

Targeted and purposeful industrial polices shaped the software industry in Jalisco, and ensured its continued relevance as an economic powerhouse. Entrepreneurs, educational institutions, and the Federal government jointly developed initiatives that would give rise to the development of the Software Industry Program (PROSOFT), which was implemented in 2002. PROSOFT's origins are associated with the software industry, but drawing on its success, it soon also expanded to include IT, multimedia or creative industries, as well as IT-based services. PROSOFT was a major trigger for industrial dynamics. The promotion of the software industry by the state of Jalisco included several agencies, programs and institutional arrangements. It should be noted that at that time, Jalisco had its own program called Information Technology, Microelectronics and Multimedia (known as TIMEMU for its Spanish acronym). PROSOFTJAL (managed by the Jalisco state government) was launched in 2004. The objective was to promote the software industry and extend this technology to the market of Information Technology, Microelectronics, Multimedia and Aerospace. Support was aimed at the formation and development of human capital, improvements in the level of quality, and innovation, the development of entrepreneurial skills, the bolstering of promotion and marketing, and the strengthening of regional capacities and business groupings.

The program was extremely valuable for all relevant actors in this industry in Jalisco, but for different reasons. The local government had additional funds to boost the development strategy of the IT industry. In a similar manner, existing businesses gained access to fresh resources, which enabled them to grow. The success of the software industry in Jalisco is the result of collaboration between enterprises, and the Federal and local governments, in particular, with the Jalisco government, which has promoted the sector through dependencies, such as COECYTJAL, IJALTI and programs such as TIMEU, which focused on the development of IT, microelectronics and multimedia.

The relevant policies and programs also benefitted international companies like IBM that managed to technologically scale up their operations in Guadalajara. Starting from the 1970s with the manufacture of typewriters, targeted industrial support to the software sector has enabled the business to shift and modernise towards it current role as a manufacturer of custom storage and software equipment. IBM has also managed to link up with universities and research centres to attract talent.

However, a wide number of the enterprises in the sector are now facing difficulties to promote continued innovation processes. This is reflected in the low capacity to undertake projects with greater technical complexity and higher embedded value-added content. This could allow catch-up processes to occur along the software value chain. This weakness has increased imports as a proportion of value added from 2008 to 2013, leading to a reduction in the employment and value-added multipliers.

It is desirable that the industrial policy for this sector keeps or strengthens its long-term vision, with a key intermediate goal of further developing professional and organisational capacities. In addition, it is essential to continue working on planning, and manufacturing with a road map fully geared towards Industry 4.0. Within this framework, it is urgent to strengthen the governance scheme of the industry in particular to facilitate the access of 'developer' companies to long-term finance, and thus equip them with greater tools to overcome the barriers to entry in the industry.

Conclusions

Despite the largely passive approach to industrial policy at the Federal level in Mexico over the last 30 years, there have been successful experiences of highly active industrial policy implementation. Interestingly, a key underlying ingredient for these successes has been the strong interaction between the government—at both Federal and state levels—academia and the private business sector. Their interaction had the explicit aim to boost key sectors of industrial activity in specific regions in the country, and tool concrete and enviable form in policies, programs with set goals.

In the case of PROSOFT, Federal and state actors joined forces to create a national software industry, while a regionalised version of the program, designed and implemented in the state of Jalisco, enabled the formation of a strategic industrial hub. In the case of the aerospace industry, the role of the federal government and the state of Querétaro combined to foster the formation of a highly successful cluster, with important linkages in the aerospace GVC.

Among the lessons that can be derived from the Mexican experience is that, in spite of the neglect or rejection of an active industrial policy at the level of the national agenda for development, there is ample room at the local level for its application if the key sector join forces towards common goals, and induce foreign investors to participate. Success in industrial policy will eventually be, as Rodrik and Hausman have stated, the result of a continuous process of experimentation, learning and design setting. In this process there is the recognition of the importance of 'learning by doing', and the acceptance of a pragmatic approach where there is not a single recipe, nor a 'one size fits all' formula for industrial policy formulation or implementation. Moreover, industrial policy cannot and should not be conceived as an activity, as a task of exclusive competence of the state, of the public sector. Far from this, for industrial policy to persist as a legitimate and dynamic process and to advance to its goals, it must include the participation of the private sector from an early stage.

Its view is indispensable to guide the policies, programs, goals and priorities according to the needs, possibilities and potential of the specific industry in case, and the regional economy as a whole. Finally, as the case studies show, the state should not be seen as a monolithic actor for the sake of industrial policies. On the contrary, the fate of such policies depends too on the coordinated and active participation of different levels of state actors. Political vision and continuity do matter for successful industrial policies to be implemented and achieve their objectives. Changes in administrations can be disruptive as they generate situations of instability in public officials and gaps in public management during the transition processes. These disruptions are always negative in the short run, but in some cases they bring new, more favourable visions of industrial polices for development coupled with more resources and better business environments for public–private partnerships. The presidential elections in 2018 in Mexico brought a MORENA, a new party, to power ending decades of only PRI or PAN administrations. So far, its approach to industrial policy at the national level, has been as orthodox as the one of the precious administrations. Trade policy is once again ruling the roost in the national development agenda, with industrial policy being virtually absent. Whether this policy orientation prevail in the next five years remaining in López Obrador's Sexenio is an open question.

Note

1 This view is radically opposed to other approaches put forward by Amsden (2001), Chang (2002), ECLAC (2012), Rodrik (2004, 2008) and Hausmann et al. (2005). Recently, Cherif and Hasanov (2019), from the IMF, have argued that a modern view of industrial policy to promote technology, innovation, and export sophistication is a legitimate, and necessary tool to build-up dynamic competitive advantages.

Bibliography

Acta Constitutiva del CLAUT (2007). *Escritura Número 5,940 del libro 114 ante el Notario Público 130 del Municipio de Monterrey, Nuevo León, Mexico.*

Amsden, A. (2001). *The Rise of "the Rest": Challenges to the West from Late-industrializaing Economies.* Oxford: Oxford University Press.

Atlas de la Complejidad Económica. (n.d.). *¿Quienes somos?* Obtenido de http://complejidad.datos.gob.mx/#/about/project-description

Banco de México. (2018). *Las Zonas Económicas Especiales de México.* Mexico.

BID and Gobierno de Nuevo León (2009). *Monterrey, Ciudad Internacional del Cono-cimiento*, Grupo Editorial Movimiento Actual S.A. de C.V.: Monterrey.

Carrincazeaux, C. and V. Frigant (2007). "The Internationalization of the French Aerospace Industry: To What Extent Were the 1990s a Break with the Past?" *Competition and Change*: 261–285.

Casalet, M. (2013). *La Industria Aeroespacial. Complejidad productiva e institucional.* Mexico: FLACSO México.

Chang, H.-J. (2002). *Kicking Away the Ladder: Development Strategy in Historical Perspective.* London: Anthem Press.

Cherif, R. and F. Hasanov (2019). "The Return of the Policy that Shall Not Be Named: Principles of Industrial Policy," *VOXEU.*

CIA. (27 de Mayo de 2019). *Central Intelligence Agency.* Obtenido de The World Factbook: www.cia.gov/library/publications/the-world-factbook/fields/381.html

Cimoli, M. and G. Dosi (2008). The Future of Industrial Policies in the New Millennium: Toward a Knowledge-centered Development Agenda. *LEM Papers Series.*

Colosio Foundation (2013). Statutes. http://fundacióncolosio.mx/content/media/ESTATUTOS.pdf

Colosio, F. (2013). *El futuro que vemos: Memoria de los encuentros por el futuro de México.* Mexico: Fundación Colosio.

Comité Nacional de Productividad. (15 de Noviembre de 2016). *Acciones y estrategias para Democratizar la Productividad.* Retrieved from www.senado.gob.mx/comisiones/productividad/reu/docs/151116_JR.pdf

Coparmex. (2017 йил 11-Diciembre). *Propuesta Coparmex de Reforma Fiscal.* Retrieved from www.coparmex.org.mx/downloads/ENVIOS/COMPILACION_PROPUESTA_DE_REFORMA_FISCAL.pdf

Cordera, R. (2012). "Manifiesto por la construcción de un nuevo modelo democrático de Estado de Bienestar," *Economía UNAM*, 9(25): 94–97.

Di Maggio, M., and Kermani, A. (2016). *The Importance of Unemployment Insurance as an Automatic Stabilizer.* Cambridge, MA: The National Bureau of Economic Research.

Díaz, M. Y. (n.d.). "Dinámica de la cadena global aeroespacial y sus factores de competitividad y estancamiento; un análisis con teoría de grafos," *Contaduría y Administración*, Issue 64, No. 64–1, enero-marzo de 2019.

Domínguez, L. and F. Brown (2018). *Fuerzas motoras y obstáculos de la cadena aeroespacial en México.* Mexico: Facultad de Economía, UNAM.

Dussel, E. (2018). *Cadenas Globales de Valor.* Mexico: Facultad de Economía.

Dutrénit, G., J. Moreno-Brid and J. Sánchez (2018). *Políticas de Desarrollo Productivo en México.* Lima: Organización Internacional del Trabajo.

ECLAC (2012). *Capital Flows to Latin America and the Caribbean. Recent Developments.* Washington, DC: ECLAC.

Esquivel, G. (2010). "De la inestabilidad macroeconómica al estancamiento estabilizador: el papel del diseño y la conducción de la política económica," pp. 35–77 in *Los grandes problemas de México.* Mexico: El Colegio de México.

Farole, T. (n.d.). *Special Economic Zones: What Have We Learned?* Washington, DC: World Bank-Economic Premises.

Farole, T. and G. Akinci (2011). *Special Economic Zones: Progress, Emerging Challenges and Future Directions.* Washington, DC: The World Bank.

Farole, T. and G. Akinci (2016). *Federal Law of Special Economic Zones.* Mexico: Mexican Government.

FEMIA/PROMÉXICO. (2012). *Programa Estratégico de la Industria Aeroespacial.* Mexico: PROMÉXICO.

FIAS. (2008). *Special Economic Zonez Performance, Lessons Learned, and Implications for Zone Development.* Washington, DC: The World Bank Group.

Finanzas Públicas (CEFP) (2016). *Indicadores socieconómicos de entidades federativas del sur y sureste consideradas por la Ley Federal de las Zonas Económicas especiales (ZEE) en México.* Mexico: Cámara de Diputados.

Gaudin, Y. and R. Padilla (2013). *Sistemas nacionales de innovación en Centroamérica.* Santiago: CEPAL.

Gobierno de México. (2012). *Pacto por México.* Mexico: Gobierno de México.

Gobierno de México. (2019). *National Development Plan 2019–2024.* Mexico: Gobierno de México.

González, F. (2015). La industria aeroespacial en México. *Comercio Exterior*: 24–29.

Hanson, G. (2012). *Understanding Mexico's Economic Underperformance.* Woodrow Wilson International Center for Scholars. Washington, DC: The Regional Migration Study Group.

Hausmann, R., L. Pritchett and D. Rodrik (2005). "Growth Accelerations," *Journal of Economic Growth*, 10(4): 303–329.

Hualde, A. and J. Carrillo (2005). *Diagnóstico de la industria aeroespacial en Baja California Características productivas y requerimientos actuales y potenciales de capital humano.* Tijuana, Mexico: El Colegio de la Frontera Norte.

Hualde, A. and J. Carillo (2007). *La Industria Aeroespacia en Baja California.* Tijuana: El Colegio de la Frontera Norte.

INEGI. (30 de Octubre de 2013). *La contabilidad del crecimiento y la productividad total en México.* Obtenido de www.inegi.org.mx/eventos/2013/contabilidad_mexico/presentacion.aspx

INEGI. (2013). *Sistema de Clasificación Industrial de América del Norte, México SCIAN 2013.* Ciudad de México: INEGI.

INEGI. (27 de Mayo de 2019). *Directorio Estadístico de Unidades Económicas.* Retrieved from www.inegi.org.mx

Leontief, W. (1986). *Input-Output Economics.* Oxford and New York: Oxford University Press.

Máttar, J., and W. Peres (1997). "La política industrial y de comercio exterior en México," in P. Wilson (ed.), *Políticas de competitividad industrial.* Ciudad de México: Siglo XXI.

Mazzucato, M. (2015). *The Entrepreneurial State. Debunking Public vs. Private Sector Myths.* New York: Public Affairs.

Miller, R. and P. Blair (2009). *Input-Output Analysis.* New York: Cambridge University Press.

Morales, A., S. Sandoval and H. Diaz (2019). "Estrategia de escalamiento en las cadenas globales de valor: el caso del sector aeroespacial en México," *Entre Ciencias*, 7(20): 35–52.

Moreno-Brid, J.C. (2013). "Industrial Policy: A Missing Link in Mexico's Quest for Export-led Growth," *Latin American Policy*, 4(2): 216–237.

Moreno-Brid, J.C. and J. Ros (2009). *Development and Growth in the Mexican Economy: A Historical Perspective.* Oxford: Oxford University Press.

Moreno-Brid, J.C. and J. Ros (2010). "¿Por qué ha sido decepcionante el crecimiento posterior al periodo de reformas?" pp. 293–330 in *Desarrollo y crecimiento en la economía mexicana.* Mexico: Fondo de Cultura Económica.

Muñoz, A. and F. Martínez (2019). Confirma AMLO desaparición de zonas económicas especiales. *La Jornada*, 25 April.

OECD. (2007). Recuperado el 02 de noviembre de 2017, de www.oecd.org/sti/inno/39374789.pdf

OECD. (2015). México. Policy Priorities to Upgrade the Skills and Knowledge of Mexicans for Greater Productivity and Innovation. *Better Policies*.

Plan Nacional de Desarrollo Industrial: bases de concertación para su cumplimiento (Diario Oficial de la Federación 19 de Marzo de 1979).

Padilla, R. (2014). *Fortalecimiento de las cadenas de valor como instrumento de la política industrial.* Santiago: CEPAL.

Pérez Castañeda, J.C. (2007). *La planeación y el desarrollo rural.* Distrito Federal: Centro de Estudios para el Desarrollo Rural Sustentable y la Soberanía Alimentaria.

Presidencia de la República. (2017). *5to Informe de Gobierno 2016–2017.* Ciudad de Mexico: Gobierno de los Estados Unidos Mexicanos.

Programa para Democratizar la Productividad 2013–2018 (Diario Oficial de la Federación 30 de Agosto de 2013).

PROMÉXICO. (2015). *Mexico's Aerospace Industry Road Map.* Mexico: PROMÉXICO.

Ríos, V. (2016). *¿Cómo crear Zonas Económicas Especiales que creen y redistribuyan riqueza en México?* Mexico: Friedrich Ebert Stiftung.

Rodrik, D. (2004). *Industrial Policy for the Twenty-First Century.* Cambridge, MA: Harvard University.

Rodrik, D. (2008). Normalizing Industrial Policy. *Commission on Growth and Development.* Working Paper, Vol. 1, Report no. 57703. World Bank, Washington DC.

Rodrik, D. (13 de enero de 2016). The return of Public Investment. *Project Syndicate.*

Romero, J.A. (2010). *La hélice Anáhuac. Un siglo después.* Retrieved from: www.uaq. mx/investigacion/revista_ciencia@uaq/ArchivosPDF/v4-n3/t4.pdf

Rubio, F. (Febrero de 2018). Entrevista a Felipe Rubio, Director del CENTA Querétaro. (G. Dutrénit, A. Vera, J. Sánchez, and A. Torres, Entrevistadores)

Ruiz Durán, C. (2013). *Nueva política industrial ¿Opción para un desarrollo sustentable e inclusivo en México?* Mexico: Friedrich Ebert Stiftung.

Sánchez Gómez, J. (2019). *México en la integración de Cadenas de Valor: el caso de la Industria Aeroespacial.* Ciudad de México: Universidad Nacional Autónoma de México.

Sánchez Juárez, I.L. and Moreno-Brid, J.C. (2016). El reto del crecimiento económico en México: industrias manufactureras y política industrial. *Finanzas y Política Económica*, 271–299.

Samaniego, N. (2008). El crecimiento explosivo de la economía informal. *Economía UNAM*, 5(13): 30–41.

Sandoval, M. (Febrero de 2018). Entrevista al ex CEO de TechBA en Montreal y ex Director Ejecutivo de Análisis Prospectivo e Innovación de PROMÉXICO. (G. Dutrénit, Entrevistador)

Secretaría de Economía/FEMIA. (2009). *Plan Nacional de Vuelo.* Mexico: Secretaría de Economía. Obtenido de www.gob.mx/cms/uploads/attachment/file/58802/Plan_Estrat_gico_de_la_Industria_Aeroespacial_junio.pdf

Secretaría de Economía/FEMIA. (2014). *Plan Nacional de Vuelo.* Mexico: Secretaría de Economía.

Secretaría de Economía. (2017). *5to Informe de Labores 2016–2017.* Ciudad de México: Secretaría de Economía.

Zeng, D.Z. (2011). *How Do Special Economic Zones and Industrial Clusters Drive China's Rapid Development?* Washington, DC: The World Bank.

6 Communes in Venezuela in times of crisis

Dario Azzellini

From the year 2000 onwards in Venezuela, popular organisations, communities and even some institutions have developed various local self-government initiatives. From those experiences arose in 2005 the Communal Councils as a form of self-administration at the neighbourhood level, followed by the Communes in 2007 as the tier of self-government above that. Both developed from below; although their massive expansion was due to formal support by the state, the laws regulating them were only devised after they had become a widespread practice. Out of the different experiences and initiatives, an outline emerges from below of what Chávez called 'the communal state', which has become the political and social project of the popular movements in Venezuela. However, since self-government arises in a context of representative democracy and private and state-owned economy, councils are constantly engaged in struggle. They have a complex relationship of cooperation and conflict with the institutions of representative democracy. The latter co-exist with the former, but maintain a dominant position in an asymmetric power relationship; even though they officially support the development of self-administration, they often interfere with it and obstruct it. Since 2013, under president Nicolás Maduro, structures of self-government have experienced decreasing institutional support, and have been displaced from the centre of government discourse in favour of institutional and party hierarchies. Following the severe economic crisis, financial support has also been significantly reduced. Nevertheless, council structures have endured and are the main organisational framework through which communities build mechanisms to resist the consequences of the crisis.

The council system

From the very early 2000s, the Bolivarian government started experimenting with mechanisms of popular participation in institutional decisions. The first examples mirrored experiments that existed in other places, such as participatory budgets.[1] They then experimented with the creation of bodies to bring together institutional (e.g. the municipalities) and grassroots representatives, the Local Councils of Public Planning (*Consejos Locales de Planificación Pública*, CLPP). Those experiments were considered a failure. The new institutions were still largely representative bodies with a very clear power inequality or asymmetry between grassroots delegates and institutional representatives. This made them inadequate for facilitating grassroots autonomy and decision-making. The difficulties in the operation of those structures were not limited to municipalities controlled by the opposition but also occurred in Chavista ones (Azzellini, 2018: 84–92).

Starting in 2005 people in Venezuela have been organising themselves in structures called Communal Councils (*consejos comunales*, CCs) although at the beginning different names were used by the various communities that developed comparable structures. CCs are a non-representative form of local self-government based on assemblies and direct democracy. After the failure of the CLPP, Chávez redirected his attention to the CCs that had been created from below and disseminated awareness of them by placing them at the centre of his public discourse. He presented them as 'good practices', visited them with his weekly TV show *Aló Presidente*, and promoted legal and institutional initiatives in their support. This gave the CCs a significant boost. As a consequence of publicising the legal initiative, CCs were created in many places. Chávez's commitment to the CCs strengthened the council form in general, so it can be argued that from 2006 onwards this communal council logic began to expand.

The first Law of Communal Councils was passed in April 2006, when some 5,000 CCs had already been formed. Informed by past experiences, the law defined CCs as small entities and independent institutions. CCs rapidly became the central mechanism for participation; as such, they were the organisational form on which the greatest expectations were placed, especially by the popular sectors. The law was reformed in 2009. According to the new law, in urban areas each Communal Council comprises between 150 and 400 households, while in rural areas around 30 and in indigenous areas 10 to 20 (LOCC, 2009). The council is the community assembly of all inhabitants. The Communal Councils form committees on different issues, depending on their needs and interests: infrastructure, health, water, sports, culture, etc. The community appoints committees, elects spokespeople for each workgroup and designates a technical organising committee for the council. Committees and spokespeople have no power of decision; all decisions are made by the CC, the general assembly of the community. Committees elaborate proposals in their respective fields, which are submitted to the CC for approval. The projects are then financed by public institutions. The financing process no longer relied on local representative institutions, which in prior structures fostered direct, unequal competition. Instead, it was linked with the national or at least regional level. This created the possibility to have more community-centred and independent projecting and decision-making (Azzellini, 2018: 93–123).

In 2007, the Communes emerged from below. A Commune is made up of several Communal Councils (around 10 in rural areas and 20 to 40 in urban areas) and other organisations within the same territory; it can develop longer-term projects and measures over a wider area, while decisions continue to be taken in the Communal Council assemblies. Communes coordinate the Communal Councils, social missions and grassroots organisations so that projects are planned, implemented and assessed jointly (Azzellini, 2017: 81–124; 243–251). As Melisa Orellana of the *Frente Nacional Comunal Simón Bolívar* (FNCSB) explains, building a Commune includes taking over various functions generally performed by the state:

> The establishment of the *Comuna* has to do with the whole community. We would like to share this experience and to strengthen it from the grassroots level on, that's how we understand people's power. Concerning the political, the economic, the cultural and the military level.
>
> *(Comuna Under Construction, 2010)*

Both CCs and Communes strive for consensus. Individual decisions are also voted on but rarely decided by simple majority. Spokespeople, coordinators, and people in charge of specific tasks are elected. They usually have no (or limited) decision-making power and can be recalled at any time by the assembly that elected them. The operation of self-administration structures has so far been satisfactory (Azzellini, 2017: 124–156; *Comuna under construction*, 2010; Interview Jiménez).

Affinity-based councils were also created (e.g. by fishermen, peasants, students, the disabled and others). They did not evolve into structures of broad participation and became mostly mechanisms that only convened on rare occasions without real delegation to discuss law initiatives. In 2007, president Chávez launched the idea of communal cities as a level of self-administration above the Communes. Communal cities consist in the coordination of Communes within a self-defined territory. Although some rural Communes started to coordinate and declared themselves communal cities, no broader public debate or law followed. To this day, the discussion—as well as the practice—revolves mainly around the Communes. By August 2018, the official number of CCs had reached 47,514, while the number of Communes was 2,424.[2] The council structure exists parallel to the structures of representative democracy. Communal councils and communes are recognised by law and, up until the massive economic crisis that began in 2014 due to oil price decrease, their projects used to be funded extensively by different state institutions (mainly from the central state level, in order to avoid dependence on local and regional governments). Nevertheless, the boundaries of their responsibilities remain unclear, while their relations with the old institutionality are variable and constantly redefined.

In 2008, CCs and Communes started to establish *enterprises of communal social production* (*Empresas de Producción Social Comunal*, EPSCs). These are cooperatives founded and administered collectively by the CC or the Commune. The necessity of forming community-controlled companies as an alternative to traditional worker-controlled cooperatives emerged in 2006. By then, as a result of institutional programs and incentives, more than 70,000 traditional cooperatives were in operation; however, these did not permit advance planning of a communal production cycle (production, processing and distribution). Their work did not necessarily correspond to the interests of the communities. Often, they did not contribute to the development of a communal economy. Over the years, thousands of EPSCs have been founded. They principally operate in sectors that respond to pressing social needs, such as food and construction materials production or transport services; textile manufacturers, agricultural companies, bakeries and shoemakers are also common. Larger EPSCs also exist, such as the ones dedicated to the production of prefabricated houses (Azzellini, 2018: 164–171, 252–258).

Many communities see the socio-productive development of the Communes as a necessity. Adys Figuera León explains: "We want to develop the Communes productively so they can truly be a communal self-government" (Interview, Figuera León, 2012). A change can be observed in the kinds of projects undertaken by Communal Councils and Communes. During their first years, most Communal Councils and Communes concentrated on repairing homes, roads, and common spaces, and in creating access to basic services. At this point productive projects began increasing, especially at the level of Communes. Institutions and state-owned enterprises began to adopt and promote this model of communal cooperative. The *Organic Law of the Communal Economic System* (LOC, 2010) provided the legal framework for Enterprises of Communal Social Property (Azzellini, 2018: 253–273).

At times, Communes and worker collectives have jointly occupied and taken over underperforming state companies or abandoned private companies. This is the case of the former Brazilian beer brewery Brahma-AmBev in Barquisimeto, Lara state, abandoned by the owners in March 2013. Sixty of its workers occupied it and 30 started managing it together with the local self-government, the 'José Pío Tamayo' Commune. They started selling filtered deep well water, established a car wash and opened a selling point for chicken supplied by another nearby worker-recuperated company, Beneagro. In 2014 they founded the EPSC 'Proletarios Uníos' (United Proletarians in the local dialect) (Teruggi, 2015). The Commune faced various eviction attempts by the oppositional authorities of the regional government. In 2016 their communal company successfully started the production of industrial animal feed.

Community as class: the shared experience of marginalisation and struggle

The residents of urban barrios and peasant communities have been, and continue to be, the most active agent of change in Venezuela. Especially the inhabitants of the urban *barrios*—popular neighbourhoods with precarious infrastructure—are the ones who constitute the strongest base for Chavismo and its more radical interpretation as a process of social transformation. Venezuela is highly urbanised with 87 per cent of its population living in urban areas. In 2008 about 14.3 million of Venezuela's approximately 27 million inhabitants lived in *barrios* (Colau, 2008: 1). There is no reason to assume that the proportion of Venezuelans living in *barrios* has changed in contemporary Venezuela. Since the cities offered no space for the newly arrived, most *barrios* were formed through the occupation of private or public land and are therefore not only precarious but also officially invisible:

> Material negation accompanies symbolic negation: the barrios are not represented in the images of the city, they don't appear on its maps, they're not listed in its land registries, don't show up on its censuses, aren't covered in its news, and are not included in inventories of heritage.
>
> (Antillano, 2005: 206)

In the urban areas of Venezuela, the *barrio* is the most important template of identification and collective organisation. Any kind of organisation, from cultural groups and alternative media to guerrilla groups has always been and can still be found at the level of the *barrio*. Because of territorial segregation, the *barrio*'s territorial identification goes hand in hand with the dimension of class.

The sharing of a collective, precarious daily life in the *barrio* or the community represents a fundamental source of identification for the lower strata, which make up the majority of the population. Facing the conditions of life is a dimension marked by struggle, solidarity and a relational network. It is not a place, nor a given community, but a vivid framework of social relations. Moreno calls it coexistence (*convivencia*), and underscores that it is not necessarily harmonious, but may also be conflictive (Moreno, 2005: 213). Coexistence, nevertheless, has to be built and constantly maintained. Many of the *barrios* look back on a long history of struggles, as for decades they have had to defend themselves against eviction, struggle to obtain services, and develop collective mechanisms of mutual aid (Antillano, 2005: 200). They are thus the result of urban marginalisation, as is the resistance against segregation, and as such, they are the guardians of alternative values.

Historical and theoretical roots of the local self-government structures

The idea of local self-administration is rooted in the historical experiences of indigenous people and Afro-Venezuelans, in the thought of Latin American Marxists, such as Peruvian José Carlos Mariátegui, in the concept of *popular power* (*poder popular*) and in different socialist and councilist experiences and currents. In the area of Barlovento, Afro-Venezuelan Communes call themselves *cumbes*, referring to the maroon communes created during slavery times. Chávez also made a connection with the early socialist Simón Rodríguez (Bolívar's teacher):

> Look at what Simón Rodríguez said, he spoke in 1847 of toparchy. In a document directed to Anselmo Pineda, February 2, 1847, Simón Rodríguez said: 'The true utility of the creation of a republic, is to see that the inhabitants have an interest in the prosperity of their ground. In that way, provincial privileges are destroyed.' (Bolívar said that in the towns there was a caste,

and he called it that of the doctors, military, and priests, which was the caste in each place). I wish that every parish would be erected in toparchy [*toparchía*]. You know, *topos* means place [...] and *arquía* is the authority or the government, as in monarchy, oligarchy, in this case it is toparchy, which is the government of the place, of the inhabitants of the place, it's the popular government, it's the communal government.

(Chávez, 2008: 43)

As of 2007, the protagonistic popular participation formulated in the 1999 constitution was officially located in a context of popular power, revolutionary democracy, and socialism, with the defined goal of bringing about twenty-first-century socialism (as opposed to the 'actually existing' socialisms of the twentieth century) in full development and debate. The process of search and construction is guided principally by such values as collectivity, equality, solidarity, liberty, and sovereignty (MinCI, 2007: 30). Chávez situated council structures of self-government and workers' self-management at the heart of the new socialism to be built.

The concrete strategy of transformation toward socialism was based on the creation of communal cycles of production and consumption, following the idea of a communal socialism. The central theoretical reference for building a 'communal system' is Istvan Mészáros, who delineates strategies for the transition to socialism in his book *Beyond Capital: Towards a Theory of Transition* (1995). Specifically, in the chapter "The Communal System and the Law of Value" (Mészáros, 1995: 739–70), he details, with reference to Marx's *Grundrisse*, the idea of a communal system (communitarian and cooperative). Chávez often made reference to the ideas of Meszaros, and the author was invited to Venezuela for talks and workshops with the government; his book *Beyond Capital* was published as single-chapter brochures and widely distributed.

The CCs and Communes are self-government mechanisms that, by maintaining the pressure of constituent power on constituted power, play an important role in what, since 2007, is being called the 'new geometry of power',[3] with reference both to the formal geography of Venezuelan democracy and the power relations within it (Massey, 2009: 20–21). This concept is based on the recognition that the country's geometries of power are highly unequal and anti-democratic, and that its territorial geopolitics needs to be reorganised. With the advent of the CCs, those who previously had no say, such as rural and urban marginal communities, now have more of a voice, and the form of participation has changed from individual, representative and passive to collective, direct and active.

In the council structures, the division into separate political, social and economic spheres tends to be abolished. As a first step towards overcoming the separation of spheres and of powers by local self-administration endeavours, the inhabitants of the communities, from the lowest level to the highest, determine the reference territory and their affiliation themselves (Azzellini, 2018: 98–100; 244–247). The new boundaries refer to the (relational) social-cultural-economic space that derives from everyday life and not to the existing political-administrative space (Harvey, 2006: 119–148). Nor do the Communes have to correspond to the official territorial divisions; rather, they can stretch across different municipalities or even states.

Chávez defined the CC as constituent communal or people power (Chávez, 2008: 15).[4] In fact, the CCs have the potential to be an institution of constituent power at the level of the community (understood as a social relation, not as an administrative entity). Popular protagonism is especially prominent in the marginalised areas of urban and metropolitan regions (Lacabana and Cariola, 2005: 29). However, political conflict, social fragmentation, and divergence of interests are also greater there. This has complicated the situation for urban constituent processes and has slowed them down in comparison with rural ones (Parada, 2007). The percentage of the population organised into CCs tends to be higher in rural areas – where the first Communes were created – than in urban areas (Romero Pirela, 2007: 136).

The CCs and Communes had far-reaching implications for the model of the state, whose public welfare function is no longer the responsibility of a specialised bureaucracy, but is realised through transfers of financial and technical resources to the communities (Azzellini, 2018: 100–107; FCG, 2008: 6). Nevertheless, local autonomy is neither isolation from state power, nor a counterweight to it; rather, it is a form of networked self-administration that overcomes the separation between political, social, and economic spheres, and renders the state in its present form partly superfluous.

The communal state

The specifically Venezuelan socialist project is grounded in the construction of 'council structures' from the bottom up in different sectors of the society. The intention is that these councilist structures of self-government and control of production cooperate and converge at higher levels of organisation, in order to overcome the bourgeois state and gradually replace it with a communal state. The state is considered an integral product of capitalism. According to this analysis, the state is not a neutral instrument or an autonomous entity, and thus cannot be the central agent of transformation in the process of constructing a new model of socialist society. It is the constituent power that occupies this central role as an agent of change and innovation. The term communal state—which seems almost an oxymoron—was coined by Chávez in January 2007. In this manner, he picked up a concern originating with anti-systemic forces and applied it more widely. As Chávez further specified in his TV program *Aló Presidente* on 19 August of the same year, the future communal state must be subordinated to popular power, which would replace bourgeois civil society. This would overcome the rift between the economic, the social, and the political spheres—between civil society and political society—which underlies capitalism and the bourgeois state. It would also prevent, at the same time, the over-centralisation that characterised the countries of 'actually existing socialism' (Chávez, 2008: 67).

The mechanisms of transformation, the structures of self-government and the solutions to prevailing problems have to emerge from the popular movements and the organised *pueblo*. The state is responsible for lending technical and economic support to the constituent power and guaranteeing the material conditions that the realisation of the common good requires, in order that the constituent power can develop the new society. In short, constituent power assumes the form of councils if it is to maintain its autonomy from constituted power.

This arrangement was declared by Chávez to be the normative orientation for the transition to socialism. Although it was shared by only a few governmental sectors, it was widely adopted and promoted by rank-and-file movements that propose a protagonistic role for constituent power in redefining state and society, thus opening up a perspective on how to overcome the logic of capital.

In the 'Organic Law of Communes', the envisioned communal state is defined as:

> [a] form of sociopolitical organisation, founded in the Social State of Law and Justice established in the Constitution of the Bolivarian Republic of Venezuela, in which power is exercised directly by the people, by means of communal self-governments with an economic model of social property and endogenous and sustainable development that permits the achievement of supreme social happiness of Venezuelans in the socialist society. The basic structural cell of the communal state is the Commune.
>
> (LOC 2010)

This implies a profound transformation of constituted power and a resignification of the state. By this definition, the communal state would be more a non-state than a state. Among the popular forces that have adopted this perspective are the biggest popular movements, such as the Bolívar and Zamora Revolutionary Current (CRBZ),[5] the movement for workers' control, the National Network of Communards (RNC),[6] and many Communal Councils, Communes and rank-and-file activists. The RNC declares among its goals:

> To progressively dismantle the bourgeois liberal state and construct on the part of the *pueblo* a new form of government, the Socialist communal state, which resembles and recuperates the historic project truncated in 1498 with the arrival of the Spanish conquistador. To develop self-management capacity as a central element in exercising revolutionary communal self-government, the government of the *pueblo*, in which decisions are made in a collective, democratic manner.
>
> (RNC, 2011)

Although the communal state was declared to be the official normative orientation and Chávez kept on promoting it, the majority of public institutions and most PSUV cadres worked effectively against it, on account of their inherent logic of power. Anacaona Marin of the El Panal Commune in the *barrio* 23 de Enero of Caracas explains:

Chavez developed a hypothesis [...]: The commune is the historical subject, the commune and its people, the comuneros, that is where the revolution really begins. [...] We were aware that the proposal and our embracing it was going to be attacked from its onset, at its genesis. [...] Self-government and economic emancipation go hand-in-hand with socialism, with a people in power. [...] It became clear to us then that there was going to be a new level of confrontation. We knew that the path towards socialism was going to be demonized, that contradictions would pop up everywhere, inside and outside. [...] Today, we are not only resisting imperialism. We are also resisting old forms of production and their diverse forms of domination: from the organization of education and affects, to the organization of the formal political sphere and the economy. [...] The communal subject is the one that affirms that capitalism is not a natural occurrence, it is an imposition. The communes are counter-hegemonic spaces with a vocation for hegemony. From our commune, we aim to show that another organization of society is possible, that power must be reorganized, and that power should be in the hands of the people. That means combining new economic relations with an exercise of power in the commune's territory.

(Pascual, 2019)

El Panal comprises some 13,000 people, who started organising self-government structures years before the Commune law was promulgated. Marin belongs to the Alexis Vive Patriotic Force, a revolutionary organisation with deep roots in a specific sector of the barrio. It is well known in Venezuela that, in historically left-leaning marginalised urban and rural areas, local revolutionary organisations represent a hegemonic organising force.

After 2010, as the rank and file pushed for a radicalisation of the transformation process, conflicts between workers and communities, on one side, and government institutions and party representatives, on the other, were on the increase, while discontent among Chavistas deepened (Azzellini, 2017). Chávez was well aware of the impasse. Less than two weeks after his re-election as President of Venezuela for the fourth time and only months before his death on 5 March 2013, he delivered a very critical speech at the Cabinet meeting. The speech came to be known as 'El Golpe de Timón' ('Strike at the Helm', Chávez, 2015) and is still the central reference for radical and rank-and-file Chavistas. Chávez offered a radical critique of the way in which the process of social transformation was obstructed, insisted on fundamental changes in the entire government structure, and advocated an immediate leap forward in the creation of the communal state.

Conflicts and contradictions

From a very early stage, the process of building local self-government structures was marked by both cooperation and conflict between constituent power and constituted power. There is an inherent contradiction between representative democracy and its institutions on the one hand and the structures of self-government on the other. Beyond all the government declarations in favour of Communal Councils and Communes and the valuable support granted—especially by and under Chávez—by constituted power for the construction and consolidation of Communal Councils and Communes, the antagonism between constituted power and constituent power is at the root of the conflicts that have arisen during the process of construction. Moreover, the power asymmetry favours the constituted power. The institutions control the finances and have privileged access to the media and other institutional actors.

In a representative system, the constituted and the constituent power obey opposing logics, even when—as is the case in Venezuela—they claim to pursue the same objectives. The institutional logic dictates to measure everything through statistics, whereas the social logic is often not quantifiable. The logic of political representation within a hierarchical framework tends to call any non-representational body into question – and vice versa. Public servants and representatives, who are mainly accountable structurally to their superiors, are wary about letting the people decide. What if the people decide wrong!? Thus, they may feel inclined to make the decisions themselves. Juan Carlos Pinto of the FNCSB, in the state of Barinas, stated during a communal workshop for building a Commune:

> Usually, state institutions come together and say: this is the project, this is the *Comuna*, this is ready, and they present everything. And then you ask yourself: When was this project ever discussed at all? This destroys the essence, because the essence is the participation of the people, and the people are writing their own history.
>
> (*Comuna under Construction*, 2010)

Representatives of constituted power tend, for the most part, to view local self-government structures as mere appendages of constituted power and to reduce them to executive bodies responsible for implementing institutional decisions. On the contrary, those who take part in Communal Councils and Communes regard them as embryonic forms of a structure that must, in the long term, replace the state and its old institutions. Local and regional administrations are therefore very often in conflict with the Communes because they see them as a direct threat. Contradictions and clashes arise especially where structures of representative democracy are in direct competition with the new forms of local self-government for influence and political control. What Adys Figuera León, from the Los Siete Pilares Socialistas Commune in Anáco, state of Anzoátegui, describes is no exception:

> Confrontations with the town halls [...] we've had them. They've called us anti-revolutionaries, troublemakers, etc., etc. Initially, when we started to do the work, we wondered, could we be wrong about this? But no, we aren't wrong because we believe that this is the right way to go. [...] Not the way

of the institutions, because the institutions are more of the same regardless of whom they put there, of whether he's a mayor of the revolution or whatever type of mayor they set up there. It's always going to be a bureaucratic institution, and that's what we need to break with, because the system that the institutions have doesn't work. Many people say, 'It's not that the staff there are no good'. No. It's the system that's there. The system is no good.

(Interview with Figuera León, 2012)

Although popular initiatives to create Communes multiplied from 2010 on, the Ministry did not register any Communes until 2012, when it was obligated to do so because of protests and popular pressure from Communes under construction. The number of registered Communes reached 1,195 in July 2015,[7] almost all of them after president Nicolás Maduro named Reinaldo Iturriza Minister of Communes in April 2013. In September 2013, Figuera León, whose Commune, Los Siete Pilares Socialistas, had at that moment been trying to register for almost two years, commented:

The Commune is still not registered. We took all the steps required by the law and solicited by Fundacomunal [the government agency responsible for funding projects by Communal Councils and Commune]. We have had a tough political struggle in the municipality, but nevertheless we keep on working and organising. We are legitimised by the *pueblo*, we meet on Saturdays as a Commune and we are constructing popular power. The struggle has been hard because the old does not want to die and the new has not been born. Above all, there are problems with the bureaucratised municipal government over funding. However, long-needed radical changes are being made in the Ministry of Communes. We hope to get registered and we keep on working and organising.

(Interview with Figuera León, 2013)

The Commune was registered two months later. The registration of Communes continued even after Iturriza was unseated as Minister of Communes in September 2014 and named Ministry of Culture (a position he held until January of 2016). According to *vox populi*, Iturriza was ceased as Minister of Communes because of heavy pressure by PSUV mayors and governors, who saw his strong support for the Communes as a threat to their authority. Civil servants who fully support the process of construction of local self-government are a minority. As bureaucratisation takes hold, those civil servants are increasingly being sidelined by the institutions.

Communes that had strong self-organisation and developed their own initiatives—many of which were organised in the RNC—met with institutional resistance at all levels, as Atenéa Jiménez describes:

We have had no substantial support from any level of government. Good relationships with the mayoralty, the regional government, some ministry or any institutional body of the state are the exception. We have tried to speak up, but we have only faced obstacles and impediments. Even with the National Assembly! When the first law of Communes was to be passed, we had to mobilise to stop it because our critical perspective was ignored. This strengthened us and allowed us to express our level of consciousness. Material reality tells us that it's impossible to keep on waiting for a minister, for an institution. It has to come from the people with the force of popular power, through their organisation, and it's going to depend on the extent to which we organise.

(Interview Jímenez, 2012)

The example of the El Maizal Commune

Rural Commune El Maizal consists of 22 Communal Councils, of which 12 are part of the municipality of Simón Planas in the state of Lara and 10 of the municipality of Araure in the neighbouring state of Portuguesa. It is located on 2,200 hectares of land expropriated under the Chávez government. It got national attention for the first time when president Chávez visited it in March 2009 with his TV program Aló Presidente. Since then El Maizal, registered officially as a Commune in 2013, became one of the main references for other Communes because of its determination in building a socialist communal system, its highly organised population, its advances in building a productive economy and its many conflicts with government institutions. Agricultural production started with 150 hectares of black beans in 2009 and 200 hectares of corn in 2010. By 2013, corn cultivation had grown to 600 hectares. The same year El Maizal stopped collaborating with CVAL, the state agricultural corporation, because of constant conflicts. By 2016 and 2017 corn cultivation had expanded to 1,100 hectares (including 68 small producers), of which 600 hectares were sown with financial support from the state and the rest were financed by the Commune. In 2018 1,300 hectares were sown with a planned harvest of approximately 9,000 tons of corn. The agricultural production of the Commune also includes coffee and various vegetables. Along with its agricultural production, the Commune built storage facilities to eliminate intermediaries. In 2011 El Maizal used government credit to launch a cattle production unit; beef and dairy products started to be sold to local Communal Councils in 2012/2013 and beyond the Commune in 2014. By the end of 2017, the cattle stock had grown to 1,150 animals. In December 2017, the monthly production of the Commune included 8 tons of beef, 1.5 tons of cheese, 800 kg of cream, 2.5 tons of coffee and 4 tons of various vegetables. At the end of 2018, the Commune built a plant that can process 2 tons of corn a day. The unit supplies the population of the Commune and nearby communities with corn flour (used for the traditional arepas) at non-speculative prices through communal food fairs. (Comuna El Maizal, 2019; Teruggi, 2018; Vaz, 2018a; 2018b)

Among the communal enterprises founded by the Commune there were also a cement block production unit set up in 2010 (which stopped production in 2016 because of the high cost of cement due to the sanctions) and the communal gas distribution company Camilo Cienfuegos, which delivers 25,000 gas cylinders per month. Moreover, in 2014, the Commune occupied and repaired an abandoned 6.6 hectares agricultural unit containing 12 greenhouses, water tanks and irrigation systems. In 2015, president Maduro officially handed over the formerly state-owned unit to the Commune. By the end of 2018, the six greenhouses repaired by the Commune were yielding 30 tons of vegetables annually (Comuna El Maizal, 2019; Teruggi, 2018; Vaz, 2018a; 2018b).

In June 2017, El Maizal occupied the state-owned pig farm Porcinos del Alba along with the workers after the administration had not delivered animal food for 28 days. The workers and the Commune accused the administration of neglecting the production facility in order to prepare its privatisation. Built with a capacity of 6,000 animals, the farm had only 350 animals in bad condition. Under administration by the Commune, the animal stock increased to 2,150. In October 2017, the Commune occupied a cattle facility belonging to the Lisandro Alvarado Centroccidental university, which had been abandoned even though the university was receiving government support for a cattle breeding program. Following a petition by the local Community Council, the facility was occupied to restart work under community control. By the end of 2018, the facility was producing 180 litres of milk and 15–18 kg of cheese daily (Comuna El Maizal, 2019).

Over the course of the past ten years, the Commune has paved roads and built power grids for communities without electricity; it has repaired five rural schools and built three new schools for 450 students, two medical centres, a communal centre, sports facilities and 284 houses. In 2018 the Commune started building a department of the J.J. Montilla Polytechnic University of Portuguesa, which will offer three study programs (veterinary science, agricultural food science, and food distribution and processing) for 300 students (Comuna El Maizal, 2019).

Despite—or because of—its impressive success, El Maizal has fallen victim to constant attacks and sabotage from all sides. Former private owners of production facilities taken over by the Commune have filed lawsuits. In early 2018 more than 200 hectares of pasture were intentionally set on fire by unknown assailants, in order to sabotage the efforts of the Commune.

In July 2017, at the height of the economic and political crisis, Ángel Prado, main spokesperson of El Maizal, was elected delegate of the Simón Planas municipality for the National Constituent Assembly (ANC) with over 80 per cent of the votes. The communal movement decided then that Prada should be a candidate for mayor for Simón Planas in the local elections in December of the same year. By stepping into the institutional space, the communal movement wanted to make it easier to coordinate institutional support for the Commune. The governing PSUV (United Socialist Party of Venezuela) denied him the possibility to run on the party's ticket. With the support of the community, Prado ran as the candidate of a small leftist party, Patria Para Todos, (PPT, Homeland for All) and was supported by several other small leftist parties that generally support the government. His candidacy continued to face obstacles: The local chapter of the PSUV asked that he be excluded from the elections; on the ballot paper the PPT was still listed as supporting the PSUV candidate, even if the electoral council had confirmed Prado as the PPT candidate; many of the parties supporting Prado did not appear as doing so on the ballot paper; and, finally, only a few days before the election, the directorate of the ANC declared that Prado could not run for elections without the explicit consent of the ANC. Despite all resistance, Prado won the local elections with 57.92 per cent of the votes. However, the National Electoral Council declared the PSUV candidate the winner because Prado did not have the authorisation of the ANC to run for elections. The communards organised a march in Caracas. Several high-ranking Chavista representatives protested that political differences should not be solved by administrative means and that the will of the people should be respected (Cardozo, 2017). However, the PSUV candidate took the mayor's seat, and a legal decision is still pending.

In May 2018, the state-owned agricultural supplies company Agropatria did not deliver the necessary supplies and corn for sowing to the Commune. The community was forced to buy them for much higher prices on the illegal market. Ironically, the supplies purchased originated from Agropatria. As soon as the community bought them, anti-extortion units of the police showed up in the Commune, arrested Prado and two more communards for buying on the illegal market and tried to confiscate the supplies. After massive protests, the communards were released without charges (Vaz, 2018b).

Nevertheless, nothing could stop the Commune's determination to advance in the construction of a socialist communal system under direct democratic and collective control of the people. Since 2017 the Commune was engaged in forming a communal city as a federation of four Communes in the two neighbouring states. This has sparked more opposition, as Prado explains:

> The communal city project is not going to be easy. The principal enemy is the right-wing, because the communal city at some point will imply 'communalising' the territory. That project involves a broader scope and more power, in particular taking charge of means of production: factories, companies, etc. So, we will be struggling for power in the face of forces that already exist. The bourgeoisie, for economic reasons, wants to put the brakes on Chavismo. Sadly, the reformist sectors in our camp are also looking to rein in on the tendencies and political currents that threaten the privileges that some politicians in our government, or people close to them, have become accustomed to.
>
> (Vaz, 2018a)

Conclusions

The construction of local self-government has been strongly embraced by the rank and file in Venezuela. With more than 47,000 Communal Councils and almost 2,500 Communes officially registered, the numbers show solid growth; local self-government has been established as the main instrument of participation.

This participation helps break down socio-spatial segregation. The population reconquers public space at three levels: collective space, living space and institutional space. Self-government enables communities and their inhabitants to expand their horizons and plan their lives, which are now more self-determined, rather than being reduced to a mere struggle for survival. It also makes it possible to develop a utopia that is not located on the far side of what is imaginable but is connected to reality. It is a 'concrete utopia' that expresses 'dreams of living together in a better way' (Bloch, 1986: 479).

However, not all Communal Councils and Communes function as democratic popular assemblies. Some stopped working as soon as economic support by the state vanished due to the crisis. In some cases, the councils work thanks to a few activists who rely on the support but not the active participation of the community, while in other cases councils truly operate based on community assemblies. Regarding the Communes, some continue to function thanks to well-organised activists who do the heavy lifting with the support of the communities, despite the assemblies meeting regularly, while others, such as El Maizal, are highly organised and boast direct democratic decision-making structures with high levels of participation.

Well-functioning Communes are among the structures that are most successful in dealing with the problems people are facing because of the crisis. There are interesting projects involving huge production facilities controlled by the community or out-of-business companies taken over by their workers and the community to establish different kinds of production. These types of experiences are very relevant in times of a very deep crisis that strains social networks by pushing people to greater individualism.

As is common in processes of deep social transformation, women have been the driving force. They make up a vast majority of the activists in the Communal Councils and Communes (Azzellini, 2018). This is recognised explicitly at the El Maizal Commune, where women are organised in the Movement of Communard Women (*Movimiento de Mujeres Comuneras*), which defines its own means and ends, and brings them into the general struggle. The Commune confirms that the majority of its activists are women, a fact that has defined the character of the Commune's endeavors, actions and victories (Comuna El Maizal, 2019).

While state support has played an important role – especially during the Chávez government – by helping disseminate and strengthen many processes of local self-organisation, it has been, at the same time, inhibiting and limiting them. Attempts at cooptation, the imposition of agendas and projects, and welfare-based paternalistic practices by the institutions constantly threaten autonomous popular organisation. The centrality of the state and its role as the entity that allocates financial resources make the relationship an unequal one.

Local self-government structures are by no means a government or a party mechanism of control. The communities regard access to the socially produced wealth as a right and insist on their autonomy vis-à-vis state institutions and parties. In implementing their ideas and decisions, Communal Councils and Communes often come into conflict with state institutions. For that reason, most CCs and

Communes regard their socio-productive development as necessary to cease being dependent on the state (Azzellini, 2018; *Comuna under Construction*, 2010).

During his 2013 electoral campaign, president Maduro acknowledged the centrality of Communes. In 2013 increasing workers' struggles and occupations forced Maduro to step in and negotiate the gradual workers' control in state-owned companies (Azzellini, 2017). Communes used to mobilise by occupying inefficient institutions and state-owned companies. However, after the violent mobilisations of the opposition intensified, internal conflicts in Chavismo were mostly not anymore openly discussed, but more often suppressed by the government and the institutions instead of opting for a negotiated solution. With the worsening of the crisis—which was equally due to the collapse of oil prices, the international siege against Venezuela, violent attacks by the opposition, economic war by private entrepreneurs, mafias and financial institutions, and errors by the government in economic and financial matters – the Communal Councils and Communes no longer occupied a central space in government discourses and the media, and the idea of the communal state disappeared completely. The 'Strike at the Helm' did not take place. On the contrary, bureaucratisation has increased, critical voices in both the party and the government have been marginalised, and the government has demonstrated diminishing support for communal self-organisation. For instance, when the Local Committees for Supply and Production (CLAP, Comité Local de Abastecimiento y Producción) were established by the government to supply the population with subsidised food as a response to the shortages, the local committees were linked to the PSUV and not to the Communal Councils or Communes. Prado from El Maizal states:

> Unfortunately, there are big contradictions inside the state, between the state and the popular social movements, and between the state and the Commune. Because the government is very powerful economically, it has the capacity to make big decisions, and sometimes with a single blow, it can put an end to interesting experiences.
>
> (Vaz, 2018a)

While a few years ago hope that the government was going to solve all problems was widespread, this is not any longer the case. Most communities are well aware that their aspirations are only going to be fulfilled if they are autonomous in their development. They are determined to continue along the road to building self-government and are increasingly developing their skills, building networks and prefiguring a new economy, a new politics and a new society. A broad popular network of Communes and Communal Council concerned with bringing about communal socialism from below and a new Venezuela, remains very much alive, as reflected in the recent formation of the Communard Union (Unión Comunera) and a regional meeting of the Unión on 24–26 January 2020, in Las Lomas farmstead, Villanueva, Morán Municipality in Lara state. At the meeting, attended by some 300 people from 60 communes, the Communard Union in a guideline document of their meeting declared its aim to become 'a large national political movement, a space that will link the struggles of the Chavista people for the definitive construction of socialism'. In the opening session, Ángel Prado, spokesman of El Maizal Commune, proclaimed the Communard Union's firmly Chavista identity. He pointed out that the goal is not to oppose the government. Instead, popular power needs to push forward and establish its own 'great pole' in the new Venezuela.

Notes

1 Although the model of participatory budgeting is known at an international level principally for its application in Porto Alegre (Brazil), were it was introduced in 1988, in Venezuela it was introduced in 1990 and implemented in a similar way by Clemente Scotto, mayor of Caroní (Bolívar) with La Causa R, one of the major leftist parties in those times (Scotto, 2003).
2 See the list of Communal Councils and Communes officially registered on the website of the Ministerio del Poder Popular para las Comunas, http://consulta.mpcomunas.gob. ve. [Accessed 17 August 2018].
3 The 'new geometry of power' is a concept employed in the debates of radical geography or social geography, as it is called by Anglophones and Francophones respectively. It was the fourth of the five 'motors' that were proposed by Chávez to revitalise the transformation process in 2007, as the basic axes of the Simón Bolívar National Project. For more on the new geometry of power, see Di Giminiani, 2007.
4 The term 'constituent power' refers to the legitimate collective creative power inherent in human beings, the capacity to originate, design, and shape something new without having to derive it from or subject it to something that already exists. The understanding of constituent power as the force that creates a new society developed in Venezuela during the late 1980s as an idea of social transformation through a continuous constituent process. As the 1990s progressed, this conception became critically important for the movements, while its affinity with the concept Antonio Negri presented in his book Constituent Power (*Il Potere Costituente)* was discovered (Denis, 2001: 143–144). This book played a fundamental role in the development of the Bolivarian project; Chávez quoted from it often, claiming to have read it in prison (Chávez, 2008: 2; 47; Harnecker, 2002: 18).
5 The Corriente Revolucionaria Bolívar y Zamora is composed of the peasant organisation National Peasants' Front Ezequiel Zamora (FNCEZ); the Simón Bolívar National Communal Front (FNCSB), which brings together Communal Councils, Communes, and communal cities; the Simón Rodríguez Center for Training and Social Study (CEFES); and the Workers Popular Power Movement (MPPO) (Azzellini 2018: 71–73).
6 The National Network of Communards (Red Nacional de Comuneros y Comuneras), which brings together several hundreds of Communes, is the most important autonomous movement pressing for the construction of Communes.
7 Ministerio del Poder Popular para las Comunas y los Movimientos Sociales [online] Available at: http://consulta.mpcomunas.gob.ve [Accessed 25 July 2015].

References

Azzellini, D. (2018). *Communes and Workers' Control in Venezuela: Building 21st Century Socialism from Below*. Chicago: Haymarket.

Azzellini, D. (2017). "Class Struggle in the Bolivarian Process: Workers' Control and Workers' Councils," *Latin American Perspectives*, 44(1): 126–139.

Antillano, A. (2005). La lucha por el reconocimiento y la inclusión en los barrios populares: la experiencia de los comités de Tierras Urbanas. *Revista Venezolana de Economía y Ciencias Sociales*, 11(3): 205–218.

Bloch, E. (1986). *The Principle of Hope*, vols.1 and 2, Oxford: Basil Blackwell.

Cardozo, J. (2017). Àngel Prado. El Chavista que revolcó al PSUV en las elecciones. *Supuesto Negado*, 13 December, [online]. Available at: https://supuestonegado.com/angel-prado-chavista-revolco-al-psuv/ [Accessed 18 March 2019].

Chávez, H. (2015). Strike at the Helm. The First Ministerial Meeting of the New Cycle of the Bolivarian Revolution. 20 October 2012. Translation J. Weiss. *Monthly Review Online*, [online]. Available at: https://monthlyreview.org/commentary/strike-at-the-helm/ [Accessed 18 March 2019].

Chávez, H. (2008). *El Poder Popular*. Caracas: Ministerio del Poder Popular para la Comunicación y la Información.

Colau, A. (2008). Los Comités de Tierras Urbanas y el proceso de regularización de tierras en Venezuela. Observatorio de Derechos Económicos, Sociales y Culturales (DESC) de Barcelona, [online]. Available at: www.descweb.org/?q=es/node/190 [Accessed 22 April 2015].

Comuna El Maizal (2019). Comuna El Maizal: en el camino de construcción del socialismo territorial que el Comandante Chávez nos encomendó. *AlbaTV*, 3 March, [online]. Available at: www.albatv.org/Comuna-El-Maizal-en-el-camino-de.html. [Accessed 22 April 2019].

Comuna under Construction. (2010). [film] Berlin, Caracas, Vienna: Dario Azzellini and Oliver Ressler.

Denis, K. (2001), "Twenty-five Years of Corporate Governance Research... and Counting," *Review of Financial Economics*, 10(3): 191–212.

Di Giminiani, D. (2007). ¿Qué es la Nueva Geometría del Poder?. *Aporrea*, 23 August 2007, [online]. Available at: www.aporrea.org/actualidad/a40153.html. [Accessed 26 May 2016].

FCG (Fundación Centro Gumilla) (2008). *Estudio de los Consejos Comunales en Venezuela*, [online]. Available at: http://gumilla.org/files/documents/Estudio-Consejos-Comunales01.pdf. [Accessed 18 March 2019].

Harnecker, M. (2002). *Hugo Chávez Frias: un hombre, un pueblo*. Entrevistado por Marta Harnecker. La Habana: Editorial de Ciencias Sociales, [online]. Available at: www.nodo50.org/cubasigloXXI/politica/harnecker24_310802.pdf. [Accessed 30 June 2015].

Harvey, D. (2006). *Spaces of Global Capitalism. Towards a Theory of Uneven Geographical Development.* London, New York: Verso.

LOC (Ley Orgánica de las Comunas) (2010). Caracas: Asamblea Nacional de la República Bolivariana de Venezuela.

LOCC (Ley Orgánica de los Consejos Comunales) (2009). Caracas: Asamblea Nacional de la República Bolivariana de Venezuela.

Lacabana, M. and Cariola, C. (2005). "Los bordes de la esperanza: nuevas formas de participación popular y gobiernos locales en la periferia de Caracas," *Revista Venezolana de Economía y Ciencias Sociales*, 11(1): 21–41.

Massey, D. (2009). "Concepts of Space and Power in Theory and in Political Practice," *Doc. Anàl. Geogr.*, 55: 15–26.

Mészáros, I. (1995). *Beyond Capital: Towards a Theory of Transition.* New York: Monthly Review Press.

MinCI (Ministerio del Poder Popular para la Comunicación y la Información) (2007). *Líneas generales del Plan de Desarrollo Económico y Social de la Nación 2007–2013.* Caracas.

Moreno, A. (2005). "Reto popular a la gobernabilidad en Venezuela," pp. 207–217 in M. Ramírez Ribes (ed.), *Gobernanza. Laberinto de la democracia.* Caracas: Informe del Capítulo Venezolano del Club de Roma.

Parada, F. (2007). Los Consejos Comunales. La verdadera explosión del poder comunal desde las bases. *Aporrea.org,* 23 February 2007, [online]. Available at: www.aporrea. org/ideologia/a31058.html. [Accessed 25 March 2019].

Pascual Marquina, C. (2019). The Commune is the Supreme Expression of Participatory Democracy: A Conversation with Anacaona Marin of El Panal Commune. *Venezuela Analysis,* 19 April 2019, [online]. Available at: https://venezuelanalysis.com/ analysis/14435. [Accessed 19 April 2019].

RNC (Red Nacional de Comuneros y Comuneras) (2011). Culminó con Éxito IV Encuentro Nacional de Comuneros y Comuneras, [online]. Available at: http://rednacionalde comuneros.blogspot.com/2011/08/culmino-con-exito-iv-encuentro-nacional.html. [Accessed 6 March 2019].

Romero Pirela, R. (2007). *Los consejos comunales más allá de la utopía. Análisis sobre su naturaleza jurídica en Venezuela.* Maracaibo: Universidad del Zulia, Ediciones del Vice Rectorado Académico.

Scotto, C.D. (2003). "La Participación Ciudadana como Política Pública. Una Experiencia en la Gestion Local," pp. 69–83 in C. Mascareño (ed.), *Políticas públicas siglo xxi: caso venezolano.* Caracas: Cendes.

Teruggi, M. (2015). Proletarios Unidos: recuperar, resistir y producir. *Cultura Nuestra,* [online]. Available at: http://laculturanuestra.com/proletarios-unidos-recuperar-resistir-y-producir/ [Accessed 16 April 2019].

Teruggi, M. (2018). "El Maizal: La fuerza de la estrategia comunera en Venezuela," *La Correo,* September, 26–29.

Vaz, R. (2018a). "The Commune Holds the Solution to the Crisis"—interview with Ángel Prado. *Investig'Action,* 24 August, [online]. Available at: www.investigaction. net/en/the-Commune-holds-the-solution-to-the-crisis-interview-with-angel-prado/.

Vaz, R. (2018b). Production and Conflict in El Maizal Commune. *Investig'Action,* 8 September, [online]. Available at: www.investigaction.net/en/production-and-conflict-in-el-maizal-Commune.

Interviews by the author

Figuera León, Adys. Facilitator of popular power, Los 7 Pilares Socialistas Commune, Anaco, Anzoátegui state. 11 February 2012.

Figuera León, Adys. 17 September 2013.

Jiménez, Atenéa. Red Nacional de Comuneros y Comuneras, Caracas, Venezuela. 14 February 2012.

Part II

Antinomies of development

Constructing an alternative reality

7 Neoextractivism and development

Maristella Svampa

In this chapter I present the key concepts that informs our critical perspective on the development process unfolding in Latin America, namely, neoextractivism, commodity consensus and developmentalist illusion. Also, I establish several lines of continuity and rupture between the concepts of extractivism and neoextractivism.

Extractivism and neoextractivism

Neoextractivism is a very productive analytical category invented or born in Latin America that has a great descriptive and explanatory power, as well as a denunciatory character and strong mobilising power. This appears both as an analytical category and as a powerful political concept, because it speaks eloquently about power relations and disputes at play, and beyond the actually existing asymmetries it refers to a set of responsibilities shared and at the same time differentiated between the global north and south, between the centre and its peripheries. Insofar as it alludes to unsustainable development patterns and warns of deepening a logic of dispossession, it has the particularity of illuminating a set of multiscale problems that define different dimensions of the current crisis.

It is impossible to fully synthesise the complex literature surrounding the concept of neoextractivism due to the profusion of existing articles and books on the subject, which includes the use that those that are directly impacted by the advance of extractive capital, the communities and social movements on the extractive frontier, have made and are making of the category of neoextractivism. But in this first approximation I am concerned to give an account of some readings that point to the multidimensionality and multiscalarity of the phenomenon. Thus, for example, all of the authors in this field of study recognise the historical roots of extractivism as a model of accumulation. For example, for the Ecuadorian economist Alberto Acosta, 'extractivism is a form of accumulation … forged some 500 years ago' and determined since then by the demands of the metropolitan centres of nascent capitalism (Acosta, 2013). Along this line, the Argentine Horacio Machado Araoz affirms that extractivism is not just another phase of capitalism, or a problem of certain underdeveloped economies on the periphery of the system, but rather it constitutes 'a structural feature of capitalism as a world system', a 'historical-geopolitical product of the original differentiation-hierarchisation of colonial territories and imperial metrópoli, the former regarded as mere spaces for the looting and plundering for the supply of the others' (Machado, 2013). Along these lines, the Venezuelan Emiliano Terán Mantovani argues that neoextractivism can be read as a particular 'mode of accumulation', especially in regard to Latin American economies that 'can be studied from the social and territorial scope encompassed by the nation-state without detriment to other scales of territorial analysis' (Terán, 2016).

Other outstanding works on this question consider extractivism as a form of development based on the extraction of natural resources and an appropriation of nature that 'feeds a sparsely diversified productive framework', which is very dependent on an international division of labour in which the peripheral economies on the frontier of extractive capital serve as suppliers of raw materials. Thus, for the Uruguayan Eduardo Gudynas, extractivism refers to a 'mode of appropriation' rather than a mode of production; that is, 'a type of extraction of natural resources', which refers to activities that extract large volumes of natural resources in unprocessed or relatively unprocessed ('primary') form for the purpose of meeting the demand for these resources on the world market—and for appropriating the surplus value and resource rents generated in the process. Throughout history, there have been successive generations of extractivism, the most recent of which is characterised not so much by the extraction of minerals and metals, and the exploitation of agricultural labour, as by the appropriation and intensive use of water, energy and resources. Also, there are differences between traditional extractivism as practiced by the most conservative or neoliberal governments in the region and 'progressive neoextractivism' where the state plays a more active role in capturing a part of the surplus as a source of additional fiscal revenues that can be directed towards the reduction of poverty—what might be described as 'inclusionary state activism'.

However, although neoextractivism or progressive extractivism has acquired a social legitimacy denied to the extractivism practised by the remaining or returning neoliberal regimes in the region, progressive extractivism has not escaped the exceedingly sharp contradictions of extractive capitalism; the negative social and environmental impacts of extractive capital and its destructive operations have been reproduced in the most progressive extractive regimes such as Ecuador under the presidency of Rafael Correa (Gudynas, 2009, 2015).

My own particular perspective coincides with much of this analysis, which is that the historical–structural dimension of extractivism is linked to the invention of Europe and the advance of capital in the development process—the expansion of capitalism as a world system. Associated with a history of conquest and genocide, extractivism in Latin America has a long pedigree. Since the conquest of the aboriginal population and the indigenous people and nationalities, Latin America has been the preserve of imperialist exploitation, destruction and looting. Rich in natural resources, the region was reconfigured again and again in the heat of successive economic cycles, imposed by the logic of capital through the expansion of the extractive frontier; a reconfiguration that at a local level led to great contrasts between extraordinary profitability and extreme poverty, as well as a great loss of human lives and the degradation of territories converted into areas of human sacrifice and despoilation. For example, Potosí, in Bolivia, marked the birth of a way of appropriation of nature on a large scale and of a mode of accumulation characterised by the export of raw materials from the periphery of the system and its subordinate insertion into the world economy. Internal specialisation and external dependence consolidated what the Venezuelan Fernando Coronil has aptly termed 'exporting societies of nature'.

However, the history of extractivism in the region is not linear; it is traversed by successive economic cycles dependent on the demands of the world market, as well as by the processes of consolidation of the national state—'especially in the middle of the twentieth century', which allowed a certain control over extraordinary incomes and revenues generated by the capitalist development of both mining and oil (the intensive exploitation of both labour and nature).

At the beginning of the twenty-first century, extractivism was loaded with new dimensions. In this context, where it is possible to register continuities and ruptures, the concept of extractivism reappeared as neoextractivism. Continuities because, in the heat of successive economic cycles, the extractivist DNA with which European capital marked the long memory of the region was also feeding a certain social imaginary about nature and its benefits. As a result, extractivism was associated not only with the dispossession and the large-scale looting of natural resources, but also with the comparative advantages and economic opportunities that emerged at the same time as the different economic cycles and the role of the state. Neoextractivism reinvigorated the developmentist illusion expressed in the idea that, thanks to the opportunities offered by the new boom of commodities and even more of the active role of the state, it would be possible to achieve development.

And ruptures, because the new phase of capital accumulation characterised by the strong pressure on natural goods and territories, even more by the dizzying expansion of the commodities frontier, opened up new political, social and ecological disputes to social resistance against the dominant developmentalist imaginary. New forms of collective action questioned the developmental illusion while denouncing the consolidation of a monoproductive model that destroys biodiversity and entails both landgrabbing, the destruction of preexisting forces of development, and the degradation of both the environment and territorial spaces for production and sustainable rural livelihoods.

Neoextractivism as a 'privileged window' on capitalist development in the region

In order to grasp the specificity of contemporary neoextractivism, I propose a reading of it at two different levels: first, a general reading in which neoextractivism emerges as a 'privileged window' that allows us to give an account of the major dimensions of the current global crisis; and second, a more specific reading in which neoextractivism appears as a sociopolitical–territorial model for understanding the dynamics of local and regional development. As I understand neoextractiivsm in the form that it has assumed over the last 15 years in Latin America, far from being a flat category it constitutes a complex concept that provides a privileged window for viewing its complexities, and at a different level the multifaceted crisis that contemporary societies are experiencing.

First, neoextractivism is at the centre of diverse contemporary accumulation dynamics. Indeed, as several authors have pointed out, the increase of the social metabolism of capital within the framework of advanced capitalism demands for its maintenance an ever-increasing quantity of raw materials and energies, which translates into greater pressure on natural resources and territories. Although the metabolic exchange between humans and nature is dealt with only marginally in the writings of Marx,[1] it has been studied systematically by several representatives of critical (and ecological) Marxism in more recent times. Both O'Connor (2001) and Foster (2000) emphasise the costs of the natural elements involved in the advance of both constant and variable capital, as well as land and resource rents, and negative externalities of all kinds. While Foster talks about 'the metabolic fracture', O'Connor calls this process 'the second contradiction of capitalism', noting that 'there is no single term that has the same theoretical interpretation as the rate of exploitation in the first contradiction' (Capital/Labour). Likewise, both authors highlight the appropriation and self-destructive use by Capital of the labour force, infrastructure, urban space, and nature or the environment.[2]

A complementary reading of the so-called 'second contradiction of capitalism' is offered by the geographer David Harvey (2003), who places the process of primitive accumulation of capital, analysed by Marx in *Capital*—that is, the expropriation and dispossession of the land to the peasantry, who are thrown into the labour market as proletarians—at the centre of the development process. The update of this interpretation in terms of the concept of 'accumulation by dispossession', often cited in the Latin American literature, highlights the importance of the dynamic of dispossession in the current expansion and the advance of capital on goods, people and territories. This reading recognises an important precedent in the work of Rosa Luxemburg, who at the beginning of the twentieth century observed the continuous character of 'original, or primitive, accumulation', rather than associating it, as Marx did, exclusively with the origins of capitalism.

Second, neoextractivism illuminates the crisis of the project of modernity, and more generally the current socioecological crisis. Certainly, the imminence that we are witnessing of major anthropogenic and sociogenic changes on a planetary scale that endanger life on the planet (Anthropocene), has led to a questioning of the current dynamics of development linked to unlimited expansion of the commercialisation frontier, as well as the dualist vision associated with modernity. Consequently, it is possible to establish a relationship between neoextractivism (as a dynamic of dominant development) and the Anthropocene (as a critique of a specific model of modernity), when examining its consequences on a planetary scale. The ecological crisis thus appears intrinsically linked to the crisis of modernity. Arturo Escobar (2005) in this regard warns us about the need to think alternatives to modernity, other paradigms that place the reproduction of life at the centre of analysis and point to the need to view and recreate the link between the human and the non-human from a critical non-dualistic perspective.

Third, neoextractivism also connects us with the global economic crisis insofar as the current model of accumulation is associated with the reforms carried out by neoliberal and financial capitalism from the 1990s onward, as well as the propensity towards crisis reflected in the global financial crisis of 2008. On the one hand, financial capital plays a fundamental role in the operations of extraction of raw materials, as well as in the organisation of the logistics of their circulation (Gago and Sandro, 2015) and of course, in determining increases and decreases in the prices of commodities in international markets. On the other hand, the crisis accentuated social inequalities, based on an economic adjustment policy that extended to the central countries and made attractive economic models that commodify nature more intensely, as an alternative to combat the recession. In this way, the so-called green economy model based on inclusion (inclusive growth and sustainable development) is being promoted from a mainstream development perspective. This model extends the financial format of the carbon market to other elements of nature, such as air, water, and processes and functions of the environment or nature (Svampa and Viale, 2014).

Fourth, neoextractivism provides a privileged window that allows us to read the development of capital(ism) in geopolitical terms, from the relative decline of the US and the rise of China as a global power. This situation of hegemonic transition is interpreted as entry into a period characterised by conflicting polycentrism and plurality in cultural-civilisational terms, the consequences of which are still to be defined. From the globalised peripheries, both in Latin America and Africa and in certain regions of Asia, the hegemonic transition brought as a correlate the intensification of exports of raw materials, which is reflected in the consolidation of increasingly unequal economic and socioecological links to economies at the centre and especially the Republic of China. In other words, in the current geopolitical context, which points to the great Asian country as a new global power, neoextractivism allows us to read the process of global reconfiguration, which from the perspective of peripheral capitalism implicates the expansion of the extractive frontier and a dizzying reprimarisation of economies on the periphery.

Last but not least, neoextractivism provides a privileged window for reading the development process in terms of the crisis of democracy, that is, the relationship between political regime, democracy and respect for human rights. Certainly, the association between neoextractivism and the weakening of democracy is indisputable: without a social licence, without consultation of the population, without environmental controls and with scarce presence of the state, or even with, the tendency marks the manipulation of the forms of popular participation, in order to control collective decision-making. On the other hand, the increase in state and parastatal violence raises the question about the always tense links between extractivism and human rights. Given the growing criminalisation of socioenvironmental protests and the increase in the murder of environmental activists throughout the world, particularly in America, the perverse equation 'more extractivism, less democracy' (Svampa, 2016) points to a dangerous slip towards political closure.

In short, extractivism covers the long memory of the continent and its struggles, and it defines a way of appropriation of nature and a pattern of colonial accumulation associated with the birth of modern capitalism. However, its updating, in the twenty-first century, brings new dimensions at different levels: global (hegemonic transition, expansion of the commodity frontier, depletion of non-renewable natural resources, socioecological crisis of planetary scope), regional and national (relationship between the extractive-export model, the nation-state and the capture of extraordinary income), territorial (intensive occupation of the territory, ecoterritorial struggles with the participation of different collective actors), in short, policies (emergence of a new political contestatory grammar, increase in state and parastatal violence).

Neoextractivism as a socioterritorial development model

Contemporary neoextractivism can be characterised as a development model based on the overexploitation of increasingly scarce, largely non-renewable natural goods, as well as the expansion of exploitation frontiers into territories previously considered unproductive from the point of view of view of the capital. It is characterised by the orientation to the export of primary goods on a large scale, including hydrocarbons (gas and oil), metals and minerals (copper, gold, silver, tin, bauxite, zinc, among others), as well as products linked to the new agrarian paradigm (soybean, African palm, sugar cane). Defined in this way, neoextractivism designates something more than the activities traditionally considered as extractive, since it includes open-pit mega-mining, the expansion of the oil and energy frontier, the construction of large hydroelectric dams and other infrastructure works such as hidrovías, ports, and bioceanic corridors, up to the expansion of different forms of monocultures or monoproduction, through the generalisation of the agribusiness model, the overexploitation of fisheries or forest monocultures.

In this vein, neoextractivism is also a useful sociopolitical-territorial model for analysis of development and resistance dynamics at national, regional or local levels. For example, the expansion of the soybean frontier led to a reconfiguration of the rural world in several South American countries: Between 2000 and 2014 alone, soybean plantations in South America expanded by 29 million hectares, comparable to the size of Ecuador. Brazil and Argentina account for close to 90 per cent of regional production, although the fastest expansion has occurred in Uruguay, and Paraguay is the country where soybean occupies the largest area relative to other crops: 75% of the total agricultural production (Oxfam, 2016: 30).

Another major feature of neoextractivism is the large scale of the ventures, which also warns us about the size of the investments, since these are mega-intensive projects, rather than work-intensive. This refers to the character of the intervening actors 'in general, large transnational corporations', although, of course, the so-called trans-Latins are not excluded, that is, national mega companies such as Petróleo Brasileiro (Petrobras), Petróleos de Venezuela (PDVSA) and even Argentina Yacimientos Petrolíferos Fiscales (YPF), among others. At the same time, this warns us about an important variable of megaprojects; the scarce generation of direct jobs (whose maximum is reached in the stage of construction of the enterprise). For example, in the case of large-scale mining, for every million dollars invested, only 0.5 to two direct jobs are created (Machado Araoz, Svampa et al., 2011). In Peru, a country par excellence of transnational mega-mining, it occupies barely 2 per cent of the Economically Active Population, against 23 per cent of agriculture, 16 per cent in commerce and almost 10 per cent in manufacturing (Lang and Mokrani, 2013).

Likewise, neoextractivism presents a certain territorial dynamic whose tendency is the intensive occupation of territory and landgrabbing, through forms linked to monoculture or monoproduction, one of whose consequences is the displacement of other forms of production (local/regional economies), as well as populations. In this line, at the beginning of the twenty-first century, neoextractivism redefined the dispute over land, which confronts asymmetrically poor and vulnerable populations with large economic actors interested in implementing transgenic crops linked to soybeans, oil palm, sugar cane, among others. According to the 2016 Oxfam report (with data from the agricultural censuses of 15 countries), together in the region, 1 per cent of the larger farms concentrate more than half of the agricultural area. In other words, 1 per cent of farms account for more land than the remaining 99 per cent. Colombia is the most unequal in regard to the distribution of land: 0.4 per cent of agricultural holdings dominate 68 per cent of the country's land, followed by Peru where 77 per cent of farms are held by 1 per cent, then Chile (74 per cent), Paraguay (71 per cent), Bolivia where 1 per cent own or manage 66 per cent of the farms, Mexico with 56 per cent, Brazil with 44 per cent of the agricultural territory for 1 per cent of the farms. In Argentina, 36 per cent is in the 1 per cent.[3]

According to Gian Carlo Delgado, the concentration of land results from the dynamics of 'accumulation by dispossession'—the appropriation of land for the purpose of:

i   monoculture, including the so-called 'wild' or flex crops and food/bioenergy/ production inputs (corn, sugarcane, African palm), and the production of non-food inputs such as cellulose;

ii   access, management and usufruct of resources such as energy and non-energy mincrals, as well as

iii access to water (or blue grabbing); and

iv conservation or the so-called green appropriation of land or green grabbing, which includes from the creation of private protected areas, to the establishment of climate change mitigation projects such as the so-called redd + (projects to reduce emissions for deforestation and degradation + conservation) (Delgado, 2016).

The commodities consensus and the developmentist illusion

In Latin America, neoextractivism expanded in a context of change of epoch, marked by the passage of the Washington Consensus, associated with financial valorisation and structural adjustment, to the Consensus of Commodities based on the large-scale exportation of primary goods, economic growth and the expansion of consumption capacity (Svampa, 2013). Indeed, unlike the 1990s, Latin American economies as of 2000–2003 were favoured by the high international prices of primary products (commodities), all of which was reflected in the trade balances and the fiscal surplus. The fact cannot be dismissed, especially after the long period of stagnation and economic regression of the previous decades, particularly the openly neoliberal period (the nineties). In this favourable economic climate—at least until 2013—Latin American governments tended to emphasise the comparative advantages of the commodity boom, denying or minimising the new inequalities and socioenvironmental asymmetries, which brought with it the consolidation of a development model based on the export of raw materials on a large scale. Along this line, all Latin American governments, regardless of ideology, enabled the return of a productivist vision of development, which, together with the developmentalist illusion, led to the denial and snatching of substantive discussions about social impacts, environmental, territorial, political, neoextractivism, as well as the devaluation of the mobilisations and emerging socioenvironmental protests.

As for the matter of consequences, the Commodities Consensus was characterised by a complex, vertiginous and recursive dynamic, which must be read from a multiple perspective. Thus, from the economic point of view, it was translated by a new tendency to the reprimarisation of the economy, visible in the reorientation towards primary extractive activities, with little added value. This 'reprimarisation effect' was aggravated by the ascension of China as a global economic power oriented towards the extraction of natural resources and the importation of these resources to meet the domestic demand for industrial inputs and consumption goods.

Latin American exports to China, as well as Chinese investment in the region, have been much more concentrated in primary commodities—especially extractive commodities—than Latin American economic relations with the rest of the world. In 2014, in the Mercosur countries, exports of primary goods as a percentage of total exports ranged between 65 per cent (Brazil) and 90 per cent (Paraguay) (ECLAC, 2015).[4] Even a country like Brazil, which has a diversified economy, suffered for this reason what the French economist Pierre Salama (2011) characterized as a phenomenon of 'early deindustrialisation'.

The Commodities Consensus can be read both in terms of breaks and continuities in relation to the previous period of the Washington Consensus. Rupture because there are important elements of differentiation with respect to the nineties, associated with the Washington Consensus, whose agenda was based on a policy of adjustments and privatisations, as well as financial valorisation, which ended up redefining the state as a meta-regulatory agent. Likewise, neoliberalism operated as a kind of political homogenisation in the region, marked by the identification with World Bank recipes. In contrast, the Commodities Consensus put the implementation of export-oriented extractive projects at the centre, establishing a space of greater flexibility and activism regarding the role of the state. But it also allowed for the coexistence of progressive governments that seriously questioned the neoliberal consensus in its orthodox version with those governments that continue to pursue a neoliberal policy agenda.

Certainly, from a progressive perspective the Commodities Consensus is associated with the agency and activism of the state, as well as a battery of economic and social policies directed to the most vulnerable sectors, whose base was the extraordinary income associated with the extractive-export model. In the new context, certain tools and institutional capacities of the state were recovered, which once again became a regulatory actor and, in some cases, a redistributive agent. However, within the framework of the theories of world governance, which point to an institutional framework based on supranational frameworks, the tendency is not precisely for the national state to become a mega-actor, or for its intervention to guarantee fundamental changes. On the contrary, the maximum hypothesis points to the return of a moderately regulating state, capable of settling in a space of variable geometry, that is, in a multisectoral scheme, of complexity of civil society, illustrated by social movements, nongovernmental organisations (NGOs) and other actors, but in close association with multinational capital, whose weight in the Latin American economies far from retreating, increased significantly. Thus, although the progressive approach has been unorthodox and has departed from neoliberalism in terms of the guiding role of the state, as noted by the Argentine economist Mariano Feliz, he was far from questioning the hegemony of transnational capital in the peripheral economy (Feliz, 2012: 24–27). This reality placed clear limits to the action of the national state as well as an inexorable threshold to the democratisation demand of collective decisions, coming from the communities and populations affected by the large extractive projects.

On the other hand, in Latin America a large part of the left and populist progressivism continue to hold a productivist vision of development,[5] which is nourished by a tendency to privilege a reading of social conflict in terms of opposition between capital and labour, minimising or paying scant attention to capital–nature relations, as well as in the new social struggles concentrated in the defence of territory and the commons. In this context, especially at the beginning of the progressive cycle, the dynamics of dispossession tended to become a blind, non-conceptualisable point. As a consequence, the socioenvironmental problems were considered a secondary concern relative to structural problems of poverty and exclusion. Thus, in spite of the fact that in the last decades Latin American left and populism carried out a process of revalorisation of the community–indigenous matrix, a large part of them continue to adhere to a productivist and efficiency vision of development, closely linked to a hegemonic ideology of progress based on confidence in the expansion of the productive forces.

Consequently, the progressive governments sought to justify the neoextractivism affirming that this is the way to generate foreign currency to the state, then reoriented to the redistribution of income and domestic consumption, or to activities with a higher content of added value. This discourse whose real scope should be analysed case by case, and according to different phases or moments, sought to simplistically oppose the social question (redistribution, social policies) with the environmental problem (the preservation of the Commons, the conservation and protection of the territory), while leaving out complex and fundamental discussions on development, environmental sustainability and democracy. In fact, in the name of 'comparative advantages' Latin American governments sought to promote a model of inclusion associated with consumption, in a plebeian-progressive key, even denying its short-term character. This transitory link between state advancement, economic growth and consumer citizen model was the condition of the possibility of electoral success and permanence in the power of the different governments (through re-election).

The confirmation of Latin America as an adaptive economy with respect to the different cycles of accumulation, and therefore acceptance of the place it occupies in the global division of labour, constitutes one of the hard nuclei that the continuity goes through without interruption. The Washington Consensus and the Commodities Consensus beyond the progressive governments have emphasised a rhetoric that claimed economic autonomy and national sovereignty, and postulated the construction of a Latin American space.

Finally, the development model was not only supported by an instrumental and productivist vision, it also implied the updating of social imaginaries linked to the (historical) abundance of natural resources (the continent's Eldorado vision). In some countries, this imaginary appeared connected with the experience of the crisis, that is, with the exclusive legacy of the nineties, which produced the increase of inequalities and poverty. For example, the end of 'the long neoliberal night', in the words of former Ecuadorian President Correa, had a political and economic correlate, linked to the great crisis of the first years of the twenty-first century (unemployment, reduction of opportunities, migration, political instability). This topic also recurrently appears in the speech of Néstor and Cristina Fernández de Kirchner in Argentina, in conditions of economic growth that represented a notable recovery from the legacy of economic crisis left by the neoliberal regime of Carlos Menem in the 1990s), a legacy that ended with the great crisis that shook that country in 2001–2002 and a cycle of progressive reforms and the search for a new model oriented towards neodevelopmentalism (inclusive development in the form of poverty reduction).

Thus, within the framework of a post-Washington Consensus on the need for the state to become more actively involved in the development process, and the advance of capital on the extractive frontier, Latin America resumed the foundational myth of progressive development—what we have called developmentalist illusion—expressed in the idea that thanks to economic opportunities provided by the primary commodities boom (rising raw material prices, growing demand, mainly from China), it would be possible to quickly shorten the distance with the industrialised countries, in order to reach that always promised but never realised development of our societies. In the discourse of dispossession (the liberal perspective) as that which aims for the state to control the surplus (progressive perspective), current development models based on the extractivist paradigm, updated the Eldorado imaginary that runs throughout the history of the continent.

Consequently, the Latin American scenario not only points towards a coupling of neoextractivism and the developmentalist illusion, expressed paradigmatically in the cases of Peru, Colombia or Mexico, but between neoextractivism, the developmentalist illusion and progressive governments in an articulated relationship with the indigenous and socioenvironmental movements. The most paradoxical Latin American scenarios of the Commodities Consensus during the apogee of the progressive cycle were Bolivia and Ecuador. This is not a minor issue, given that it was these countries, within the framework of a participatory development process, where new concepts such as the plurinational state, autonomies, *buen vivir* or *vivir bien* and the rights of nature, were born, and in the case of Bolivia and Ecuador reflected in the construction of new constitutions that established the formation of a multiethnic and plurinational state. However, with the consolidation of these progressive regimes, other issues, linked to the export of raw materials and their relationship with economic growth, began to assumed importance.

As I understand it, the Commodities Consensus also has a political–ideological charge and content, because it alludes to the idea that there would be a 'tacit or explicit' agreement about the irresistible nature of the current extractivist dynamics, product of the growing global demand for primary goods. As happened in the golden years of the neoliberal era, in the 1980s and 1990s, when the dominant discourse affirmed that there was no alternative to neoliberalism, from 2000 on the political elites of the region (both progressive and conservative) also argued that there was no alternative to extractivism, aiming thereby to constrain or dampen the collective resistance on the basis of the 'good sense and reasonableness' that different versions of progressive capitalism would offer, while installing a new historical–comprehensive threshold with respect to the production of alternatives. As Mirta Antonelli argues, the imposition of a single narrative and with it a single possible world, seeks to control and neutralise logics that sustain other arguments, other reasonings, other memories and feelings, other societal projects (Antonelli, 2011: 11).

Consequently, critical discourse or radical opposition, driven by some NGOs or foreign agents, is inserted in the field of irrationality, antimodernity, and the denial of progress and the rights of nature (Pachamama). So, unlike the 1990s, when the continent appeared to be under the sway of the neoliberal model viewed as the only way forward—there is no other way, Thatcher was famously or infamously reported to have declared—the new century has been marked by a set of tensions and contradictions that are difficult to process. The passage from the Washington Consensus to the Commodities Consensus has meant new problems and paradoxes that has reconfigured the horizons of Latin American critical thinking.

Notes

1 Michael Lowy (2011) points out in his writings that this critical perspective linked to a metabolic exchange between the human being and nature (which gives rise to the ecological crisis) is dissociated from the productivist side of Marxism predominant in the twentieth century. On this see Sacher (2016) and also Delgado (2016).
2 In this vein, already in the 1970s, Marxist authors such as Henry Lefrèvre stressed the need to expand our readings on the dynamics of capital. Thus, in the face of the 'ossified dialectic of capital and labour', the French sociologist made an appeal to a dialectic of capital, labour and land, not only referring to the powers of nature but the agents associated with it, including the state, which exercises sovereignty over a national territory. Quoted in Coronil (2002).
3 Oxfam data, released in November 2016, clarified that these refer to farms and not to people. Therefore, it does not count landless peasants and provides very little information about collective property (for the cases of Bolivia, Colombia and Peru).
4 According to Burkhardt, it is necessary to distinguish three regional dynamics in the context of expansion of the extractive economies in Latin America. On the one hand, there are those countries, such as Ecuador and Venezuela (oil), Peru and Chile (mining) and Bolivia (gas), that stand out for the tendency to mono-production through the export of raw materials. Then there are those countries that have a diversified economy, but that have effectively increased the extractive sectors, as is the case of Brazil with mining, soy and now oil through the pre-salt. Finally, there are the countries of Central America and Mexico, which during the first phase of the Commodity Consensus had not fully committed to extractivism, but they are clearly moving in that direction (Burchardt, 2016: 63).
5 Productivism is based on the idea of indefinite growth and implies a non-recognition of the planet's sustainability limits. An excellent definition is provided by Joaquin Sampere, who uses the term 'productivism' to designate any social metabolism that does not respect the limits of ecological sustainability because it considers that the human species can afford to exploit at will and without limits of natural resources (Sampere, 2015).

References

Acosta, Alberto (2013). "Extractivism and Neoextractivism: Two Sides of the Same Curse," pp. 61–87 in M. Lang and D. Mokrani (eds), *Beyond Development. Alternative Visions from Latin America*. Amsterdam: Transnational Institute- Rosa Luxembourg Foundation.
Antonelli, M. (2011). "Megaminería, desterritorialización del Estado y biopolítica," Astrolabio 7. https://revistas.unc.edu.ar/index.php/astrolabio/article/viewFile/592/3171.
Burchardt, H-J. (2016). "El neo-extractivismo en el siglo xxi. Qué podemos aprender del ciclo de desarrollo más reciente en América Latina," pp. 55–89 in Has-Jürgen Burchardt, Rafael Domínguez, Carlos Larrea and Stefan Peters (eds), *Nada dura para siempre. Neo-extractivismo despúes del boom de las materias primas*. Ecuador: Abya Yala.
Coronil, F. (2002). *El Estado mágico. Naturaleza, dinero y modernidad en Venezuela*. Venezuela: Consejo de Desarrollo Científico y Humanístico de la Universidad Central de Venezuela-Nueva Sociedad.
Delgado, G.C. (2016). "Configuraciones del territorio: despojo, transiciones y alternativas," pp. 51–70 in M. Navarro and D. Fini (eds), *Despojo capitalista y luchas comunitarias*

*en defensa de la vida en México, Claves desde la Ecología Polít*ica. Mexico: Universidad Benemérita de Puebla.

ECLAC (2015). *Foreign Direct Investment in Latin America and the Caribbean 2015.* Santiago: ECLAC.

Escobar, A. (2005). "El post-desarrollo como concepto y práctica social," pp. 17–31 in D. Mato (ed.), *Políticas de Economía, ambiente y sociedad en tiempos de globalización.* Caracas: Facultad de Ciencias Económicas y Sociales, Universidad Central de Venezuela.

Feliz, M. (2012). "Proyecto sin clase: crítica al neoestructuralismo como fundamento del neodesarrollismo," pp. 13–44 in edited by M. Feliz et al. (eds), *Más allá del individuo. Clases sociales, transformaciones económicas y políticas estatales en la Argentina contemporánea.* Buenos Aires: El Colectivo.

Foster, J.B. (2000). *La Ecología de Marx: materialismo y naturaleza.* España: El Viejo Topo.

Gago, V. and M. Sandro (2015). "Para una crítica de las operaciones extractivas del capital, Patrón de acumulación y luchas sociales en el tiempo de la financiarización," *Nueva Sociedad*, núm. 255.

Gudynas, E. (2009). "La ecología política del giro biocéntrico en la nueva Constitución del Ecuador," *Revista de Estudios Sociales*, 32: 34–47.

Gudynas, E. (2015). *Extractivismos. Ecología, economía y política de un modo de entender el desarrollo y la naturaleza.* Bolivia: ClAES-CEDIB.

Harvey, D. (2003). *The New Imperialism.* New York: Oxford University.

Lang, M. and D. Mokrani (eds) (2013). *Beyond Development. Alternative Visions from Latin America.* Amsterdam: Transnational Institute- Rosa Luxembourg Foundation.

Lowy, M. (2011). *Ecosocialismo. La alternativa radical a la catástrofe ecológica capitalista.* Buenos Aires: Editorial El Colectivo-Ediciones Herramienta.

Machado Aráoz, H. (2013). "Crisis ecológica, conflictos socioambientales y orden neocolonial. Las paradojas de Nuestra América en las fronteras del extractivismo," *Revista Brasileira de Estudos Latino-Americanos*, 3(1): 118–155. http://rebela.edugraf.ufsc.br/index.php/pc/article/view/137.

Machado Araoz, H. and M. Svampa (eds) (2011). *Colectivo Voces de Alerta mitos y realidades sobre la minería transnacional en Argentina.* Buenos Aires: Editorial El Colectivo-Ediciones Herramienta.

O'Connor, J. (2001). Causas naturales. Ensayo de marxismo ecológico. Buenos Aires: Siglo xxi. http://theomai.unq.edu.ar/Conflictos_sociales/oconnor_2da_contradiccion.pdf.

Oxfam, (2016). *Unearthed, Land, Power and Inequality in Latin America.* www.oxfam.org/sites/www.oxfam.org/files/file_attachments/bp-land-power-inequality-latin-america-301116-en.pdf.

Sacher, W. (2016). "Segunda contradicción del capitalismo y megaminería. Reflexiones teóricas y empíricas a partir del caso argentino". Tesis doctoral. Flacso-Ecuador.

Salama, P. (2011). "China-Brasil: industrialización y 'desindustrialización temprana'," *Open Journal System.* www.revistas.unal.edu.co/index.php/ceconomia/article/view/35841/39710.

Sampere, J. (2015). Sobre la revolución Rusa y el comunismo del siglo xx. https://centenarirevoluciorussa.wordpress.com/2015/05/01/31/.

Svampa, M. (2013). "Resource extractivism and alternatives: Latin American perspectives on development," pp. 117–144 in M. Lang and D. Mokrani (eds), *Beyond Development. Alternative Visions from Latin America.* Amsterdam: Transnational Institute-Rosa Luxembourg Foundation.

Svampa, M. (2016). *Debates Latinoamericanos. Indianismo, Desarrollo, Dependencia y Populismo.* Buenos Aires: Edhasa.

Svampa, M. and E. Viale (2014). *Maldesarrollo. La Argentina del extractivismo y el despojo.* Buenos Aires: Editorial Katz.

Terán, E. (2016). "Las nuevas fronteras de las commodities en Venezuela: extractivismo, crisis histórica y disputas territoriales," *Ciencia Política*, 11(21): 251–285.

8 Paradoxes of development in the Andes and Amazonia

Fernanda Wanderley, Horacio Vera Cossio and Jean Paul Benavides

We are undergoing a period of epochal change. The COVID-19 pandemic swept across the world, ignoring geographic and political borders, and wove together the individual and collective experience of our condition of humanity that inhabits a single common house: our planet. At the same time, it exposed economic, social and political inequalities between and within countries. The unexpected health crisis for the majority and more dramatic for some than for others, but universal in the most precise sense of this word, made visible the unsustainability of the capitalist system as we know it today.

The pandemic made it clear that if all the inhabitants of a country, a region and the planet are not healthy and do not have a decent life, we are all at risk. Health and dignified living conditions are a common good and, as human rights, must be guaranteed by states. Eradication of poverty through respectful development of ecosystem balances and fair distribution of wealth is central to the sustainability of life and the economy.

This crisis came to reinforce the citizen mobilisations that increasingly demand answers to today's great dilemma: how to meet the needs of the present without compromising the needs of future generations in a democratic and social justice framework. The novelty of the twenty-first century is the search for new paradigms of development that harmoniously articulate the production and distribution of goods and services for the sustainability of life in conditions of equity and democracy.

We are witnessing the construction of new global agreements that are moving forward with significant difficulties. In 2015, Pope Francis published the encyclical *Laudato Si*. That same year, the United Nations approved the 2030 agenda for sustainable development that proposes new development goals that need to be met on a global scale. Both documents recognise the seriousness of the social and environmental crisis, and point to the close relationship between, on the one hand, the persistence of social exclusion, poverty and social inequalities, and, on the other hand, climate change, loss of biodiversity and pollution of the earth, water and the air. Global goals to address deep environmental and social imbalances establish an urgency to transform the current pattern of production, distribution and consumption. While this is a global challenge, regions and countries across the world face differentiated dilemmas. These depend on the specificities of the ecosystems of their territories, the characteristics of their economic and social structures, the institutional frameworks and disparate power correlations both nationally and internationally.[1]

In the light of the concept of sustainable development, this chapter articulates the social, environmental and economic outcomes of Bolivia, Colombia, Peru and Ecuador in the Latin American context in the first two decades of the twenty-first century. These Andean-Amazonian countries share a mega-diverse biozone with an exceptional environmental heritage. Despite this great natural potential, Latin American economies failed to overcome a dependence on the exploitation of minerals, hydrocarbons and food from colonial times to the present day. The main dilemmas facing the region are low long-run economic growth, the persistence of high levels of inequality and social exclusion, and the acceleration of the predation of its ecosystems. There are also problems associated with economies primary goods exporting economies subordinated to global demand and commodity price cycles.

The intensification of global demand for renewable and non-renewable natural resources placed these countries at the heart of the new cycle of dispute over access and control of strategic raw materials at the beginning of the twenty-first century (Rojas, 2015). The expansion of exports of primary goods, mainly energy and mineral resources from the Andean countries, at rates higher than the Latin American and Caribbean average, led to the extraordinary economic bonanza between 2004 and 2014 with exceptional rates of short-term economic growth and easy access to additional fiscal resources. This led to significant improvements in social indicators mainly of poverty and inequality, a trend that stalled and even receded with the slowdown in the world economy from 2014 on. Also, the significant environmental cost of this short-term growth and these social achievements also need to be taken into account, considering the impact of local environmental imbalances: deforestation, loss of biodiversity, the high intensity of water and energy consumption, and pollution of the soil, water and air.

These impacts and imbalances are reflected in and associated with new social conflicts in the territories. In addition, ecological imbalances have broad effects throughout the region and across the world: intensification in the occurrence of drought, floods and extreme natural events, as well as global warming. It is also surprising that these results occurred against the backdrop of legal and regulatory advances in environmental protection and the collective rights of indigenous peoples in the Andean countries.

With the end of the economic bonanza of high commodity prices, the persistent Latin American debate on overcoming the extractivist growth pattern based on the intense exploitation of a large volume of natural resources (minerals, hydrocarbons and commodity monocultures), aimed at the export of raw materials with low added value, has been renewed (Gudynas, 2015). This situation is much worse with the COVID-19 pandemic. This debate has been enriched by the incorporation of new dimensions and themes that have sharpened an awareness of the paradoxes of extractivism and associated academic and public policy challenges. New contributions were added from the perspective of ecofeminism associated with the ethics of care and depatriarchalisation, the struggle on the extractive frontier to reclaim territorial rights, indigenism linked to the collective rights of indigenous peoples and to notions of *vivir bien* or living well, and social and political ecology (Svampa, 2016).

This chapter analyses some dimensions of these paradoxes in the Andean region over the past two decades. The articulation of the economic, social and environmental axes of these paradoxes offers several elements as to how to think about the dilemma facing the Andean region in the Latin American context. In particular, how to articulate ways of transforming the economic structures that have sustained continuous improvements in social welfare while sustainably exploiting its environmental heritage? Although we do not propose a conclusive answer to this complex question, we seek to provide evidence of the results achieved by Andean countries that have adopted divergent policy orientations and suggests ways forward.

At the beginning of the century the new governments of Bolivia and Ecuador generated great expectations about profound transformations in their development strategies in regard to harmony between human beings and between them and the other living beings that cohabit nature. In contrast, the governments of Peru and Colombia that did not participate in the 'pink wave' of progressive regimes, did not surprise the world with disruptive proposals regarding the neoliberal policies implemented in previous decades.

The chapter is organised in three parts, in addition to the introduction and conclusions. The first part presents a comparative regime analysis in the evolution of poverty and inequality, and the factors that explain these results. It also analyses tax structures and their role in moving towards and achieving social justice in the long run. The second part analyses the environmental heritage of the Andean region, the acceleration of deforestation and the loss of biodiversity, and the role of protected areas and indigenous territories in the sustainable management of ecosystems. The third part reviews the salient trends in the four economies in regard to the recent economic boom in both the Latin American and the global context. And it discusses the policies that can be used to promote sustainable diversification. Finally, we present the conclusions.

Extractivist economic growth and social achievements

Latin America is one of the most unequal regions on the planet with high levels of poverty and inequality, as well as limited and fragmented social protection systems, with marked differences between countries (Ocampo and Gómez-Arteaga, 2017). However, significant social gains were made in the period of economic growth attributed to high international commodity prices from 2002 to 2013. With the slowdown in the global economy as of 2014, many of these countries have experienced stagnation in regard to social progress and, with COVID-19 pandemic, setbacks in the exercise of rights by the most vulnerable populations are anticipated.

What is the progress in poverty and inequality in the region during the period of the economic boom?

Countries in the Andean region have experienced a higher pace of extreme and moderate poverty reduction compared to the Latin American average. Between 2000 and 2017, in the Andean region the incidence of extreme poverty was reduced by 24.6 percentage points, versus 14 percentage points for Latin America overall. However, it is important to remember that the Andean region began with higher average rates of extreme poverty (34.8 per cent vs. 23.8 per cent for Latin America), down to 10.2 per cent and 9.8 per cent respectively in 2017.[2]

Bolivia is the country in the Andean region that showed the largest reduction in extreme poverty between 2000 and 2017—from 41.4 per cent to 11.8 per cent—which meant a total reduction of 29.4 percent. The second largest reduction was in Colombia—with 36.6 per cent of the population living on less than 3 dollars and 20 a day in 2001 but only 10.8 in 2017 (a total reduction of 25.8 percentage points). Ecuador then rose from extreme poverty levels from 30.1 per cent in 2003 to 8.7 per cent in 2017 with a total reduction of 21.4 percentage points. Finally, in Peru, the country that began the 2000s with a poverty rate of about 30.5 per cent, the rate of poverty fell to 9.8 in 2017, a total reduction of 20.5 percentage points. These trends allowed for differences in the incidence of extreme poverty to narrow between the four countries. However, the most striking and surprising aspect of these figures is that the policy regime—progressive in the case of Bolivia and Ecuador, and more or less neoliberal in the case of Peru and Colombia—did not seem to be a major factor. This contradicts the common understanding derived from a comparison between the South American countries that were part of the progressive cycle in Latin American politics, a cycle that paralleled the primary commodities boom-bust cycle, with Mexico, which continued to hoe the neoliberal line (Veltmeyer and Petras, 2014).

To put this issue in perspective we need to take a closer look. First, looking at the decrease in poverty over the period in question, there are differences between countries. In Peru, the period with the greatest poverty reduction was 2005–2012 (2.6 percentage points per year). In Bolivia, as in Peru, the largest poverty reduction also occurred over this period—with a fall of 2.5 percentage points per year on average, on par with the experience of Peru. Third, there is Ecuador where the incidence of poverty was reduced at an annually averaged rate of 2.0 percentage points. As for Colombia the rate of poverty reduction over this period was at an annually averaged rate of 1.1 percentage points. In the period 2012–2017 the rate of poverty reduction slowed down in all of the countries except for Bolivia, which continued to post high rates of economic growth. This coincided with the slowdown in economic growth across the region since 2013; 2012 in the case of Brazil, where the rate of economic growth fell from a ten-year average of over 5 per cent down to zero. In Bolivia and Colombia the annual decrease was on average 0.6 points, and in Ecuador and Peru 0.5.

Inequality is a complementary condition to poverty, indeed a fundamental cause,[3] and expresses how far societies are from an ideal income distribution among all members of society. Despite the gains in poverty, the reductions in inequality experienced at the turn of the century have not been enough to improve the global ranking. Latin America, the report notes, remains the most unequal region in the world, where even more than half of countries had a Gini Index greater than 0.5 in 2017.

The decrease in inequality measured by the Gini Coefficient in the Andean region was higher than in Latin America between 2000 and 2017. At the beginning of the period, the most unequal Andean country was Bolivia, with a Gini Index of 0.62, followed by Ecuador and Colombia, both with 0.56, and Peru, with 0.53 (World Bank, n.d.). Between 2007 and 2011 there was the largest reduction in Bolivia, Ecuador and Peru, coinciding with the boom in international commodity prices. During this period Bolivia rose from 0.55 to 0.46; Ecuador from 0.53 to 0.46 and Peru from 0.50 to 0.45. In the following years Bolivia and Ecuador are receding in the positive trend. Bolivia experienced increasing inequality until 2014 and Ecuador until 2013. From these years they return to the path of decline until 2017 when they recorded G indices of 0.44 and 0.45, respectively. The third country in the Andean region with the greatest reduction in income inequality is Peru. Since 2007, there has been a gradual but sustained decline from a Gini Index of 0.50 to 0.45 in 2014. Starting this year, it stalled to close at 0.43 in 2017. It is important to note that Peru is the country with the lowest income inequality in the Andean region in the entire period. At the other end is Colombia that maintained higher rates of inequality and was the country with the worst performance in reducing income inequality over the entire period ending, concluding with an index of 0.50 in 2017.

What are the most important factors in reducing inequality and monetary poverty in the Andean region?

The Andean region differs from Latin America as a whole in that the greatest contribution to reducing extreme poverty between 2007–2017 came from labour income, followed by non-working incomes and, finally, the demographic bonus (the largest proportion of 15 to 69 years and the relationship of dependence between the non-working-age population and the working-age population). Labour incomes contributed to 82 per cent of the reduction of extreme poverty in Bolivia, 42 per cent in Colombia, 49 per cent in Ecuador and 43 per cent in Peru. The phenomenon of the expansion of work and remuneration in activities that require less qualification of workers was one of the most important factors for the reduction of income inequality in this period (Wanderley and Vera Cossio, 2018). Thus, any role that macroeconomic or social policy might have had in explaining the achievements of number of countries at the level of poverty reduction, should be viewed with this lens.

Despite the increase in real wages for lower-skilled workers, working conditions in Andean countries did not improve significantly in the economic bonanza period. The majority of the population in the four countries remains employed in jobs outside of labour regulation and low productivity. In terms of labour regulation coverage, in 2015, 84 per cent of the occupied population was informal in Bolivia, 69 per cent in Peru, 62 per cent in Colombia and 58 per cent in Ecuador, reaching an average of 68.25 per cent in the four countries this year. It is also noted that the percentage of informal employment in Colombia, Ecuador and Peru followed a declining trend, while in Bolivia over this period the trend was in a contrary direction.

Another critical factor in regard to the link between poverty and labour income is education, and thus social spending on education via the impact of these expenditures on productivity. In this regard, reducing social expenditures on education as in some neoliberal policy regimes, is a barrier to increased productivity as it both reduces the value added by labour to production and reduces the incentive of workers to qualify for the labour market. In terms of productivity per worker, regardless of the level of public expenditures on education—or perhaps because of it—Bolivia has the worst performance of the four countries, while Colombia the best in 2017: USD16,370 and USD32,510, respectively. Second is Peru (USD26,715) followed by Ecuador (USD25,418). For a non-Latin America reference point, the Republic of Korea in the same year showed productivity of USD77,860, while Chile, recognised as a regional leader in public social expenditures, productivity was measured at USD55,961. Neither public expenditures on education nor working conditions in the Andean countries changed significantly in the following years.[4]

Non-working income includes public transfers, remittances, pensions, and other non-working income. Non-working income made a contribution to poverty reduction, but with differences between the four countries. Bolivia was the country with the lowest incidence of non-working income with 21 per cent, followed by Colombia with 26 per cent. In Ecuador and Peru, the contribution of non-working income was similar to that of labour income, respectively 45 per cent and 42 per cent. The lower incidence of this factor in Bolivia is striking considering high social spending relative to GDP. The reverse situation is seen in Peru, the country that allocated a lower share of GDP to social spending (Wanderley et al. 2018).

The factor with the least impact on the reduction of extreme poverty was the so-called demographic bonus, which suggests that the window of opportunity for still young working-age people is not being adequately exploited. Colombia was the country that showed the greatest impact (14 per cent) between 2007 and 2017, followed by Ecuador (10 per cent) and Peru (9 per cent). In contrast, the impact of the demographic bonus was zero in Bolivia, despite being the country with the lowest percentage of young people who do not study and do not work (NiNis)[5] in 2017. With an aging population, this opportunity is shrinking, while the pressure to improve retirement benefits and social policies such as care policies is increasing (Wanderley, 2019).

What is the role of the tax system in the sustainability of social achievements?

It can be concluded from our data analysis that between 2000 and 2014 labour market dynamics and the expansion of social protection were important for poverty reduction and inequality in Latin America, although with this progress the challenges change. It is necessary to maintain a continuous and sufficient flow to ensure access to the opportunities that were conquered. As commodity prices declined and with this economic growth prospects, this becomes more difficult to sustain through transfers. The tax system needs to be changed so that the burden does not fall on people whose income is most exposed. The comparative description of tax structures will allow us to analyse how Andean countries have made progress towards mitigating this risk.

Direct taxes (i.e. taxes on people's income, land income taxes, capital or natural resources, property, etc.) are considered to generate greater social justice. On the one hand, they introduce fewer distortions about the relative pricing system; on the other hand, they open up the possibility of establishing tax refund mechanisms and exemptions more clearly related to the economic status of households. In this sense, if the weight of direct taxes is higher the system tends to be more progressive. In contrast, indirect taxes (i.e. specific consumption taxes, value added tax, trade tariffs) directly affect relative prices, thereby taxing consumption and affecting households that spend a greater proportion of from their income to the purchase of goods. In this sense, when the weight of indirect taxes is higher and if more than subsistence is taxed, the tax system penalises less-favoured strata more.

With this in mind, countries in the region showed regressive tax systems, as they obtained their income mainly from indirect taxes (IDB and CIAT, 2017). The tax pressure related to indirect taxes in 2015 was higher in Bolivia (14.4 per cent), followed by Ecuador (10.5 per cent), Peru (8 per cent) and Colombia (7.4 per cent). The trend observed between 2000 and 2015 indicates that Bolivia was the country with the highest increase in indirect taxes by 2.4 points of GDP; Colombia (1.7) and Ecuador (1.2). Unlike other countries, indirect taxes reduced by 0.7 points of GDP in Peru in the above-mentioned period. According to Lustig's study (2017), the effects of net indirect taxes nullified the equalising effect of direct taxes and money transfers in Bolivia.

On the other hand, Colombia and Peru show tax systems that could be fairer in the future, as they reveal a higher proportion of direct taxes on tax collection. In these two countries, the direct tax contribution increased at a faster rate than indirect taxes. In 2015, the direct taxes collected make up 7.4 per cent of GDP in Colombia and 6.2 per cent in Peru; Ecuador (5.2 per cent) Bolivia (4.7 per cent). Direct tax collection in Colombia in 2015 has become as significant as indirect tax collection. In Peru and Ecuador, direct taxes are the government's second source of funding. By contrast, direct taxes in Bolivia are the fourth most important source of financing, which goes hand in hand with the informality of the labour force and the taxes on exploitation of resources as the main source of financing.

In conclusion, despite the potentially regressive systems in all countries, Peru, Ecuador and Colombia showed progress towards fairer outcomes. Meanwhile in Bolivia, despite the increase in direct tax collection, the greatest variation was in indirect taxes.

The loss of environmental wealth in the period of the economic boom

As analysed in the previous section, in the first 15 years of the twenty-first century, the Andean region has intensified its role as a commodity exporter for the world economy achieving significant growth and improvements in poverty and inequality indicators. However, this growth pattern had a high environmental cost in one of the world's most forested and biodiverse regions. The degradation of environmental heritage in this period also contrasts with legal advances in the protection of indigenous rights and the environment mainly through two instruments: Protected Areas and Indigenous Territories.

What is the environmental heritage of the Andean region?

The natural wealth of Bolivia, Colombia, Ecuador and Peru is exceptional. Globally these four countries contain about 13 per cent of all species (counting only birds, mammals, reptiles, fish and vascular plants). At the Latin American level, these countries host 35 per cent of biodiversity. Colombia is more biodiverse than China, the United States or India. Ecuador with its 255,000 km^2 occupies the 76th position of countries ordered by area, but is more biodiverse than the ten largest countries in the world, with the exception of Brazil. As Andean-Amazonian countries, Bolivia, Colombia, Ecuador and Peru are rich in forests, on average more than 50 per cent of their territories are covered with these.[6] These account for 22 per cent of the world's forests and 30 per cent of global tropical forests. They contain 49 per cent of the carbon stock above the soil of the tropics. In addition, Andean countries are responsible for approximately 27.7 per cent of the Amazonian biome. However, this coverage has been declining in recent years in all countries as reported by data from the Global Forest Watch portal and a number of sources (FAO, 2015, RAISG 2015).[7]

The Amazon is an interrelated system that crosses political boundaries. Their role is paramount to the environmental functioning of the planet: they affect rains in and out of the same continent so they are key to agricultural production beyond its limits. On the other hand, its carbon sequestration capacity is essential to prevent climate change. Examples of these connections and exchanges can be easily multiplied. Thus, if the potential can be harnessed by each country, the negative effects of their destruction can be regional, continental and global. More than 33 million people live in the Amazon, including 385 indigenous peoples, with a total population estimated at 1.4 million people and inhabiting 2,344 indigenous territories. In addition, indigenous peoples living in urban areas, peoples living in voluntary isolation belonging to approximately 71 groups and finally thousands of traditional communities that depend on the biodiversity of the Amazon for their livelihood (RAISG, 2015).

How did indicators of deforestation and biodiversity loss evolve?

Biodiversity loss is a global problem, but the impact of this phenomenon is greater in the tropics where a higher concentration of species is found. The Tropical Andes is the hotspot with the most globally threatened species (Mittermeier, 2004). Nearly 500 species between birds, mammals and amphibians are threatened with extinction, or nearly 21 per cent of all species are endangered due to habitat change caused by deforestation.[8]

In general, Andean countries are experiencing increasing rates of deforestation. Deforestation accumulated in the Amazon region between 1970 and 2013 over a territory originally of 6.1 million km^2 (or 609,978,800 ha) affected 9.7 per cent of the region up to 2000, and since 2013 this percentage rose to 13.3 per cent, an increase of 37 per cent in 13 years. According to RAISG (2015) 27 per cent of the total deforestation took place after 1970. Only Colombia showed a reduction in the loss of coverage over these years. The other countries—Bolivia, Ecuador and Peru—have maintained an increasing rate of forest loss since 2001. This trend has been exacerbated since 2016, the year of the signing of the Paris agreements, until 2017 in all the countries here treated. In 2018 while Colombia continued to show a high rate of deforestation in both Peru and Bolivia the rate of deforestation decreased while remaining at a relatively high level. Overall, the rate of deforestation in 2015 and 2016 doubled and continued to increase thereafter. Bolivia, less populated and with less forest area than Peru and Colombia, proportionally loses more hectares of forests per year (above 400 thousand hectares) than the latter. That is, its contribution to deforestation is higher whether one considers total forest area or per capita. Bolivia is followed by Peru. In recent years, Colombia joined Bolivia in leaving the category of a moderate rate of deforestation, doubling its rates of deforestation.

What are the social dynamics and economic activities that affected deforestation and biodiversity loss?

The history of deforestation is similar in all Andean-Amazonian countries. It began in the past centuries as a history of the colonisation of the forested area of the Amazon, understood as a virtually uninhabited or uncivilised and very underpopulated space. Indigenous peoples were invisibilised and not taken into consideration, albeit having had to confront their governments and colonisers. All Andean countries have sought the integration of this forest area into the national level with the desire to exploit non-renewable natural resources and expand the agricultural frontier, dominating in general an agricultural vision of development in which the forest has no value other than that of its transformation as land for the cultivation or the rearing of livestock.

Recently the most important player in deforestation is the large agricultural industry. In Peru and Bolivia, agribusiness has played a greater role in deforestation levels in recent decades compared to Ecuador and Colombia. In Bolivia, essentially industrial products are soy, sugar, sorgo, sunflower. In Peru and Ecuador there has been significant growth in oil palm extensions. In general, commercial agriculture became the leading cause of deforestation in Latin America and the Andean region. This production is driven by the demand for international markets and less with the food consumption of national populations. In the same way, extensive livestock farming has developed contributing to deforestation and is a growing trend with the prospects for meat exports. This production occurred mostly outside the hotspots, but the most developed areas affect the Cerrado, an area of high plant endemism. Similarly, Ecuador has since 2006 an increase in large-scale livestock production, mainly in the southern part of Ecuador, in the centre of the hotspot Andes Tropicales (Tapia-Armijos et al., 2015).

Also linked to international markets is deforestation led by illegal activities. First, the cultivation of coca leaf, important in Colombia, Peru and Bolivia is also related to illegal and highly conflicting forces that make it difficult to design forest conservation policies when the presence of the state is contested and contested. The peace process in Colombia has resulted in an increase in levels of deforestation. Similarly, illegal gold exploitation responds to a similar scheme: high international demand, poor national control capacity, strong local interests, and ill-known deforestation and pollution effects. This is especially the case in Peru and is on the rise in Bolivia.

In the same vein, hydropower plants will continue to contribute to deforestation and biodiversity loss. In general, dam construction is presented as a clean energy source, however, this is questionable. Thus, in the headwaters of the Amazon there are 117 hydroelectric plants in operation and 246 planned or under study; 69 of these are found in the Andean countries (44 in Peru, 14 in Bolivia, ten in Ecuador, and one in Colombia) which are the main contributors of the Amazon basin (RAISG, 2012), and where most of the nutrients that are fundamental to the configuration of ecosystems and biodiversity of the basin come from (Hoorn, et al., 2010). In addition, the construction areas of the dams correspond or are close to the areas of greatest biodiversity. There are few studies on the impact of these dams on the headwaters of the Amazon, but in the case of Brazil they show that hydropower contributes to deforestation, although to a lesser extent compared to other activities such as agriculture and livestock, but they produce other important socioenvironmental impacts: greenhouse gas emissions, in addition to the disruption of fish migration, the elimination of ecosystems by reservoirs, changes in the flood system, displacement of populations and life systems (Fearnside, 2006, 2014, 2016).

What is the role of protected areas and indigenous territories in the protection of environmental heritage?

Two environmental management instruments stand out for environmental protection and the rights of indigenous peoples in the Andean region: Protected Areas (PA) and Indigenous Territories (IT). The creation of Protected Areas is considered one of the most important strategies for environmental protection. In addition to their objective of protecting endangered species, they also ensure or protect ecosystem services and biological resources. This is why they have become essential components in climate change mitigation plans and for meeting the sustainable development goals (SDGs 14 and 15).[9]

Indigenous Territories have been institutionalised at the international level in the ILO Convention 169 (1989) regarding Indigenous Peoples. It establishes the concept of the territory of Indigenous Peoples as a right over the ancestral spaces they have historically occupied. This territory refers to the significant symbolic, cultural, social and economic geographical area in which its culture and ethnic identity have been forged. A distinction is then drawn between social appropriation and individual ownership of land. All the countries covered by this report have signed this Convention and these are mandatory. In the region since the 1980s there has been a massive process of land titling in favour of indigenous peoples, through constitutional reforms: Colombia in 1991, Peru in 1993, Bolivia in 1994 and Ecuador in 1998 (Fajardo, 2006, 1999).[10]

In the Amazon, Protected Areas cover about 1.4 million km^2 (or 104 million Ha) and Indigenous Territories about 1.9 million km^2 (or 109 million Ha). These occupy 45 per cent of the Amazon and other wooded areas, therefore, they are important actors in designing sustainable development strategies, policies in the face of climate change and biodiversity conservation. Although often invisibilised in the context of the landgrabbing associated with the advance of extractive capital in Indigenous Territory indigenous groups and nations occupy 25 per cent of the Amazon's total area. Protected areas cover about 20.9 per cent of the Amazon's total landmass. Although many APs overlap with IT, they together cover 45 per cent of the Amazon (RAISG, 2015). Among the Andean countries analysed, Colombia has the highest proportion of its lands under some form of protection (35 per cent). This compares to 31 per cent for Peru, 24% for Ecuador and 26% in Bolivia. However, if we were to include marine areas Ecuador has a greater protection coverage than the other countries.

The future for Amazon forests is not encouraging. In light of deforestation levels, APs and IT seem to act as clear tools to ensure the continued provision of ecosystem services to society and to the functioning of the planet's process systems. But they face increasingly strong pressures from the extractivist sectors of the economy—oil, gas, hydropower, agribusiness and extensive livestock (RAISG, 2012).

Bolivia is the only country where levels of deforestation within IT have increased between 2000 and 2013. And yet, since the 1990s it has been an international example of the return of the right to manage and recognition of property rights of lowland communities and peoples (White and Martin, 2002), in particular since constitutional changes and normative advances for the recognition of their rights. However, national policies implemented mainly since 2010 encourage the expansion of the agricultural border and consequently deforestation (Land Foundation, 2019; McKay, 2018). In Peru, deforestation in the Indigenous Territories is higher than in The Protected Areas, but with a declining trend between 2000 and 2013. Despite this Peru has officially initiated a policy of zero deforestation, betting on the mechanism of Reduction of Deforestation and Degradation REDD+ with the participation of local communities.

The overlap between Protected Areas and Indigenous Territories with oil lots is not a marginal issue. In Peru it is 49 per cent; in Bolivia it is 23 per cent; and in and Ecuador it is 17 per cent, regardless of the work phase in which they are located. In Peru 66 per cent of IT has on position. Intangible zones (in Ecuador) or territorial reserves (in Peru), both intended for indigenous peoples in isolation, are superimposed with oil lots on 71 per cent of their area. On the other hand, oil lots overlap by 95 per cent with the new territorial reserves demanded in the Peruvian Amazon. In Bolivia, approximately 20 per cent of ITs overlap with oil lots, but this hides a particularly worrying situation in the country's highest biodiversity area. For example, Madidi Park and Pilón Lajas Biosphere Reserve Park and Indigenous Territory were 7 per cent and 85 per cent internally opposed to oil concessions respectively (Jiménez, 2013; RAISG, 2012).

In the face of these threats, the resilience of indigenous peoples is reduced. Its economic and organisational resources are even smaller compared to the resources held by the interests of oil, gas, livestock and land. Government actions were generally contradictory. On the one hand, they supported the creation of protected areas and indigenous territories and on the other they violated or did not implement the laws. For example, in Ecuador, in the same year of the creation of the Yasuní National Park (1979), the government opened roads through it facilitating colonisation in the face of the protest of the people. The conflict around TIPNIS in Bolivia since 2010 is another example of contradictory government actions in which the construction of the road through TIPNIS violated principles of the Political Constitution adopted in 2009 (Fundación Tierra, 2018). In the face of helplessness, abuse becomes stronger. The recent report *Extractivismos and Rights in the Andean Region*, prepared by four institutions for the defence of the environment and human rights, gives an account of the patterns and mechanisms of the abuses of power against environmental and indigenous rights defenders in Bolivia, Colombia, Ecuador and Peru in the framework of the consolidation of extractive activities (Aprodeh, Delen, Cajar, Cedib, and Cedhu, 2018).

Exporting primary economies and degrees of diversification

The counterpart of economic growth and social achievements was the accelerated loss of environmental heritage at the beginning of the twenty-first century. The structural cause of this paradox lies in the export-based growth pattern of raw materials that has characterised Latin American economies since the colony. Overcoming the regional position as a commodity bidder in global economic dynamics is one of the central themes of the Latin American debate in the last seventy years (Bárcena, 2016). Comparative analysis of the economic structures of Bolivia, Ecuador, Peru and Colombia in the Latin American and global context is part of the approach of economic complexity as the expansion of knowledge of countries and regions to produce greater diversity value-added goods and services (Hausmann and Hidalgo, 2010). Critical criticism of this perspective and the challenges of sustainable and inclusive productive diversification in the Andean region are being made.[11]

What is the position of the Andean countries in the global economy at the beginning of the twenty-first century?

Based on the Economic Complexity Index, it is clear that Latin America is made up mostly of simple economies in the sense of productive structures that lack complex networks of knowledge and a diverse set of knowledge-intensive products. However, the differences[12] between countries are significant. Colombia stands out in 61st place along with Uruguay (60) and Brazil (53). At the other end of this rank order, out of 122 countries Bolivia, Ecuador and Peru occupy 109th, 103rd and 94th positions respectively in 2016.

In recent decades, the gaps between Latin American countries and the leading countries of Asia have widened. While in 1995 the level of complexity of leading economies in our region, such as Brazil and Uruguay, placed them above China and a few steps from the Republic of Korea, the former underwent a gradual process of backwardness and stagnation at the beginning of the twenty-first century, similar to that of the rest of the countries in the region. Differences in the income of Latin American countries and the Asian leaders of China and the Republic of Korea can be understood as expressions of the knowledge gap that exists between them. As we will see below, the investment gap in productive capacities as measured by indicators of technological intensity (level of investment in research and development, appropriation of knowledge through patents and scientific publications) has significantly widened since the 1980s when Asian economies experienced increased exports of knowledge-intensive products. By contrast, the region's economies had slower income growth, in line with a lower sophistication of their productive structures.

The result is expressed in the levels of education demanded by the productive structures of the different countries. For example, in advanced countries such as Japan and Switzerland, characterised by a high of complexity in the structure of production, it is common for a high percentage of the workforce to have received advanced education or training. In the case of Japan. for example, in 2016 up to 48.5 per cent of the workforce had received advanced education and training in the acquisition of knowledge and skills—accumulating 'human capital (in the discourse of development). In contrast, the four countries of the Andean region, the highest proportion of workers has basic (primary) and intermediate (secondary) levels. The country with the highest proportion of workers without schooling (lower than basic) was Bolivia (31 per cent), followed by Peru (18.4 per cent) and Ecuador (13.2 per cent). Colombia had less than 5 per cent of its workers without schooling. At the other extreme, the proportion of workers with advanced training stands out first In Colombia (27.3 per cent), followed by Peru (19.3 per cent), Ecuador (16 per cent) and finally Bolivia (12.1 per cent).[13]

What are the factors that explain the divergences in productive diversification between countries?

An important literature has studied the factors that explain the convergences and divergences between countries especially in the last 70 years. Comparative studies highlight political, institutional and public policy factors. It is verified that most of the countries that transformed their productive structures shared institutional characteristics, regulatory frameworks and productive promotion policies aimed at promoting public and private investment (domestic and foreign) driving productive diversification. The strong investment in education, research, technological development and innovation stands out for the increase of economic complexity. They converge in pointing out the importance of long-term public policy concertation and coherence within the framework of a market economy (Evans, 1995; Freitas and Paiva, 2015; IDB, 2009; Wade, 2018; CAF, 2006).

A wide range of literature shows that the development of new communication technologies such as mobile phones, GPS and biotechnology in the US and Europe, as well as *clusters* such as Silicon Valley, benefited substantially from public resources and productivity promotion policies (Mazzucato, 2015; Block and Keller, 2011; Sabel, 2009). The importance of productive policies in the Asian miracle was also extensively analysed (Amsden, 2001; Wade, 1992; Orrù, Biggart and Hamilton, 1997). The same thing happened in leading countries in Latin America in the twentieth century (Wanderley, 2011). One of the lessons of late diversification experiences was the ability of development strategies to advance trends in the global economy and promote investment and technological development in sectors and activities with great potential for the future.

To what extent is the decline in productive diversification homogeneous between Latin American countries?

To analyse the diversification differences of Andean countries, the Relative Export Diversification Index (IDRE) developed by Meller (2013) is useful, disaggregating the number of categories exported. According to this index, while confirming the high concentration of hydrocarbon and mineral exports in the countries of the Andean region, it also notes that Colombia would become the country of the region with the greatest diversification of exports, with more high value-added products among its main ten products (e.g. medicines, plastics products, authorised chemicals and perfumery). Primary products such as coffee, flowers and bananas also stand out.[14]

By contrast, the main exports of Bolivia, Ecuador and Peru were concentrated in primary products. It highlights the potential for diversification of the Ecuadorian economy towards the production of food such as crustaceans and molluscs, fish, flowers and cocoa, palm oil, wood and coffee. For its part, in Peru there is the production of grapes, coffee, clothing, fresh vegetables such as asparagus and tropical fruits, as well as meat and fish flour not suitable for human consumption. Bolivia is the country with a less diversified export basket with the export of cake and flour of oilseeds, vegetable oils, coconuts and cashew nuts, and jewellery. These differences are reflected in the position of these countries in the international ranking of economic complexity mentioned above.

However, this diversification in low-complexity economies remains mainly focused on *commodities.* Many of these primary products have very negative environmental impacts such as deforestation, biodiversity loss, accelerated soil erosion and water pollution and environmental services. Of note is that the most important products in terms of export value are not food-oriented and conflict with family production aimed at ensuring adequate and healthy eating (McKay, 2018; Earth Foundation, 2015; Detsch, 2018). According to the Food and Agriculture Organization, up to 80 per cent of the world's food in terms of value is produced by households (FAO, 2014).

What are the new paths of sustainable productive diversification in the Andean region?

The above considerations expose the need to think about diversification not simply in terms of product exports. Rather, services and products intended for the internal and external market should be incorporated. This also leads us to question the same available indices on diversification that do not consider environmental and social issues. By broadening the perspective beyond exports and incorporating environmental sustainability and social impacts, new chains and sectors with great potential are emerging in the Andean region. These include ecological tourism, agroecology, gastronomy, pharmaceutical and disease control products, the technology sector, and environmental services among other value-added products and services anchored in the environmental and cultural heritage of the Andean-Amazonian territories (Flowers, 2018; Bovarnick et al., 2010; Alayza and Gudynas, 2011; Campero, 2016; Cartagena, 2018; Malky and Mendizábal, 2018; UNDP, 2008).

From these criticisms, new studies based on the theory of economic complexity are advancing the incorporation of environmental sustainability and social implications. Based on classifications of environmentally friendly goods, Mealy and Teytelboym (2018) have constructed the Green Complexity Index (GCI). Their study shows that countries with the highest levels of GCI have the highest percentage of environmental patents, lower levels of carbon emissions, and stricter environmental policies. In this way it can be foreseen that the relationship between complexity and economic growth in the following decades will depend on the accumulation of environmentally sustainable productive capacities (e.g. clean energies, monitoring and internalisation of environmental costs by companies, innovation and technological development of efficient use of natural resources and reduction and reuse of waste, among others).

Considering that the challenges of sustainable development are more complex, it is legitimate to inquire about the relevance of lessons from experiences of productive diversification in the nineteenth and twentieth centuries based on activities classified as brown economics, who are responsible for the current environmental and social crisis. Recent studies converge in the conclusion that the path of productive diversification based on knowledge expansion (prioritisation of education, science and technology) remains even more valid. This is because the degree of complexity of countries not only exposes the set of capacities they have, but also anticipates the difficulties of diversifying their productive structures, and thus their economic development. This is because the creation of new production chains, and consequently the transformation of the patterns of the productive structure, is conditioned on the set of productive capacities that an economy has.

Equally important is confirmation of the importance of next-generation productive promotion policies. These include changes in institutional arrangements and regulatory frameworks inducing private and public investment towards productive sectors and chains that, on the one hand, integrate and respect the biophysical boundaries and regenerative capacity of ecosystems and, on the other hand, generate quality jobs and contribute to collective well-being. From a long-term perspective, the quality of investment is measured not by the amount[15] per se, but by the degree of contribution to the expansion of the knowledge envelope, the preservation of the environment, the generation of employment and the productive chains that it promotes. If investments are concentrated in few low-value-added sectors, it destroys environmental heritage, does not create quality jobs, and does not contribute to knowledge and increased productivity, these may favour high growth rates in the short term, but may not contribute to overcoming extractivism and, therefore to the comprehensive and sustainable development of countries.[16]

How far are we making progress in the direction of productive diversification?

In relation to the quality of investment, we focus on trends in foreign direct investment (FDI). Colombia was the country with the highest FDI in the region followed by Peru, Ecuador and Bolivia. However, in all countries, the most important target sectors of foreign investment were *commodities* (mining and hydrocarbons). Bolivia is the country with the highest concentration of FDI in these sectors, while Peru and Colombia have greater diversification of Retail target sectors (Wanderley et al., 2018). The environmental damage and social conflicts of this type of investment, analysed in the previous section, outweigh the short-term benefits. The challenge persists in the region to generate institutional and public policy conditions to attract quality foreign investment.

The low priority of research in our countries, which results in low public and private investment in research and development as a percentage of GDP, is striking. Based on World Bank data in 2014, Brazil led with 1.17 per cent, followed by Argentina, 0.59 per cent. In contrast, the Andean countries had the lowest levels of current and capital expenditure (public and private) on research and development relative to GDP. Ecuador increasing from 0.06 per cent to 0.44 per cent and Colombia from 0.14 per cent to 0.25 per cent between 2002 and 2014. The data for Peru and Bolivia are very incomplete. However, they show stagnation in the case of Peru between 2002 and 2014 (0.11 per cent) and decline in Bolivia between 2002 and 2009, from 0.28 per cent to 0.16 per cent, this being the last year of available data. To get a comparative idea, in 2014 the Republic of Korea invested 4.23 per cent, North America 2.79 per cent, China 2.07 per cent, while Latin America invested 0.77 per cent.

One indicator to approximate the state of the productive capacities of the Andean countries is the contribution to scientific knowledge, both in the areas of the social sciences as well as in the biological sciences, technology, art and humanities. According to the bibliographic indicator of the number of publications per inhabitant recognised in the SCOPUS bibliographic database, the differences between the Andean countries are marked.[17] Colombia shows a significant increase in annual publications per capita, from 2.16 in 2000 to 21.00 in 2016. The same is true in Ecuador with the increase in its per capita publications from 1.13 to 14.62 in the same period. Third, there is Peru that rose from 1.04 to 7.50. The largest contrast is observed in the case of Bolivia—from 0.85 to 3.00 over the same period.

This situation is confirmed by an analysis of the appropriation of knowledge in terms of the indicator of patent applications per million inhabitants. According to the WIPO Statistics database, the differences between Latin American countries are considerable, with Brazil, Chile, Argentina and Colombia at the top with 25, 22, 20 and 11 patent applications per million inhabitants, while Bolivia, Ecuador and Peru, had a share of only one, two and three patent applications per million inhabitants, in recent places in 2016. The contribution to technological development in these countries was significantly low compared to that of emerging economies in Asia. For example, the Republic of Korea had 3,189 patent applications per million inhabitants and China 874. The trend in the global share of patents granted as a percentage of the total between 2004 and 2016 indicates a decline in Latin America and the Caribbean (2 per cent to 1 per cent of the total), while Asian countries, led by their emerging economies, expanded considerably (from 41 per cent to 57 per cent).[18] These figures also have a qualitative meaning. Technological advancement must meet local needs. Therefore, to the extent that a country is unable to generate more patents, it is less likely to have technology that responds to the problems it confronts.

In short, the poor effort to promote research and low production and knowledge appropriation help us to understand the significant lag of the region compared to emerging countries in Asia, as well as differences between countries Latin American in the ranking of economic complexity. With the increasing importance of knowledge to address the challenges of sustainable productive diversification, the urgency of changes in development strategies in the Andean region is clear.

Conclusions

Criticism and debate of the concept of development since its conception in the 1950s has been intense with the constant renewal of paradigms, knowledge and practices. At the end of the twentieth century new theoretical and political currents emphasised the need to recognise and integrate the biophysical boundaries of the planet and the regenerative capacity of ecosystems as enabling conditions of development, and consequently, of the systemic balance vital to living beings. In this more complex horizon of sustainable productive diversification, countries and regions face dissimilar challenges depending on ecosystems, the degree of knowledge and technological development, the type of social welfare regime, and institutional frameworks and political coalitions. Specifically, countries exporting natural resources with low productive diversification face not only the growing distances of knowledge and technological development relative to industrialised countries, but also international commodity pressures in the expansionary cycles of the global economy. This knowledge gap is not only quantitative, but also calls for reflection on the needs of the knowledge generated, as well as understanding that the need expressed by international demand for goods does not necessarily coincide with those of the producing countries.

The data and studies reviewed in this chapter counter-intuitively suggests that in the current context of the capitalist development process, a system in crisis caught up in the vortex of conflicting forces of change, political discursive orientation is not the most critical factor in the determination of a country's achievement at the level of social development and progress in the direction of protecting and advancing human and territorial rights and bringing about a more an alternative reality, another world that is more equitable, inclusive and environmentally sustainable. For example, our findings in regard to social and environmental advances in the Andean region—for e.g. the reduction of poverty and protection of the integrity of the ecosystem—do not correspond to the classification of countries according to political orientation. The advances or achievements made by Ecuador and Bolivia, both countries with a progressive orientation towards inclusive and sustainable development, and Colombia and Peru, with a more liberal orientation, do not fit this classification. In the current or recent context of fiscal revenues and higher incomes derived from the export of natural resources, each of these countries benefited from the high rates of resource-led economic growth and achieved a significant reduction in the incidence of poverty. And with the slowdown in the world economy each of these countries have fallen victim to a slowing down of this trend.

Our conclusion is that the effect of labour income in an international context of expansion of commodity prices was the main factor explaining the decline in poverty and inequality. The effect of non-working income included in public transfers was much more significant in Peru and Ecuador compared to Colombia and Bolivia. At the same time, Colombia and Peru have less regressive tax systems than Ecuador and Bolivia. In terms of deepening the pattern of extractivist growth, Bolivia and Ecuador regressed the most. Environmental predation was a common denominator in the region. The pattern of these developments raises a number of questions that arise from the contradictions between, on the one hand, discursive and legal advances for the protection of the rights of indigenous peoples and the environment, and, on the other hand, non-compliance and even violation thereof.

Over this period, labour dynamics stopped rewarding those workers with the most educational training in all countries in the region. The decrease in real wages for the most skilled workers at the university level resulted in a decrease in income inequality as measured by the Gini coefficient. Despite the increase in working income, working conditions of high informality and low productivity did not significantly change. Added to this is the regression of tax systems in the Andean region; i.e. the poorest contribute more of their income than the richest, constituting a barrier to the more equitable distribution of wealth by the agency of the state. On the other hand, over the period under study some progress was made in this regard, although again this progress did not correspond to the classification of countries by political orientation or development model. As it turned out, in Colombia and Peru tax systems became less regressive than in Ecuador and Bolivia.

However, both the high annual growth rates and social achievements made in the first two decades of the new millennium, were based on the advance of extractive capital in the development process, and extractivism was also behind the resulting intensification of the rate of predation of the Andean-Amazonian countries' exceptional environmental heritage. In addition to the intensification of deforestation and loss of biodiversity, other equally devastating environmental impacts, such as high intensity of water and energy consumption, and soil, water and air pollution, were added. It is difficult to measure the scope and extent of the predation and destruction of the Andean-Amazonian ecosystems given the multiple services that forests provide for both human well-being and for the functioning of the earth as a system. These systems are important for climate regulation, for the circulation and supply of water throughout the territories, contribute to the prevention of natural disasters, and play an important role in the provision of clean air. This is why the dynamics of resource-led economic growth are unsustainable, and to dramatically reduce deforestation rates and create conditions for forest recovery and growth, both existing economic structures and macroeconomic policies need to be urgently and radically transformed.

Other social and economic impacts of deepening extractivism at the beginning of the century are equally significant. In social terms, alliances formed between large multinational corporations in the extractive sector, governments reliant on the investments and operations of these companies, and other social actors in the private sector, have led to a deepening of both the landgrabbing phenomenon and the pillage of the region's wealth of natural resource wealth. (on these dynamics see Veltmeyer in this volume). The advance of capital on the extractive frontier of the development process, and the resulting displacement of rural peasant and indigenous communities and the wholesale violation of the territorial rights of both indigenous communities, has also released powerful forces of resistance in the form of a socioenvironmental protest movement.

In economic terms, the extraordinary natural wealth of the Andean-Amazonian countries, now threatened by unsustainable management of natural resources and ecosystems, has an as-yet unknown or immeasurable economic value. From a long-term perspective, over-exploitation of biodiversity resources and ecosystem services has a high opportunity cost for new paths of productive diversification and, consequently, development. In this context, those sectors with the potential to move towards environmentally sustainable and job-generating economies are intrinsically connected to the economic opportunities represented by the rich environmental and cultural heritage of the Andean-Amazonian region. Examples include ecotourism, biotrade, medicine, agroecology, new frontiers of environmental services and the benefits of clean energy. The accumulation of knowledge and innovations are the keys to productive diversification at the beginning of the twenty-first century within the framework of a new generation of sustainable productive policies. The territorial dimension is particularly relevant in these new policies. Likewise, the integration of environmental management tools and the protection of the collective rights of indigenous peoples are fundamental in particular the Protected Areas and Indigenous Territories in the Andean region. The preservation of biodiversity and ecological balance will only be ensured while preserving the diversity of cultures and vice versa.

Looking ahead, the paving of sustainable development roads in the Andean region is founded on two structural pillars: on the one hand, in sustainable productive transformation with quality employment generation and, on the other hand, in the expansion of universal social protection. These two pillars complement each other to advance more prosperous societies, fair and harmonious with their environment. Today what citizens in different countries are calling for is the strengthening of democracies, the generation of quality employment, the construction of environments for the equal exercise of rights and, correlatively, the provision of quality public goods and services such as health, education, transport and dignified retirement. Aspirations are much more complex and express a desire to belong to communities free of discrimination and violence of all kinds, social solidarity, and both environmental and social justice.

Notes

1 For a more detailed analysis of the construction of international agreements and evidence of the environmental and social crisis, see Zuazo (2018).
2 The poverty line of $US 3.2 per person per day, 2011 PPP, which is specific for Latin America, will be used throughout our analysis. based on Lac-equity-lab data, worlbank.org. Last visited on 8 October 2019.
3 Editor's note. On the link between inequality and poverty, and between inequality and neoliberalism, see UNDP (2010). The UNDP reported that there existed a 'direct correspondence between the advance of globalization, neoliberalism, and the advance

of poverty social inequality, social inequity'. The 'most explosive contradictions', the report continues, 'are given because the advance of [neoliberal] globalization marches hand in hand with the advance of poverty and social polarization'. Furthermore, 'it is undeniable that the 1980s and 1990s [were] the creation of an abysmal gap between wealth and poverty' and that this gap constitutes the most formidable obstacle to achieving human development (UNDP, 2010: xv).

4 The analysis takes into account labour productivity per person occupied in US dollars in 2018. Data from The Conference Board Total Economy Database (Adjusted version), April 2019.

5 Bolivia has 12 per cent, Ecuador and Peru 17 per cent and Colombia 21 per cent NiNis. Data ILOSTAT. NiNis are youth that neither work nor study (*ni* trabajan, *ni* estudien).

6 The Amazon's forests cover 92 per cent of the continent's forested cover, representing 35 per cent of the total Latin American territory. These account for 22 per cent of the world's forests and 30 per cent of global tropical forests. They contain 49 per cent of the carbon stock above the soil of the tropics. In addition, Andean countries are responsible for approximately 27.7 per cent of the Amazonian biome.

7 www.globalforestwatch.org/

8 The concept of hotspot refers to a region with a large amount of biodiversity present and which, in turn, is in danger of disappearing (Myers, Mittermeier, Mittermeier, Da Fonseca, and Kent, 2000).

9 Protected Area is a clearly defined, recognised, dedicated and managed geographical area through legal or other effective means to achieve the long-term conservation of nature together with the services of the systems and associated cultural values (Dudley, 2008).

10 The countries that signed this Convention in the region are Mexico (1990), Bolivia and Colombia (1991), Costa Rica and Paraguay (1993), Peru (1994), Honduras (1995), Guatemala (1996), Ecuador (1998), Argentina (2000), Brazil, Venezuela and the Dominican Republic (2002) and Chile and Nicaragua (2010).

11 According to this perspective, the distance of economic prosperity between countries is strongly linked to the diversification gap of the respective productive structures: countries with the highest per capita income have productive capacity significantly more diversified and high technological development, while countries with lower per capita incomes are more specialised in lower-value-added primary goods, low technological development, and productivity.

12 Although these indices have limitations, they allow for international comparison of the degree of diversification of economies. Built on information from international trade, it excludes transable services (e.g. software exports) and non-transable services (e.g. restaurants and communication) that not only result from complex networks of specialised knowledge, but also play an increasingly important role in the economy of countries (Hausmann, 2018). On the other hand, because trade patterns do not necessarily reflect local competencies due to the vertical fragmentation of international production chains that characterises more sophisticated industries, such as the automotive industry in these industries, exported products from this segmentation do not necessarily represent the competences or technologies of countries (ECLAC, 2015b).

13 ILOSTAT data from the ILO.

14 Based on ECLACSTAT data.

15 To deepen the discussion on new productive policies, see Mealy and Teytelboym, 2018; Aghion, Boulanger and Cohen, 2011; Rodrik, 2014; Hallegate, Fay and Vogt-Schilb, 2013; Hubertand and Zachmann, 2011; ECLAC, 2015a.

16 An interesting work on regulatory frameworks for attracting foreign direct investment that favours the development of national productive fabrics is Cumbers, 2010.

17 Online data in www.scopus.com/

18 Online data: www3.wipo.int/ipstats/index.htm.

References

Aghion, P., J. Boulanger and E. Cohen (2011). Rethinking industrial policy. *Technical report, Bruegel Policy Brief No. 4*, June. www.researchgate.net/publication/277257099_Rethinking_industrial_policy_Bruegel_Policy_Brief_201104_June_2011

Alayza, A. and E. Gudynas (2011). *Transitions: Post-extractivism and Alternatives to Extractivism in Peru.* Lima: Peruvian Center for Social Studies.

Amsden, A.H. (2001). *The Rise of "the Rest". Challenges to the West from Late-industrializing Economies.* New York: Oxford University Press.

Aprodeh, Delen, B., F. Hurtado Caicedo, and R. Hoetmer (eds) (2018). *Abuses of Power against Human Rights, Territory and Environmental Defenders. Report on Extractivism and Rights in the Andean Region.* www.aprodeh.org.pe/informe-sobre-extractivismo-abusos-de-poder-y-derechos-en-la-region-andina/

Bárcena, A. (2016). "ECLAC's Economic Thinking: Past and Present," *Reflections on Development in Latin America and the Caribbean: Key Lectures 2015 (LC/G.2677).* Santiago de Chile: Economic Commission for Latin America and the Caribbean (ECLAC).

Block, F. and M.R. Keller (2011). "Where Do Innovations Come From? Transformations in the US Economy, 1970–2006," *Working Papers in Technology Governance and Economic Dynamics* No. 35. Norway, The Other Canon Foundation.

Bovarnick, A., F. Alpizar and C. Schnell (eds) (2010). *Latin America and the Caribbean. A Biodiversity Super Power.* New York: UNDP.

CAF-Andean Development Corporation. (2006). *Road to Transformation Latin America. Economics and Development Report.* Caracas: CAF Publications Unit.

Campero Nuñez del Prado, J.C. (2016). "The Fourth Industrial Revolution in Bolivia?" *Analysis* No. 1/2016. La Paz: Fredrich Ebert Stiftung.

Cartagena, P. (2018). "Sustainable Food Production: New Visions," in F. Wanderley and J. Peres-Cajías (eds), *The Challenges of Productive Development in the 21st Century. Diversification, Social Justice and Environmental Sustainability.* La Paz: UCB, Plural Editors and FES.

ECLAC—Economic Commission for Latin America and the Caribbean. (2015a). *Education, Structural Change and Inclusive Growth in Latin America.* Santiago: CEPAL.

ECLAC. (2015b). *Economic Study of Latin America and the Caribbean, 2015.* Santiago: CEPAL.

Cumbers, A. (2010). "North Sea, State and Development Trajectories in the United Kingdom and Norway," *Thresholds. Journal of the Multidisciplinary Postgraduate In Developmental Sciences*, 267.

Detsch, C. (2018). "The Social-ecological Transformation of the Agricultural Sector in Latin America. Key Steps and Actors," Friedrich Ebert Stiftung-New Society Working Paper. Mexico City: FES.

Dudley, N. (2008). *Guidelines for Applying Protected Area Management Categories: Iucn.* Gland (Switzerland): IUCN.

Earth Foundation. (2015). *Marginalization of Peasant and Indigenous Agriculture. Local Dynamics, Security and Food Sovereignty.* La Paz: Earth Foundation.

Earth Foundation. (2019). *Special Report. Fire in Santa Cruz. Balance of forest fires 2019 and their relationship with land tenure.* La Paz: EARTH Foundation.

Evans, P. (1995). *Embedded Autonomy: States and Industrial Transformation.* Princeton: Princeton University Press.

Flowers, G. (2018). "Bolivia Can Switch to a Clean and Diversified Economy. Sustainable Development as a Challenge and Opportunity," *Analysis* No. 18. La Paz: Millennium Foundation.

Freitas, E., and E.A. Paiva (2015). "Diversification and Sophistication of Exports: A Product Space Application to Data from Brazil," *Revista Econômica do Nordeste*, 46(3): 79–98.

Fajardo, Y. (1999). Constitutional recognition of indigenous law and special jurisdiction in Andean countries (Colombia, Peru, Bolivia, Ecuador). *Pena and State Magazine* (4): 129.

Fajardo, R.Y. (2006). "Milestones of the Recognition of Legal Pluralism and Indigenous Law in Indigenous Policies and Andean Constitutionalism," pp. 537–567 in *Indigenous Peoples and Human Rights*. Bilbao: University of Deusto.

FAO. (2014). *Hacia una agricultura familiar más fuerte.* Washington: Food and Agriculture Organization of the United Nations.

FAO. (2015). *Global Forest Resources Assessment 2015: How are the World's Forests Changing?* Washington: Food and Agriculture Organization of the United Nations.

Fearnside, P.M. (2006). "Dams in the Amazon: Belo Monte and Brazil's Hydroelectric Development of the Xingu River Basin," *Environmental Management*, 38(1): 16–27.

Fearnside, P.M. (2014). Impacts of Brazil's Madeira River Dams: Unlearned Lessons for Hydroelectric Development in Amazonia. *Environmental Science & Policy*, 38, 164–172.

Fearnside, P.M. (2016). "Environmental and Social Impacts of Hydroelectric Dams in Brazilian Amazonia: Implications for the Aluminum Industry," *World Development*, 77: 48–65.

Gudynas, E. (2015). *Extractivism. Ecology, Economics and Politics of a Way of Understanding Development and Nature.* Cochabamba: CEDIB.

Hallegate, S., M. Fay and A. Vogt-Schilb (2013). "Green Industrial Policies: When and How," *Policy Research Working Paper*. Washington, DC: Word Bank.

Hausmann, R. (2018). "Economic Complexity in Short," in F. Wanderley and J. Peres-Cajías (eds), *The Challenges of Productive Development in the 21st Century. Diversification, Social Justice and Environmental Sustainability.* La Paz: UCB, Plural Editors and FES.

Hausmann, R. and C. Hidalgo (2010). *Country Diversification, Product Ubiquity, and Economic Divergence.* Boston: Center for International Development at Harvard University.

Hoorn, C., F.P. Wesselingh, H. Ter Steege, M.A. Bermudez, A. Mora, J. Sevink and P. Figueiredo (2010). "Amazonia through time: Andean uplift, climate change, landscape evolution, and biodiversity," *Science*, 330(6006): 927–931.

IDB—Inter-American Development Bank; CIAT—Inter-American Center for Tax Administrations. (2017). Database on tax pressure for Latin America and the Caribbean.

IDB. International Development Bank. (2009). *The Age of Productivity – Transforming Economies from the Bottom Up.* New York: Palgrave MacMillan.

Jiménez, G. (2013). Indigenous Territories and Protected Areas in the Crosshairs. The Expansion of the Frontera was of Extractivist Industries. *Petropress*, 4–10.

Lustig, N. (2017). "The Impact of the Tax System and Social Spending on Income and Poverty Distribution in Latin America. An implementation of the Methodological Framework of the Commitment to Equity (CEQ) Project," *The Economic Quarter*, 84(335): 493–568.

Malky Harb, A. and C. Mendizábal (2018). "Forests, water and biodiversity in Bolivia," in F. Wanderley and J. Peres-Cajías (eds), *The challenges of productive development in the 21st century. Diversification, social justice and environmental sustainability.* La Paz: UCB, Plural Editors and FES.

McKay, B.M. (2018). "The Politics of Agrarian Change in Bolivia's Soy Complex," *Journal of Agrarian Change*, 18: 406–424.

Mazzucato, M. (2015). Building the Entrepreneurial State: A New Framework for Envisioning and Evaluating a Mission-Oriented Public Sector (January 2, 2015). Levy Economics Institute of Bard College Working Paper No. 824. Available at SSRN: https://ssrn.com/abstract=2544707 or http://dx.doi.org/10.2139/ssrn.2544707

Mealy, P. and A. Teytelboym (2018). "Economic Complexity and the Green Economy," *INET Oxford Working Paper* No. 2018–03, 1–57.

Meller, P. (2013). *Natural Resources and Export Diversification. A Look for the Future for Latin Aérica.* Santiago: CIEPLAN-CAF.

Mittermeier, R.A. (2004). *Hotspots revisited: Cemex.* www.researchgate.net/publication/275651117_Hotspots_Revisited_Earth%27s_Biologically_Richest_and_Most_Endangered_Terrestrial_Ecoregions

Myers, N., R.A. Mittermeier, C.G Mittermeier, G.A.B. Da Fonseca and J. Kent (2000). "Biodiversity hotspots for conservation priorities," *Nature*, 403(6772): 853.

Ocampo, J.A. and N. Goméz-Arteaga (2017). "Social Protection System, Redistribution and Growth in Latin America," *CEPAL Review*, 122: 7–30.

Orrù, M., N. Woolsey Biggart and G.G. Hamilton (eds) (1997). *The Economic Organization of East Asian Capitalism.* New York: Sage Publications.

UNDP United Nations Development Programme. (2010). *Human Development Report 2010 The Real Wealth of Nations.* New York: UNDP.

UNDP United Nations Development Programme. (2008). *Human Development Report. The Other Frontier: Alternative Uses of Natural Resources in Bolivia.* Peace: UNDP.

RAISG. (2012). *Amazon under Pressure.* Retrieved from www.raisg.socioambiental.org.

RAISG. (2015). Deforestation in the Amazon (1970–2013). Retrieved from www.raisg.socioambiental.org

Rodrik, D. (2014). "Green Industrial Policy," *Oxford Review of Economic Policy*, 30(3): 469–491.

Rojas, D.M. (2015). "The Andean Region in the Geopolitics of Strategic Resources," *Political Analysis*, 28(30): 88–107.

Sabel, C. (2009). *What Industrial Policy Is Becoming: Taiwan, Ireland and Finland as Guides to the Future of Industrial Policy.* New York: Columbia Law School.

Svampa, M. (2016). *Latin American debates. Indianism, development, dependence and populism.* Cochabamba: CEDIB and Edhasa.

Tapia-Armijos, M.F., J. Homeier, C.I. Espinosa, C. Leuschner and M. de la Cruz (2015). "Deforestation and Forest Fragmentation in South Ecuador since the 1970s – Losing a Hotspot of Biodiversity," *PLoS One*, 10(9): e0133701. The Conference board economy database. www.conference-board.org/us/

Veltmeyer, H. and J. Petras (2014). *The New Extractivism: A Post-Neoliberal Development.* London: Zed Books.

Wade, R. (1992). "East Asia's Economic Success: Conflicting Perspectives, Partial Insights, Shaky Evidence," *Word Politics*, 44(2): 270–320.

Wade, R. (2018). "The Developmental State: Dead or Alive," *Development and Change*, 49(2): 518–546.

Wanderley, F. (2011). "Productive Transformation, Economic Plurality and Equity Social," in F. Wanderley (ed.), *Development in Question: Reflections from Latin America.* La Paz: CIDES-UMSA; Plural.

Wanderley, F. (2019). "The Care Policies in Latin America – Articulating Women's, Children, Adolescents, Older Adults and People with Disabilities," *Working Document* IISEC-UCB No. 2/2019.

Wanderley, F., H. Cossio, J.P. Benavides, M. Gantier Mita and K. Martínez Torrico (2018). *Towards Sustainable Development in the Andean Region. Bolivia, Peru, Ecuador and Colombia*. Peace: UCB-IISEC/FHS.

White, A., and A. Martin (2002). "Who Owns the World's Forests. Forest Tenure and Public Forest in Transition," *Working Paper Forest Trends*. Washington, DC: Forest Trends.

World Bank (n.d.) LAC Equity Lab. Base data. www.worldbank.org/en/topic/poverty/lac-equity-lab1

Zuazo, M. (2018). "Sustainable Development and Governance from the Global South," in F. Wanderley and J. Peres-Cajías (eds), *The Challenges of Productive Development in the 21st Century. Diversification, Social Justice and Environmental Sustainability*. La Paz: UCB, Plural Editors and FES.

9 Uchronia for living well

René Ramírez Gallegos

Is *time money or is time life?* The answer to this question is at the heart of both the debate that has run through the conceptual discussion about *buen vivir* in Ecuador (Ramírez, 2018) and the political dispute over two different conceptions of social order on a global scale. The hegemonic social order of capitalism is based on a particular temporal order in which time is money because money is time when it is configured as a driving mechanism of the acceleration of production, circulation and consumption of goods and services to serve the purpose of capital accumulation. From the academy, this configuration of the common sense that 'time is gold' or 'time is money' has been leveraged in analytical frameworks such as neoliberal economic utilitarianism that has come to dominate both academia and help to shape the social consciousness of the average citizen (i.e. the dominant ideology).[1] We elaborate on this point below.

The prevailing social order undermines and undoes life by trying (in fictional terms) to equate time with speed or acceleration, this being the most effective instrument of capital accumulation. In this context, this chapter proposes that the utopia of the *society of buen vivir*, proposed by a collective social intellect (the Ecuadorian society) needs to be re-constructed on the basis of a uchronia[2] in which time is recovered as life—not any kind of life, but *life* understood as living well in solidarity and harmony with nature. This uchronia must be thought within the framework, both theoretical and methodological, as an alternative epistemology that accompanies the disputes involved in constructing an alternative reality whose achievement will imply the birth of a different social episteme. To this end, this chapter—born out of the depths of a social mandate—outlines a framework of conceptual, methodological and empirical analysis based on the study of *time* to serve such an historical specificity. To this end the chapter advances a number of theoretical and methodological principles derived from what we might term a *political socioecology of living well*,[3] an approach that facilitates the analysis, evaluation (distances and/or proximity) and proposes alternatives action to advance in the construction of the society in which people are able to live well—or, in the worldview of the Quichua peoples of the Andes to live according to the principle of *sumak kawsay*.[4] Why? Because time is life (to whom time is given, life is given) and in the quality of time is the configuration that implies whether this life is well-lived or not. Following the general postulate of Elias (2015) the chapter argues that in the dispute of the sense (objective and subjective) lies the dispute of the very sense of existence; that is, of life itself. That is why a different social order such as *the society of buen vivir* needs a different temporal order such as the *time for living well*. This argument is constructed with reference to the main conclusions of my book, *Life and Time. Notes for a Uchronic Theory of the Good Life Drawn from the Recent History of Ecuador* (Ramírez Gallegos, 2019), which demonstrates that time can function as a *proxy* for living well, serving as a compass for disputing the construction of a society based on the *buen vivir* principle.

The next part of the chapter analyses the 'Good Life Expectancy' (EVB) index[5] as a means of deconstructing the social, economic and ecological relations that are in force today—interrogating them as a point of departure for the project of constructing an alternative reality, another social order. The third part presents the 'time for living well' as a critical concept with which it is possible to highlight the reality and perverse oppressions lived by so many people today in the form of patriarchy, colonialism and capitalism. Finally, the chapter ends with an epilogue that opens the debate on chronopolitics for the construction of other possible social uchronias: 'other worlds are possible' as long as other temporal orders are constructed. As such, the dispute for the sense of time can also involve a dispute for social emancipation.

Towards a political socioecology of time for living well

Hardly under the analytical and methodological framework of mainstream welfare economics (utilitarianism) would it be possible to apply the proposal made by the Ecuadorian society regarding the principles of *buen vivir*. In fact, it could be argued that applying the perspective and tools of mainstream welfare economics where time only has meaning as a commodity, that is, in terms of its exchange value, would lead to the alienation rather than the affirmation of life. We argue to the contrary that a suitable *proxy* for constructing a *society of buen vivir* is time for living well. Analysing time is analysing life, and analysing the quality of time is to study the extent to which life is a well-lived life or a dignified life. This section advances empirical evidences that demonstrate that an analysis of the *political socioecology of time* is a good prism through which to visualise (and measure) 'closeness or remoteness' in the efforts taken to achieve a *society of buen vivir* in Ecuador.[6]

Human life as a time of existence: The first component of living well is life itself. In this sense, it is related to the time of human existence. In general, the average lifetime in a given territory is an expression of the presence or absence of the necessary and objective materiality needed to satisfy basic human needs and to secure the rights of a given political community. Life or time, being the opposite to mortality, reflects the adequacy of health and basic sanitation services, the nutritional and food state of its inhabitants, the level of security, the environmental quality or educational level of the population. As a society, avoiding preventable premature deaths after birth or increasing a population's life expectancy has its own value.

The average life expectancy of Ecuadorians today is 62.3 years. From 1997 to 2014 it increased by 11.5 years. This is not irrelevant given that over this same time span a number of countries saw their life expectancy slow down, and in few cases declines were even observed.[7] Turning to the question of gender, we note that women live on average seven years longer than men. Also, at a more general level, it is evident that the high levels of unmet basic needs (especially in basic services), high levels of inequality or low rates of school attendance negatively affects the average years of life of the Ecuadorian population. In turn, if the municipality is predominantly agricultural or has a population dedicated to manufacturing, the average life expectancy is higher. This is very different from the cantons where mining predominates. Indeed, if the municipality has a population predominantly engaged in the mining sector, the average life expectancy is shorter, sometimes dramatically so. Likewise, it emerges that poor environmental quality and those territories with higher population growth have a higher probability of living fewer years.

Time for living well: The dispute over the construction of an alternative social order is a struggle for an emancipated life. It is not enough to have more lifetime; it must be a well-lived life, a life worth living. Referring to living well or a good life necessarily involves analysing the 24 hours of a day, seven days a week and 365 days a year. Following this premise, it is important to analyse how time is distributed in Ecuadorian society, emphasising time for living well. It has been argued that Ecuador's new constitutional pact seeks to break with the possessive individualism of neoliberal society. The guarantee of rights or needs should not be the product of the law of the strongest where 'my' quality of life is exclusively based on a competitive struggle and a zero-sum game, self-interested and solitary, where some individuals flourish at the expense of others. The citizen of a *buen vivir* society is a republican, has rights and obligations to the 'other', recognises and coexists with diversity as part of his or her self-realisation, and works for the union of the political community to build a shared future. In other words, at the heart of the coexistence pact of 2008 is the return of the 'other'; gregariousness is restored as a human essence conducive to the flourishing of individuals, that is, as part of genuine sociability. As an analytical category, this return of interdependence for flourishing involves putting the production and enjoyment of relational goods at the heart of the debate. Time for living well is time for the flourishing of relational goods. Nevertheless, this relational time should not be interpreted as an expression of postmateriality. The materiality necessary for the living well must be constructed within the framework of the creation and enjoyment of the relational good.[8]

Relational goods can only be co-generated and co-enjoyed within the framework of a mutual agreement. And, since they depend on interaction with other human beings they are appreciated only insofar as they generate shared reciprocity on an equal footing. Methodologically, the time for living well, or relational time, is time in which citizens realise themselves and live moments with the other and/or for the other. To have time for living well is to have autonomous time to build more democracy, to participate in public, political and civil affairs; to nourish *the philia and the eros with 'the other'*; to liberate self-contemplation within the framework of emancipatory labour.

Based on the fact that time is not accumulative, the increase in relational time implies that time for living well has been more evenly distributed and that at the same time alienated time has decreased. As an alternative to a society in which citizens and workers are alienated from both their own labour power and their consumerist behaviour—and as Marx argued in a different context, from the 'human essence' ('man as a social being')—the *society of buen vivir* is ordered according to time for living well.

In a normal week, the average Ecuadorian dedicates 74 hours a week (44% of the total time available) to satisfy its biological needs. At the same time, the average citizen works 64.3 (38.3%) hours of the week (38.3% of time), with large differences in time between paid and unpaid work. Indeed, of the total hours worked by all citizens, 39.1 hours per week is unpaid work and 25.21 hours is salaried labour. While women work 28.5 hours more per week than men in unpaid work, men work 17.3 hours more than women in paid work.

The question then is: how much time does an Ecuadorian have to co-produce and co-enjoy time for living well? Without taking into account sleeping hours, an Ecuadorian enjoys a little more than one day of the week (26.7 hours per week) to live well. This is tantamount to saying that an average Ecuadorian enjoys relational goods for only 16% of his life. Of the total amount of time available for the good life, 17 hours are dedicated for enjoying free time; 9.3 hours are for love and friendship and 0.41 hours are devoted to democratic or civil participation. Finally, only between 2.3 and 3.4 hours of emancipated work per week can be added to the total of relational time mentioned above. In Ecuador, it seems that alienated labour is one of the main limits and constraints on living well.

Without taking into account sleeping hours, the average Ecuadorian lives fully a little more than one day a week (26.7 hours per week). This is the equivalent of saying that only 16% of his life an average Ecuadorian enjoys relational goods. Of the total time for living well, 17 hours are for enjoying free time; 9.3 hours of his time is dedicated to love and friendship and 0.41 hours a week is dedicated to democratic or civil participation. Finally, to the relational time mentioned, only 2.3 to 3.4 hours of emancipated work per week should be added to the total time worked. In Ecuador, it seems that alienated work is one of the main limits of living well.

The concentration or inequality of well-lived time: One of the structuring principles of living well has to do with equality and freedom, seen not only as non-interference but also as non-domination. To analyse the distribution of emancipated time for living well is to study both equality and freedom; it is to analyse how well or poorly freedom for human flourishing is distributed. If an individual—for example—for seeking work does not have time to cultivate the principle of *buen vivir*, clearly his or her freedom is limited. Freedom of thought, of expression, free participation in deliberative processes, requires among other issues a material basis, namely, time. If only a few have time for *buen vivir*, and many can barely decide what to do with their time because they lack the possibility to make such a choice—this is what we describe as an alienated life.

The distribution of time for living well under this perspective is the distribution of emancipated life. Unfortunately, Ecuador shows that there is a deep stratification in this regard. In Ecuador, while the richest 20 per cent 'concentrate' 39.4 per cent of well-lived time, the poorest 20 per cent enjoy barely 5 per cent of total relational time or well-lived time in a year (Gini coefficient of 0.32). If we analyse the extremes of the temporal strata we can realise that the richest 10 per cent in terms of time enjoys, in one week, 2.4 more days (57.6 hours per week) of relational time than the poorest 10 per cent. Having said that, if we study the main components of time for living well, it can be seen that these are also unevenly distributed. The decile with the highest temporal wealth has 50 more hours a week to dedicate to enjoying art, music, reading, contemplation, sports, etc., than the poorest 10 per cent. Similarly, the richest decile in terms of time dedicates 50.5 more hours per week to public, civil or political participation than the poorest decile. Although the distances are smaller when considering the time for philia and love, the difference between the two extreme deciles of time is not smaller either. In fact, the difference between the richest and poorest deciles in terms of relationship time for the enjoyment of being with friends, family or partners is 26 hours in favour of those on the upper end.

At the same time, the composition of the economic stratification does not necessarily coincide with the temporal one. Indeed, of the richest quintile by income, only 30 per cent belongs to the quintile with the highest level of well-lived time measured by the relational time variable. At the other end, almost 30 per cent belongs to the two 'poorest' quintiles calculated according to the time they spend living well. That is, the rich in terms of income do not necessarily enjoy and value time for living well. In other words, from a temporal perspective it is possible to identify a 'poor living' of the affluent. By changing the unit of analysis from money to time, the description of reality changes and with it the gaze towards social intervention.

The geography or spatiality of time for living well: The distribution of time can also be appreciated as a function of its allocation over the national territory. Ecuador has four geographic regions that have configured the country's political economy. As regards to life expectancy, the extent of territorial injustice is striking: the municipality with the highest average life expectancy (Oña) is almost 40 years older than the territory with the lowest average life expectancy (Taisha). It is no coincidence then, that the municipalities with the lowest average life expectancy can be found in the Amazon or in the canton with the largest Afro-Ecuadorian population. Also, it should be noted that in the Central Sierra and the Amazon the suicide rate is four times higher than the average for the rest of the country.

What are the territorial differences that come to focus through the analysis of living well? Our empirical research has found that in terms of relational time there are also significant spatial inequalities. The region with the longest time for living well is the Coast, with the exception of the province of Esmeraldas (a mostly Afro-Ecuadorian territory). The Central Sierra and the Amazon are the territories with the shortest time for living well. In terms of provinces and the main cities of the country, the territory with the most relational time is Cuenca, which has almost 11 hours more a week of time for living well than citizens living in Bolivar. It is important to note that there are territories that have seen their average relational time decrease in the period analysed, mainly the territories north-west of Quito (the capital of the Republic): Esmeralda, Pichincha and Imbabura.

Time well lived in time: Does Ecuador's population have more or less autonomous time for living well? Taking time as a unit of analysis for living well also means studying whether or not society has distributed the time for living well in such a way so as to increase the time available per person for the creation and enjoyment of relational goods within a given period. While average life expectancy in Ecuador has increased systematically, freedom understood as autonomous time for living well has decreased. Between 2007 and 2012 relational time per person was reduced by 2.3 hours. In other words, each year Ecuadorian citizens spent 6.6 million hours less time on socialisation, democracy, public and civil participation, leisure or emancipated labour. The reduction mainly concerns the time devoted to enjoying sociability (being with friends, family, partners) and public participation. At the same time there is a slight increase in the time devoted to contemplation, self-knowledge or liberating leisure. The time for sociability is 'captured' primarily by time spent on mobilising to work and school, and on spending more time satisfying personal needs (especially sleep). Such a situation occurs even though there is a reduction in the time spent on work, both salaried and non-wage.

From a territorial perspective, whether you look at the average life expectancy or the time available for living well, it is possible to verify a spatial convergence: that is, the worst-off territories in 2007 saw their conditions improve more rapidly in terms of time for living well, with the largest advances in the territories of the Central Sierra and the Amazon. The above-mentioned north-western provinces are an exception to this situation.

The macro-structuring of time well lived: Time distribution is not an exclusively individual choice, there are socioeconomic conditions that structure it. While all of us have 24 hours to distribute time, social conditions configure the time available for living well. It is no coincidence that the poorest municipalities according to unsatisfied basic needs (NBI) contains the populations with the shortest life expectancy. It is also not incidental that population groups with the highest number of NBIs have ten hours less a week of relational time than those who can meet all their basic needs; nor is it that the richest 20 per cent according to income have five hours more time for living well than the poorest income quintile.

In the case of so-called 'developing' countries such as Ecuador, improvements in material and living conditions lead to increases in the time for living well. In turn, it can be shown that decisions on macroeconomic structure also have an impact on daily life. Indeed, different macroeconomic 'models' have different impacts on working time, which has an impact on the potential time for living well. Indeed, in the macroeconomic model that promoted the liberalisation of the economy (period 1993–2001), which was accompanied by labour flexibilisation, temporary freezing of salaries, rising unemployment, citizens compensated by increasing working hours. Thus, the years of the greatest crisis in the history of Ecuador corresponded to the largest peak in the hours worked for wages, reaching an average of 45 hours a week. By contrast, in the years 2007–2016, when public policies had a more endogenous development orientation, including policies that sought to reduce labour precarisation,[9] the time spent on work was reduced by approximately five hours. Indeed, under the progressive regime established by Rafael Correa, there was a systematic reduction in working hours, closing the period with an average of 39 hours of salaried work per week. It is also worth noting that the hourly wage between 2007 and 2016 grew almost three times more in real terms than in the period from 1993 to 2001. The conclusion is clear: with an awareness of an inverse relationship between working time and relational time (Ramírez, 2012), macrostructural decisions reflected in public policy shaped the agency of individuals in making decisions and freely choosing what to do their time. After the 1999 crisis, it took the country a decade to return to the number of hours of work before the period of liberalisation.

The temporality of space (Nature or Pachamama): One of the most important changes in social terms included in the Ecuadorian coexistence pact of 2008 (to establish conditions of living well) is the transition from an anthropocentric to a biocentric ethics. Such a perspective involves building a society that puts life at the heart of value and seeks intertemporal (social and environmental) justice by protecting the rights of nature and thereby ecosystems that ensured the reproduction and future of existing generations and species, both human and non-human.

In the face of methodological individualism, the political socioecology of living well posits the recovery of the 'other', understood not only as the need for humans to co-create and co-enjoy relational goods with other humans but also with Nature. In this sense, we are not only interdependent but eco-dependent. In this context the 'Life Expectancy of Nature or Pachamama' (LEN) is a methodological proposal that allows us to evaluate the life of nature or Pachamama in temporal terms, that is, according to time. LEN proposes to study the age and the rate of regeneration of life, and the stage of maturity of an ecosystem, as part of the analysis of the condition *buen vivir*, or *sumak kawsay*. If we compare two territories with equal social conditions, we could say that the greater life expectancy of Pachamama per person, the better human and non-human populations live.

To posit the existence of the rights of Nature implies an epistemological and ontological break with the Western worldview, but this is not the case for the Andean cosmovision where time and space are two sides of the same coin.

Indeed, the Inca civilisation connected natural cycles with temporal cycles in very precise ways; and from such a relationship they organised their cities, rituals, agricultural processes and social relations. For this reason, for the indigenous cosmovision, the word Pachamama conjugates both time and space.

The analytical input of reflecting and studying the temporality of Pachamama allows for a break from a monolithic epistemological perspective that defends the proposition that there is only one temporality in time. This allows us to peer beyond the analytical framework that, from a southern epistemological perspective, is viewed as the *monocultural logic of linear time*:[10] "Under the terms of this logic, Western modernity has produced the non-contemporaneity of the contemporary, the idea that concurrency or simultaneity hides the asymmetries of historical times that converge in it ... a simultaneous encounter between the non-contemporaneous" (Santos, 2011: 30). At a specific time, several temporalities can converge, including the non-human temporality of nature. It could be argued that the problem of ecocide in our era is the result of not understanding that at the same time different temporalities coexist, thus generating decouplings between human temporality and Pachamama. As such, the need arises to analyse other temporalities of different nationalities or peoples, such as indigenous, Montubian or Afro-Ecuadorian ethnic groups. The analysis of time in this framework allows us to study and understand the epistemic diversity of building and living together in a plurinational and multi-ethnic state. The *tempos* of time are sharp edges that can also be indicators of the extent to which a society of living well of *buen vivir* (as evidenced by the analysis of the temporality of space or of the Pachamama). Following Santos, a sustainable human democracy consists in the coexistence of the plurality of temporal ecologies.

Time and subjectivity: Does the allocation of time impact subjective well-being? While, as we have argued, happiness is an inadequate indicator or measure of well-being—mainly because it can hide serious structural problems such as adapting preferences to conditions of misery—we cannot set aside analysis of subjectivity in its relationship to time. Welfare economists argue that happiness is based on maximising the consumption of the greatest amount of goods and services, considering a given budgetary constraint. Easterlin's paradox has, however, participated in the theoretical invalidation of these hypotheses by demonstrating that 'money does not buy happiness'. In the trail of this work, other studies emerged in regard to specifying the determinants of people's happiness. For example, Van Praag and Ferrer-i-Carbonell (2004) estimated that the cumulative function of happiness depends on the multiple satisfactions that an individual has in each of the sub-activities he or she performs. In other words, general happiness with one's life depends on happiness in the fields of work, family, education, health, etc.

The analysis of time and subjectivity in Ecuador is also political in nature. In the 'paradox of objective well-being and subjective malaise' (Ramírez, 2017) it was noted that, even though material conditions in the country improved between 2007 and 2016 (in terms of consumption, income, the satisfaction of basic needs, etc.), the non-poor middle class feels (subjectively) poorer. This is not a widespread phenomenon in society since, for example, in indigent or poor populations (who objectively also improved their living conditions) subjective well-being improved and the subjective feeling of poverty was reduced. This creates a fundamental issue for debate. Material changes do not necessarily produce subjective changes, or if they do they can be pro-hegemonic, which limits the possibility of structural social change.

The concept of a *society of buen vivir* entails the proposal of a new social order. New common senses can hardly be shaped if people's subjectivity does not change. In this context, in addition to the emphasis on analysing the relationship between satisfaction with life and time, it is important to analyse whether or not the distribution of time can influence the subjectivity of citizens. Non-influence would be a big problem in going forward with the study of time as a theoretical and methodological instrument to evaluate and construct senses based on the philosophy of *buen vivir*. This is why it is so important to assess the effectiveness of time as an instrument for gauging the impact on subjectivity.

It was indeed possible to find that time, and its distribution, have an effect on people's subjective well-being. In fact, it was possible to corroborate empirically that satisfaction with life, while based on sub-satisfactions in different spaces of life, depends on the time allotted to each subdomain. That is, satisfaction with life in general is a function of the distribution of time in each space of life. The time dedicated to family, friends, education, etc., significantly impacts the happiness that family, friends, education produce; and the total distribution of time influences the overall level of subjective well-being with life.

The hegemonic sense of life will hardly be disrupted if one only has time to work (most of the time in an alienated way) or if free time is only dedicate to consuming alienated entertainment and not to contemplating art, participating in public spaces—in *mingas*,[11] or to sharing with friends, etc. The distribution of time also includes a political-historical sense of time. Beyond what is in dispute as regard to time, it was possible to show that time impacts subjectivity, which is why the distribution of time can constitute an appropriate heuristic tool for seeking a new temporal order according to the precepts of the society of *buen vivir*.

Good life expectancy (GLE)[12]

Without the desire to simplify time analysis, it is necessary to propose synthetic indicators that allow for the questioning of hegemonic monetary indicators such as the Gross Domestic Product and to move closer to the principles and precepts of *buen vivir*. A proposal designed for Ecuador is the GLE index (Good Life Expectancy—*Esperanza de Vida Buena*), which was constructed as an alternative indicator and assessment tool that uses time as a unit of analysis.

This indicator consists of four fields: life, what is good in life (including emancipatory work), that what allow citizens to flourish (education and health), and the inequality in the distribution of time. This indicator puts at the heart of the debate not the accumulation of money but the flourishing of living well. Increased life expectancy must be lived healthily and well, seeking to reduce the distance that separates us from the 'other'. The GLE seeks to define what proportion of life (on average) each territory has dedicated to knowledge, contemplation, leisure or emancipatory work, love, friendship, public participation (civil or political) and democratic participation in a healthy way. This indicator can be weighted by the subjective satisfaction that time generates for living well.

An average Ecuadorian lives 32.4 well-lived years, meaning that 52.9 per cent of his life has been lived worthily. Excluding sleep hours in the time well lived, the GLE falls to 10.6 years. Over the last five years, GLE has had an annual growth of 1.6 per cent. Nevertheless, the distribution of well-lived time has been mixed. While there are territories or communities such as Cuenca that have a GLE of 36 years; others in the Amazon do not reach 25 years.

Similarly, an inverse relationship between inequality and GLE could be observed, the concentration of time as well as that of income impacts on the time for the living well of Ecuadorians. Furthermore, economic inequality coexists with temporal inequalities; that is, territories with high income inequality are also territories with a high concentration of time for living well. Finally, it has been proven that while there are different rates of change between cities and provinces, these converge in the period analysed; that is, in the lagging territories the Expectancy of Living Well grew at a faster rate than in those who were better in 2007, reducing territorial inequality.

The Expectancy of Living Well should be understood as concomitant to the Life Expectancy of Pachamama or Nature. *Sumak kawsay*; a well-lived life, cannot be understood without reference to humans living in harmony with Pachamama. In this respect, relational goods refer not only to relations of social solidarity and interdependence but also to the eco-dependence that guarantees the plurality of lives that coexist in Pachamama.

While one of the nodal debates in our democracy is how much the GDP grows from year to year, what should be discussed are questions related to public issues such as: how much did the GLE grow? Why did it vary? What territories are lagging behind, and where is there backtracking? What is happening in regard to the GLE of indigenous peoples, Afro-Ecuadorians or Montubios? Has the time well lived increased? Has Pachamama's Expectancy of Living Well been reduced or has it regenerated? A discussion along these lines would imply that that the common sense of what is socially valued would be a shift from a focus on 'money' to 'living well'.

Capitalist economies are systems of commodity production, which is why their reproduction requires money as a fundamental unit of analysis as well as a core value. An alternative form of society focused on *buen vivir*, as we have suggested throughout these pages, needs time/life as a focal variable to emerge. That is why it is necessary not only to build a supportive theoretical–political apparatus but also a methodological–empirical one. In fact, it has been shown that just using time and not money as a unit of analysis not only allows us to describe the same historical moment from another prism (with a different lens and another perspective), but that this new narrative would lead to alternative proposals of social intervention linked to the common goal of *sumak kawsay.*

For example, when the goal of education is to increase job returns, it creates a zero-sum game in which the advance of some is at the expense of others: 'it is better that fewer people have access to education because this increases the financial return of one more year of schooling'. By putting education at the centre of the construction of fraternal human beings and citizens, we have instead a positive sum game: the more individuals are educated, the more individuals and society flourish.

From the excluded and exploited of history: Living well as an uchronia

As Santos (2011) points out in his analytical framework of the epistemologies of the South, although critical theory has appropriated a vast set of concepts, in recent decades it has become distinguished by adjectives that qualify the ideas of conventional theories: if conventional theory speaks of development, critical theory refers to alternative, democratic or sustainable development; if conventional theory speaks of democracy, critical theory seeks radical, participatory or deliberative democracy. The same applies to cosmopolitanism, which takes the form of subaltern, oppositional or insurgent rooted cosmopolitanism; and human rights, which become radical, collective, intercultural human rights (Santos, 2011: 25).

The use of adjectives, as Santos reminds us, 'allows us to enter into a debate but does not allow us to discuss the terms of the debate and much less discuss why the option is for a given debate and not another' (Santos, 2011: 25). In this way, hegemony (cultural domination, ideological control) places limits on what to discuss.

It can be argued that the concept of 'Living Well' or *sumak kawsay* is a critical but mostly utopian/utopian noun. It should be understood that critical theory does not necessarily become a theory for action and therefore not for transformation either. Great diagnoses of what capitalism or colonialism imply have been constructed, but these constructions do not automatically or necessarily translate into proposals for political *praxis*. The defence of living well life as a noun can be achieved from three standpoints: epistemic ethics, philosophy and the intergenerational justice demanded by the socially excluded.

From the epistemic ethic position, living well or *sumak kawsay* is the main social issue that the Ecuadorian people have deliberately decided to put at the heart of the political debate. Something born as the will of the people cannot be 'an adjective', precisely because it is a social mandate. The citizenry is the subject and agent that establishes the frame of reference for the current public debate on how and in what direction to move forward, and Living Well is the noun that underlies and informs this debate.

In philosophical terms, following Martha Nussbaum (2007) it has been argued that there are two thresholds that allow us to characterise a life as human. The first has to do with the capabilities that human beings possess to realise themselves and operate within society. If there are people below that threshold, we might agree that their life strictly speaking should not be called human. The second is that the functions and capabilities should not be so minimal or so reduced so that, although we could consider it to be a human life, we could not claim that it is a condition of living well, or that it is a life worthy of being lived. Clearly, a new social contract should not be based solely on avoiding death (at a minimum) or prolonging years of life, but must conquer a life worthy of being lived (to a maximum): living well. In the biocentric ethics posed by the 2008 constitution, what applies to human beings also corresponds to Pachamama. In this context, the dispute is about the extensive critical and utopian/uchronic noun: living well, or *sumak kawsay, of both humans and Pachamama.*

However, living well as a whole, must be defended in the context of doing historical justice in relation to its absences and silences, in order to translate into future action.

One of the sub-questions of this research interrogates to what extent using time as a unit of analysis allows us to capture patriarchal, colonial and capitalist power relations; that is, relations of exploitation, domination and alienation. In the analysis of the 24 hours of a day, it is less likely that the absences are not made visible since one has to read not only what happens at work and consumption but also what happens in the domestic space, in democracy, in the social meeting spaces that are generated, in the actions carried out (or not) to live in harmony with nature, etc.

It has become evident throughout these pages that an analysis of time reveals the worst injustices of our time. If we study average years of life, the first injustice that comes to light is that 'luck' (which ultimately has nothing to do with luck) makes a difference in how many years one person will live in relation to another. For example, an Ecuadorian born in a predominantly indigenous territory is likely to live 12 fewer years than someone who is born in a territory in which citizens self-define as white-mestizo, a situation that reveals an exclusionary, discriminatory and racist social structure.

Now, is it a sufficient ethical condition to seek to equalise the years of life? In analysing the sexual division of labour or the exploitation of precarious work we can certainly point out that the noun is not only life but a life worthy of being lived.

While women in Ecuador live seven years longer than men, if we look at the quality of their lives it is much worse than that of men. Indeed, while women are spending 38.4 hours a week in unpaid labour, men are spending only 9.9 hours a week in the same type of activity. By combining the time spent on paid work, it can be shown that women work almost 11.23 hours more per week than men, with the greatest amount of their time (69%) being unpaid. It is no coincidence in this context that women have three hours a week less of emancipatory autonomous time compared to men to enjoy creative leisure, art, sport, share with friends, enjoy music, participate in *mingas* or in public spaces. Nor is it a coincidence that 69 per cent of total hospital discharges are women and 31 per cent men; that an unpaid domestic worker has 6.5 hours less of a well-lived time than an employer; that a worker with appointments has 8 hours more relational time than a citizen working for a day job; or that at a time of economic crisis such as

Ecuador experienced in 1999 it was workers without social security affiliation who had to compensate more hours of work for their income losses compared to insured workers.

From an ethnic point of view, indigenous people not only live fewer years but those years of life are of lower quality than non-indigenous people: those who self-define themselves as white and mestizos have almost 6.3 hours more relational time. Further, while the indigenous spend 18.5 hours to take care of their health, non-indigenous people spend 11.6 hours a week. In other words, from a full week, indigenous people spend almost seven hours more sick than non-indigenous people.

Cynically, in the face of such discussion, orthodox economists would suggest: How much money would be required to compensate for the lower life expectancy of indigenous people, or the bad life that women lead, or of workers exploited throughout their existence? Chrematistic economics is not only incomplete but also immoral.

In the analysis of time, the most structuring asymmetries of power in our society are revealed because they deal with life itself: colonialism, patriarchy and capitalist relations of production. A new temporal order involves realising the constitutional mandate to build a new sexual division of labour, a plurinational and multiethnic state, and a social and solidarity economy that breaks with the exploitation generated by the capital–labour duality.

Although linguistic grammar subordinates the adjective 'well-lived' to the noun 'life' (an adjective without a noun usually has less meaning), the semantics of ethics and history demand that the well-lived should not be subordinated to life. For women, indigenous people, the precarised, the exploited, those discriminated against and socially excluded, the utopian/uchronic struggle is for the well-lived life as a noun!

Epilogue: uchronias and chronopolitics

'Getting up early doesn't make dawn earlier', goes a popular saying. The race against time is the most absurd race humanity is waging. The age of acceleration that we live is leading to the pursuit of *speed* to the detriment of living *time,* which is life. Such self-competition for searching in every moment mechanisms for further accelerating time is killing time itself, which is nothing more than murdering our own existence. It could be argued that the imaginary of linear time has stopped to make way for the image where the human being resembles the caged *hamster* running on a wheel to exercise its muscles, and seeks to do it faster and faster without becoming aware that it is still motionless in the same place: we go faster but we don't know if we move forward; or, if we believe we are moving forward, we don't know where; it is even quite likely that we are receding or going backwards.[13]

Ironising what Jeremy Rifkin said in the aforementioned work, although *Homo sapiens* are the only animal that can 'subjugate time'; we would add that it is the only animal that can be subjugated by time.

From a philosophical point of view we could say that—on a human scale—time is being assimilated with movement, but 'time is not movement', as Aristotle (Aristóteles, 1994) pointed out. Furthermore, as argued so well by Heidegger (1996), life is ultimately time and time is the existence of life.

The *general intellect*, which makes reference to Ecuadorian society as an entity, decided in 2008 to challenge common sense and put at the centre of the debate the social question, the question of living well in solidarity and harmony with nature. Such a question implies a structural change of the social order from its roots, which entails contesting the current temporal order and building another linked to the social aspirations raised in the new social pact for coexistence; that is, to realise the uchronia of other times so as to live well.

Throughout history, conflict over the pace of life has always been one of the centres of power struggle. To dispute another rhythm and temporal order is to contest hegemonic power. The new social order proposed in Ecuador, therefore, implies another chronopolitics; that is, a policy that disputes the order and sense of time in the social, economic, ecological and cultural spheres. Based on the reflection of what is written in these pages, within the framework of the pursuit of the construction of a new temporal order and being aware of the incompleteness of the same, we propose a decalogue of uchronias to dispute the concreteness and meaning of the construction of the society of *buen vivir*:

Uchronia I: the expectancy of living well not dependent on chance. It is necessary to continue building a temporality where life expectancy continues to grow but above all where the population of any territory has an equal life expectancy (average). The uchronia is related to living time that does not depend on the randomness of one's place of birth or one's gender, ethnicity, social class, or religion. An *expectancy of living well* ensures a dignified death, starting with having decent conditions to bury our dead according to the customs of each people.

Uchronia II: another temporal order involves a new sexual division of labour. Sexual workload gaps, especially in the area of the care economy, structure autonomous time for living well in society. Respecting the diversity of *tempos,* the uchronia is based on an equal distribution of paid and—above all—unpaid working time between the two sexes. In the labour market sphere, this implies equal wages between men and women and that the so-called 'labour cost' recognises at the time of wage negotiation that the condition of material possibility of wage working time is non-working time. This second uchronia implies, for example, that paternity and maternity time are the same (as well as its burdens with respect to the reproduction of the infant's life) and that the necessary non-market supply of services and resources for the care of children, the disabled and the elderly for families in need is provided.[14] Although the utopia should be that there are no undesirable jobs, in the meantime, the undesirable jobs should be distributed democratically in society without any distinction. Uchronia II is a feminist temporal order where patriarchalism is abolished.

Uchronia III: moving towards a productive system where time is not valued as a resource and relational goods are not instrumentalised. In this uchronia time ceases to have exchange value and the relationship itself is constituted as good (not bad). Socially, no minute or second of life has supremacy over another minute or second of life. Such a perspective implies breaking the split between the world of work and the world of life. As long as we have a Kant, Buñuel, Marie Curie, Einstein or Alice Munro who produce their masterpieces not in working time but outside of it, we will hardly say that there may be a time of work that is not alienated. As it has been demonstrated for the Ecuadorian case, at best, about nine out of ten citizens do not achieve self-realisation in their employment. Uchronia is not about working less but about the possibility of the individual to flourish at work and in life. Such a situation implies new forms of organisation and ownership of the economy where none of its members work can be appropriated/exploited by another. In the case of Ecuador, such a productive system involves building a social and solidarity economy.

Uchronia IV: the horizon must be an ecology of uchronias. The new temporal horizon in the society of *buen vivir* must build an uchronia with room for a plurality of uchronias; that is, it must build a temporality that allows for the equal coexistence of multiple cultural and social temporalities. Respect for a plurality of coexisting temporalities, not only implies recognising subjectivity in the intensity of time, but also that the generation and enjoyment of relational goods depends on unrestricted respect for the fact that, in the simultaneity of history, there are different temporal rhythms. In other words, it implies accepting that there are many *tempos* at the same time. Welcoming a coexistence of uchronias is a necessary condition for the construction of a plurinational and multiethnic state and society, and for constructing a truly democratic *chronos*.

Uchronia V: a new temporal order to guarantee an intertemporal justice of human life in harmony with that of nature. The chronopolitics of the fifth uchronia has at least four aspects. The first alludes to the need to ensure the equal coexistence of different human temporalities in the present as referred in the fourth uchronia. However, in the context of history and the future, intergenerational justice involves, second, to ensure justice for groups historically excluded either by patriarchy, colonialism or the capitalist system. Third, in the context of possible futures, we seek to build a system for future generations to enjoy the same amount of time or more for living well. Finally, justice with future generations also involves guaranteeing respect for the rights of nature, i.e. the guarantee that there can be a harmonious life between the temporality of humans and that of nature. In other words, uchronia V starts from the awareness that humanity is interdependent in generational terms and that such interdependence implies an ecodependence of human temporality with that of nature.

Uchronia VI: building a system of equal ecotemporal exchange relationships. The political socio-ecology of time should not only be conceived in terms of each political community. This must also be rethought within the framework of the world community. If uchronia puts life at the centre, a fairer international system in the exchange of material life (human life, biodiversity and biophysical resources that guarantee the reproduction of life) and intangible life (education, culture, ideas, science, knowledge, innovation) must be pursued. This implies chronopolitics that call for the payment of the ecotemporal debt of the countries at the 'centre' to those on the 'periphery' of the world capitalist system. In turn, it implies the world's recognising that Nature's greatest life expectancy is in the countries of the South, which is a guarantee that there will be a future. On the other side, chronopolitics involves contesting the distribution of intangible life in the form of knowledge; that is, recovering the public and common character of them, through new institutional engineering of intellectual property and other management with regard to the creation and appropriation of knowledge, science and technology. Knowledge, in the end, is the temporal accumulation of humanity's many *general intellects* throughout its history. In other words, uchronia also refers to an equitable distribution from a perspective of intergenerational (past, present and future) justice of what has been accumulated for generating material (biodiversity) and intangible (knowledge) life throughout its history.

Uchronia VII: construction of a uchronic spatiality. Spaces made unsafe by violence, neighbourhoods ingulfed in fear, the massification of a private transport system, few public parks and empty ones, are the antithesis of what would imply a spatiality designed to produce a uchronia for living well. If there are insufficient common meeting spaces or if they exist but no one uses them out of fear or because of their price, that spatiality does not lead to another temporality. If more hours are wasted on mobility than the time spent sharing lunch with friends or family; or if access to spatiality is such that the possibility of creation and enjoyment of culture is exclusionary and elitist, then such city or territory is not being thought of in accordance with the construction of relational goods. Space should be designed to facilitate the encounter and flowering of living well.

Uchronia VIII: the right to time for living well. Utilitarian society has organised life according to conditions of production and consumption. Uchronia VI involves contesting this chronopolitics so that human activities are centred on time for living well. In the transition, the conditions must be built so as to guarantee the right to a base of hours each day dedicated to living emancipating time for living well. However, the objective is that life itself is constituted in emancipated (and emancipating) time for the good life. The uchronic construction of an autonomous time for living well that includes emancipating work in which human beings can flourish, involves breaking with any state of need. This brings us back to a debate that must be placed at the forefront of the public sphere: building a social pact for a tax and social-security system that guarantees the right to a universal-citizen income or dividend (Van Parijs, 1996).[15]

The demercantilisation of work relations and emancipation in the same, can only be achieved if the individual is not in a state of need or survival. Likewise, immaterial life (knowledge, know-how, ideas, ingenuity, scientific production) must have as its end not the accumulation of capital but the liberation of time for the enjoyment living well. Such a situation implies regaining the public and common sense of knowledge in the context of a plurality of existing knowledge and guaranteeing the sovereignty of our peoples. Finally, the chronopolitics of uchronia VI involves not only pursuing for non-alienated work but also non-alienated free time. The 'occupation' of free time and 'boredom' are clear signs of alienated free time. In other words, if society or an individual does not know what to do with free time, it is a symbol of an unemancipated time that would wrongly be called free. In this sense, life is well-lived as long as it is genuinely free.

Uchronia IX: another temporal subjectivity for Living Well. With the subjectivity generated by capitalism about time, another uchronia can hardly be built. This subjectivity begins with another distribution of time. But that is not all; a new temporal order must be articulated with a new common sense regarding the new disputed temporality.[16] The subjectivity of time must be transformed so that it ceases to be an instrumental mechanism for the accumulation of capital, so as to build a uchronia that recovers time as living well, while recognising the convergence of a plurality of uchronia.

Uchronia X: from chronos to kairós or from clock time to time for living well. According to (ancient) Greek philosophy, while *kairós* is qualitative in nature, *chronos* is quantitative. *Chronos* is sequential time, *kairós* is the moment of maximum plenitude. Metaphorically, we can say that the era we live in is the era of *chronos*, the quantitative era, the era in which the nanosecond is more important than the second because what matters is the accuracy of clock time (because time is money) and the extent to which accuracy helps to produce greater acceleration (to generate greater capital accumulation).

One of the deepest alienations occurs when a common citizen lives for and by the clock without having control over the time of his or her life. The clock is time and life is clock time. In this context, the reinvention of time as uchronia is also the reinvention of the appropriation of the meaning of a clock. (Could we imagine a society without a clock[17] or with an alternative clock?)[18] A new temporal order must retrieve other *chronos*. A *chronos* that does not serve as an instrument of surveillance of our bodies but allows the enjoyment of them. A *chronos* that does not serve to order a system for the accumulation of capital, but one that helps to de-order time for living well and for the flourishing of life. A *chronos* that does not restrict the options of how to organise our lives, but one that expands the range of options over them. A *chronos* that is not thought without its corresponding *kairós*. A *chronos* that does not limit but enhances other uchronias. In short, the tenth uchronia seeks to recover a sense of time that is not that of speed in its constant search for acceleration but that of time itself; that is, of life, of the event, of the full, dignified, well-lived existence.[19]

Will we be able as a human species to reinvent new uchronias, new temporalities, new ways of organising and giving meaning to time, which is nothing more than rethinking the very existence of life? The uchronic decalogue is presented as a thesis to rethink another temporal order. If the alienation of time is the alienation of life, the dispute over emancipated time is the dispute over emancipated life. This will not be possible without a new temporal order since in the structuring and meaning we give to time we are dealing with life itself. This research proposes to contribute to the debate on the sense of time—time for living well, because the urgency of an alternative future demands it!

Notes

1 Editor's note. Both Karl Marx, and after him the Italian Marxist philosopher Antonio Gramsci, presupposed and argued that the social consciousness of the average citizen is shaped by ideas that are manufactured by the ruling class, ideologies that represent and advance their class interests. They also argued that the 'ideas that dominate thinking in a particular epoch (i.e. the ideas of the ruling class) results in 'false consciousness' within the working class—an inability to perceive the world as it is viewed from a rational universalistic standpoint or the vantage point of their own class interests. Karl Manheim, a founder of what might be described as the 'sociology of knowledge', argued the same point from a rather different (non-Marxist) perspective that ideologies are representative of the true nature of a society, but that in seeking to achieve a *utopia* (an imagined society possessed of highly desirable or nearly perfect qualities for its citizens) the dogmas of *ideology* distort a scientific understanding of the world as it is.

2 For an explanation of the meaning given to the concept of uchronia see: http://alice. ces.uc.pt/dictionary (Ramírez, 2019).

3 For a detailed analysis of the political socioecology of *buen vivir* see Ramírez (2012) and Ramírez (2018).

4 An idea of life that is community-centric, ecologically balanced and culturally sensitive (Acosta 2012; Caria and Domínguez, 2016; Chuji, Rengifo and Gudynas, 2019). The Kichwa (Kichwa shimi, Runashimil in Spanish *Quichua*) term s*umak kawsay* in Ecuador is translated as *buen vivir*; in Bolivia as *vivir bien*.

5 Good Life Expectancy (EVB) is a macro-social indicator that serves as a proxy measure of living well viewed through Time as the unit of analysis. It departs from the monetarist approach of neoclassical economics, based on the codifier life as money synthesised in the concept of the Gross Domestic Product (GDP), which, given its level of abstraction involved makes it difficult if not impossible to measure advances related to the construction of societies that value living well.

6 The results presented here correspond to the research carried out in Ramírez (2018), cited above.

7 In fact, the US Centre for Disease Control and Prevention (CDC) notes that America's life expectancy has fallen since 1993.

8 It is no coincidence that the 2008 constitution of the Republic also restores the need to build a democracy not only in representative form but a participatory and deliberative democracy, and in the realm of production, it clearly expresses the need to build a social and solidarity economy vis-à-vis a market economy.

9 This include among other measures suspending labour outsourcing and hourly recruitment, establishing a 'living wage' according to which no company could distribute profits to its shareholders if its workers did not earn a wage equal to the cost of a *canasta básica* (literally, basic basket—of goods needed for subsistence—a measure of the poverty line); adding domestic workers to the group of workers who by law must receive a minimum basic wage; penalising non-social security affiliation; and extending the period of paternity and maternity leave.

10 It is worth noting that the concept of linearity should be nuanced. What is lived today is also a time of acceleration that brings to mind the image of a *hamster* running faster and faster on a wheel (Concheiro, 2016).

11 *Minga,* also *mingaco* or in Spanish *faena*, derives from *quechua* (*mink'a*), which refers to an Inca tradition of community work and voluntary collective labour for purposes of social utility and community infrastructure projects. In the current context it also refers to collective struggle.

12 For a detailed analysis of the methodology used in the calculation of GLE see Ramirez (2012) and Ramirez (2018).

13 The British newspaper *The Independent* in October 2016 published an important article titled: "Children of the Thatcher era have half the wealth of the previous

generation"(www.independent.co.uk/news/uk/politics/margaret-thatcher-generation-80s-children-wealth-half-amount-ifs-study-a7338076.html). The Report of the *Institute of Fiscal Studies* concludes: *"people born in the early 1980s are the first post-war generation to suffer smaller incomes in early adulthood than those born 10 years before"*. As noted above, in the United States life expectancy seems to be declining for the first time since 1993.

14 In the same way, universal policies should be sponsored, as these promote gender-focused policies, and eliminate social policy conditionality from targeted programs that increase time pressure on women, since they are usually responsible for complying with them (Damián, 2014: 296).

15 On the most unequal continent on the planet, poverty is not the result of a lack of resources but of excessive inequality. In Ecuador, with less than 5 per cent of its population's wealth, all the country's poverty could be overcome (Ramírez and Burbano, 2012). This sparsely given debate in the region must be placed on the public agenda to dispute the meaning of time in a new era.

16 A new contra-hegemonic subjectivity cannot be coopted by the capitalist system. Faced with the acceleration of life, the proposals to build slow cities seemed like an alternative. However, these ended up being good business opportunities, because they sought to meet social needs via a capitalist logic.

17 The physicist Rovelli states that 'the fundamental equations of quantum gravity are, in fact, elaborated in this way: they do not have a time variable, and they describe the world by pointing to possible relations between varying magnitudes' (Rovelli, 2018: 90). In modern quantum physics, not only is the world analysed without measuring anything with a clock, but time as a variable disappears.

18 Levine suggests that, 'part of the French Revolution was a rather radical attempt at temporal change. In 1793, the French National Convention established a 'revolutionary calendar' to replace the Gregorian. Among other things, the new calendar declared that the year of 1792 of the Christian era would be year one of the new Republican calendar; each new year was to begin on the 22nd of September of the old calendar; the months would be thirty days, and five days would be added at the end of the year; the months would be divided into three ten-day cycles; days would be divided into units of ten, instead of 24 hours. It was pronounced that time, from that moment on, would be measured in units of decades (decimal minutes and decimal seconds' (Levine, 2006: 110).

19 On a non-human scale and from the perspective of modern quantum physics, the world is made of events, not things. 'The world is a network of events. One thing is time with its many determinations, and another is simply the fact that things are not': they happen. The difference between things and events is that things stay in time. Events, on the other hand, have a limited duration.

References

Acosta, A. (2012). *Buen vivir sumak kawsay: Una oportunidad para imaginar otros mundos.* [Good living sumak kawsay: An opportunity to imagine other worlds]. Quito: Abya Yala.

Aristóteles. (1994). *Ética a Nicómaco.* Madrid, España: Instituto de Estudios Políticos.

Caria, S. and R. Domínguez (2016). "Ecuador's *Buen Vivir*: A New Ideology for Development," *Latin American Perspectives*, Issue 206, 43(1): 18–33.

Chuji, M., G. Rengifo and E. Gudynas (2019). "Buen Vivir," in A. Kothari, A. Salleh, A. Escobar, F. Demaria and A. Acosta (eds), *Pluriverse. A Post-Development Dictionary.* New Delhi: Upfront.

Concheiro, L. (2016). *Contra el tiempo: filosofía práctica del instante* (1. ed). Barcelona: Editorial Anagrama.

Damián, A. (2014). *El tiempo, la dimensión olvidada en los estudios de pobreza*. Mexico: Colegio de México. Retrieve from www.jstor.org/stable/j.ctt14jxq6r

De Santos, B. (2009). *Una epistemología del Sur: La reinvención del conocimiento y la emancipación social*. Mexico DF: Siglo XXI editores.

Elias, N. (2015). *Sobre el tiempo*. Fondo de Cultura Económica.

Heidegger, M. (1996). *El ser y el tiempo* (2.a ed.). Mexico: Fondo de Cultura Económica.

Heidegger, M. (2008). *El concepto de tiempo (Tratado de 1924)*. Barcelona: Herder. Recuperado de http://site.ebrary.com/id/11059663

Levine, R. (2012). *Una geografía del tiempo. O cómo cada cultura percibe el tiempo de manera un poquito diferente*. Buenos Aires, Argentina: Siglo XXI editores.

Nussbaum, M.C. (2007). *Las fronteras de la justicia: consideraciones sobre la exclusión*. Grupo Planeta (GBS).

Ramírez Gallegos, R. (2019). "Ucronía," *Dicionário Alice*. https://alice.ces.uc.pt/dictionary/?id=23838&pag=23918&id_lingua=1&entry=25627. ISBN: 978-989-8847-08-9

Ramírez, R. (2018) La vida y el tiempo. Apuntes para una teoría ucrónica de la vida buena a partir de la historia reciente del Ecuador, Tesis doctoral en "Sociología de las relaciones de trabajo, desigualdades sociales y sindicalismo", Coimbra: Centro de Estudios Sociales-Universidad de Coimbra [*mimeo*].

Ramírez, R. (2010). *Socialismo del Sumak Kawsay o biosocialismo republicano*. Quito, Ecuador: SENPLADES.

Ramírez, R. (2012). *La vida (buena) como riqueza de los pueblos*. Quito: IAEN.

Ramírez, R. (2017). *La gran transición: en busca de nuevos sentidos comunes*. Quito: CIESPAL-UNESCO. Recuperado de http://reneramirez.ec/la-gran-transicion-rene-ramirez/

Ramírez, R. and R. Burbano (2012). "Good bye pobretología, bienvenido ricatología: estimación de la línea de riqueza a partir de la línea de pobreza en el Ecuador," pp. 27–50 in *¡A (re) distribuir! Ecuador para todos*, first edn. Quito: Secretaría Nacional de Planificación y Desarrollo.

Rovelli, C. (2018). *El orden del tiempo*. Barcelona: Anagrama.

Santos, Boaventura de Sousa (2011). "Épistémologies du Sud," *Études Rurales*, 187: 21–50.

Van Parijs, P. (1996). "Justice and Democracy: Are they Incompatible?" *The Journal of political Philosophy*, 4(2): 101–117.

Van Praag, B. and A. Ferrer-i-Carbonell (2004). *Happiness Quantified. A Satisfaction Calculus Approach*. Oxford: Oxford University Press.

10 Disputes over capitalism and varieties of development

Eduardo Gudynas

In recent decades, Latin America has been noted for its diverse debates on capitalism and development, and for the various political strategies presented as alternatives. While some persisted in defending capitalism others questioned and opposed it, even presenting themselves as socialists. Above all the controversy was superimposed a discussion about *buen vivir*, whose origins can be located on a horizon well beyond any type of development.

This chapter discusses some of the highlights in these experiences that took place in the context of a progressive cycle of regime change in South America—the so-called 'progressivism'. Some contradictions between their rhetoric and the political practice of these the governments suggest that what finally prevailed was reformism. Departing from the idea of varieties of capitalisms the concept of varieties of development is introduced, and the chapter explains why they could not break with background problems such as the faith in progress, the allocation of values or the separation of society from Nature. Instead, the claims of *buen vivir* in its original sense, proposed alternatives that go beyond development in all of its diverse forms.

Between acceptance and criticism

As of the end of the twentieth century, multiple positions on capitalism ranging from defence to rejection were deployed in South America. Recognising that the concept was understood in many different ways, and setting aside evaluations of each of these interpretations, this diversification is undeniable.

Governments that can be classified as conservative or politically located on the right, and with the support of various actors such as politicians, entrepreneurs and academics, rallied in support of capitalism as necessary for development and to achieve citizen welfare. Examples of these positions are the administrations of J.M. Santos and I. Duque in Colombia and those of Sebastián Piñera in Chile or Mauricio Macri in Argentina.

In other cases, capitalism was questioned from the stance of electoral triumphs of groupings that described themselves as leftist—the new left or 'progressives' (see, for example, Philip and Panizza, 2011). This shift resulted from citizen resistance to neoliberal-inspired capitalisms in the 1980s and 1990s.

The importance of this cannot be minimised. Let us remember that, in the 1990s, the idea that 'there is no alternative' seemed to be firmly consolidated; history was supposedly at an end, and globalisation spread to all of the planet. Therefore, these political changes allowed us to break with that unanimity, and everything could be discussed.

Rhetoric, such as speeches, plans or program announcements, which focus in particular on the capital–labour relation, or positions taken on the environment, should be considered first. Two trends became apparent in the discourse of progressivism, between two extremes, ranging from criticism with a reluctant acceptance of capitalism to repeated rejection.

As for reluctant acceptance, while capitalism was questioned it was understood that conditions for breaking away from it were not available, and instead critics bet on reforming it. Examples of this position include the so-called proto-socialism of Uruguay's first *Frente Amplio* (Broad Front) government headed by Tabaré Vázquez, *novo desenvolvimento* (neodevelopmentalism) currents inside the government conducted by the Workers' Party (PT) government led by 'Lula' da Silva in Brazil, and the brief presidency of Fernando Lugo in Paraguay. A more incisive rhetoric took place in Argentina in the form of the so-called national and popular developmentalism (also known as 'nac and pop' strategies) advanced by the governments of Néstor Kirchner and Cristina Fernández de Kirchner.

At the other extreme in the critique of capitalism, the position of outright rejection has to do with administrations that repeatedly cited Marx or Lenin, or explicitly invoked socialism. This includes the case of the Citizen's Revolution in Ecuador under the presidency of Rafael Correa, supported by the Alianza PAIS movement, as well as the *Movimiento al Socialismo* (MAS—Movement Towards Socialism) administration led by Evo Morales in Bolivia, and the '21st Century Socialism' regime led by Hugo Chávez and Nicolás Maduro in Venezuela.

Towards the end of the first decade in the new millennium, South American progressivisms dominated the political landscape; and capitalism was questioned by governments, the academic world, and on the streets, while many others on other continents looked at these experiences with admiration. At issue in this climate of harsh questioning was what was described as neoliberal capitalism, attacking issues such as market reductionism, the privatisation of social policies, and the subordination of the state. These critics conceived of development as, above all, a political issue that had to be arbitrated by the state, with a concern to bring about a more inclusive form of development based on poverty reduction. The concern was to seek the participation of previously marginalised groups such as peasants and indigenous people, returning to the invocations of the people or the nation, and political diversification which created space for ideas such as *buen vivir*.

Rhetoric and practice: politics, economics and justice

The next step in analysis requires examining whether the rhetoric that challenged capitalism resulted in actions that went in the same direction. But we need to make clear that progressive governments and their support bases implemented heterodox strategies in various sectors and policy innovations that on the whole cannot be classified as conservative or neoliberal. However, it is also necessary to address the question of whether the declared aim and purposes and announcements actually corresponded to concrete alternative actions in regard to capitalism.

To this end, some key elements can be considered without seeking a definitive review but as a contribution to a necessary reflection. These include the permanence of extractivist modes of appropriation such as conventional oil and fracking, mega-mining, or export monocultures such as soybeans. The first point here is that in general terms progressives conceived of these activities as an indispensable source of capital and partly as a generator of employment opportunities, and thus none of them broke with such activities. However, because extractivisms depend on international markets for both physical trade and the flow of capital, they are necessarily embedded in capitalism. Progressives sought to resolve this issue by organising it in other ways, generally with the participation of the state (e.g. through state-owned enterprises), increased capture of economic surpluses in some sectors (especially oil), and to legitimise them as necessary to finance anti-poverty measures (Gudynas, 2020). But its negative social, territorial and environmental impacts were maintained.

Some social movements, especially those involving trade unions and academics, postulated that it was possible to break with capitalism but maintain extractivisms through a change in ownership of the resources or the agents who extracted them. Thus, for example, if mining companies were nationalised it would be a non-capitalist extractivism. However, they did not realise that even state extractivism for a number of reasons impose and implicates a return to capitalism, especially because of its insertion into global markets; nor did they explain that this did not solve its negative socioenvironmental local impacts.

In these and other ways, extractivist practices faces several contradictions with the discourses of progressivisms. As a way out of this, in several cases there was a shift in the debates, abandoning reference to extractivisms as part and parcel of capitalism, to move on to defending them as indispensable for development. For example, Venezuela's then-president, Hugo Chávez, in 2006, stated that oil would serve 'justice, for equality, for the development of our people' (Chávez, 2007).

The progressives did not give up on their own industrialisation, as claimed by the Latin American Left of the twentieth century. Rather, they assumed that industrialisation could serve as a counterweight to extractivisms, or that the extracted natural resources should feed national industries. Governments such as Argentina and Brazil implemented industrial promotion programs, and in Bolivia it was converted into a constitutional mandate. However, these measures had no concrete effects on boosting industrial sectors or stopping deindustrialisation; the most notorious case in this regard was Brazil, as discussed in Azevedo et al. (2013).

Progressives also engaged in an intense rhetoric regarding labour, but with very different practical applications. Some of them, such as those applied in

Argentina, Brazil and Uruguay, were successful in strengthening various workers' rights, but others (as could be observed in Bolivia and Ecuador), by supporting allied trade union organisations and punishing opponents ended up with discretionary actions; or, as happened in Venezuela, dismantling some unions (see, for example, Ermida Uriarte, 2007). In parallel, while many trade union organisations could question capitalism, at the same time they defended capitalist development strategies such as extractivisms. Some even participated in them through their pension funds, resulting in what was described as 'unionist conciliation capitalism' in Brazil (Moraes, 2011).

In progressive countries there was an impactful reduction in poverty,[1] which was presented as a success of progressives in reversing one of the contradictions and negative impacts of capitalism. The management of the Lula da Silva administration on more than one occasion was presented as a global example of successful reforms in promoting social welfare and the expansion of the middle class. This is understandable since during these governments an estimated 35 million people ceased to be poor and instruments such as conditional cash transfer programs, which, in the form of *Bolsa Familia*, came to support 13 million people (see Valencia Lomelí, 2008).

Today we have more detailed reviews of this process, including those of Lena Lavinas (e.g. Lavinas, 2017). Their analyses show that while the improvements made were documented, inequalities such as access to safe water or sanitation were not resolved; human rights violations persisted or worsened in cities and in the countryside, and urban violence did not stop. According to Lavinas (2017), the neodevelopmental 'covenant for growth with social inclusion' in the markets became a 'covenant for growth with mass consumption'. These social policies were captured by financialisation in sectors such as health, housing and education, and an expansion of the banking sector. For instance, similar situations occurred in Ecuador and Uruguay. Social justice was monetised and consumption in turn was mediated by market inclusion, reinforcing the commodification of social life, a basic feature of capitalism.

Regarding economic policies, Venezuela explored all sorts of measures in line with its rhetoric of rejection of capitalism and the construction of socialism, including the elaboration of so-called 'socialist development plans' (see also Alvarez, 2009; Dieterich, 2005; Serrano Mancilla, 2014). But it failed to reverse basic conditions such as dependence on oil revenues or management and corruption problems, which in addition to international harassment, became decisive factors for the crisis in the country (Alvarez, 2013).

A different situation is found in Bolivia, where an economic form of 'socialism' was presented as an alternative to capitalism in which the state 'is the engine of the economy, the planner, the investor, the banker', as described by its well-known Minister of the Economy, Luis Arce. But at the same time orthodox measures, including extractivisms subsidies, foreign investment facilities, bank protection, were implemented (see also Arze Vargas and Gómez, 2013; Wanderley, 2013). Similar situations were repeated in Ecuador, although it is also striking that there was no attempt to abandon the dollar and recover the national currency as would be expected from the socialism invoked by Rafael Correa (on this see also Cuvi, 2014, and Acosta and Cajas Guijarro, 2018).

These examples show that while there were some attempts towards socialism, in many cases what ended up prevailing were reforms. Economic management sought to ensure conditions such as monetary stability, inflation control, liberalised exchange rates, protection of foreign investment, state subsidies to sectors such as extractivisms, various facilities for banks, and gradual external indebtedness (Carneiro, 2006; Kulfas, 2016; Kerner, 2017; Wainer, 2018).

As for international policies, progressives advocated greater integration within Latin America by prioritising political agreements and rejecting Free Trade Agreements schemes. This explains the attempts to strengthen agreements such as the Union of South American Nations (UNASUR) or to seek closer regional cooperation as encouraged by Venezuela by means of the Bolivarian Alliance for the Peoples of Our America (ALBA). The intention was invaluable, and also served to halt the US trade liberalisation project in the region, and made very clear differences with the positions of countries such as Mexico, Colombia, or Peru. However, since all countries competed with each other to export raw materials, they failed to establish productive or economic coordinations, thus adding another dislocation between discourses and real actions. The rhetoric focuses on latinamericanisms, sometimes including invocations to anti-imperialism. But at the same time the countries were very dependent on globalisation, and thus lapsed and fell back into capitalism.

Another flank of tensions involved the performance of the state. During the economic growth phase, the state expanded and strengthened in several countries, and this was seen as an alternative welcome to conventional capitalism. But as the economic bonanza began to lag behind (with the end of the primary commodities boom), complaints about constraints on efficiency grew, clientelistic practices persisted, and, as in the case of Argentina and Brazil, several cases of corruption erupted.

Progressives achieved state power and formed governments by the means of democratic elections, a very valuable attribute. Moreover, even the harshest critics of capitalism insisted on democracy and the defence of human rights. Over the years, however, these qualities deteriorated in several countries. An analysis of this dynamic is beyond the scope of this chapter, as is the economic collapse in Venezuela under conditions of external harassment and what the government (and much of the political Left) sees as the intervention of US imperialism. But it should be noted that in all cases there was a deterioration in the enforcement of rights and the quality of democracy.

These contradictions can be illustrated by the case of Bolivia. Beyond invocations of plurinationality and popular participation, the safeguarding of human rights and democratic quality were affected. In considering the situation in regard to extractivism a recent review found that 20 essential rights listed in the country's constitution, covering the quality of life and the environment, and citizen participation in territorial control and the management of natural resources, found that all of them without exception were violated by extractivist activities (Campanini et al., 2020).

Violations of rights and violence are increasingly tolerated on the continent, and the democratic delegation and hyper-presidentialism dependent on a leader with messianic qualities were accentuated. This explains that as in the case of Ecuador, local analysts understand that a conservative restoration was underway (Cuvi, 2014). Tensions and contradictions were also evident in other strategies in sectors such as agriculture, health and security, and in all cases there was a political dimension. These dimensions and this situation are discussed and illustrated in several studies cited above, but also in studies such as Webber (2011), Singer (2012), Ospina Peralta (2013), Gervasoni and Peruzzotti (2015), Kulfas (2016), Singer and Loureiro (2016), Kerner (2017), Pucciarelli and Castellani (2017), and Munck (2018).

Contradictions between discourses and actions also occur in conservative administrations but there they are not elaborated in them as criticisms of capitalism. It is therefore essential to analyse this problematic in the case of progressivism.

While this review is schematic, and therefore of necessity incomplete, the diversity of speeches and strategies, and even heterogeneity within the same progressive administration where radical could coexist with orthodox and conservative measures, are immediately apparent. In turn, there are multiple disjunctions between rhetoric and practice. The emerging pattern is that progressives questioned capitalism but in their concrete actions, and partly in their later discourses, they came to accept or come to terms with it and so the emphasis shifted to reforming capitalism.

This was taken for granted by some on the Left, but others were forced to reluctantly accepted it because no other option was available or because the attempts to move beyond capitalism did not succeed. Even in countries such as Venezuela or Bolivia, experimentation in the direction of transformative change or postcapitalism were repeated, with steps taken forward but followed by setbacks. It was a back and forth that is partly due to the impossibility in modifying basic internal as external political structures and relationships. Adherence to strategies such as extractivism was minimised, which in turn was conditioned many other public policies. The shift towards reformism in some cases was presented as a long-term response but in others as a temporary measure until there were other conditions for a non-capitalist turn.

The questioning of capitalism dealt with external restrictions and internal conditioning. Among the former were the type of trade and financial integration of the region, the dependence on capital and external technologies, and even the impositions or influences of other nations (such as those of the US on Venezuela or loans granted by China to several countries). But there were also multiple internal conditions in the relationships with social sectors with different agendas, political parties, and the ongoing reorganisation of groups of power like entrepreneurs, latifundistas, and the armed forces. In different ways, progressives insisted on the redistribution of wealth as consistent with the tradition of the Latin American Left, but in conceiving of development as an essentially economic issue they were forced into promoting economic growth, and thus returned to capitalism. Likewise, as Wainer (2018) warned in the case of Argentina, it is not enough in dependent economies to distribute part of the surplus, as this does not resolve the external constraints or supplant the need for substantive transformation in the productive and political structure of each country.

The possibilities of these changes were in turn narrowed because progressives came to power based on alliances of very different groups, and their willingness to break with capitalism is also diverse. There were sectors that demanded more substantive change but many others were content with a conventional capitalism that would improve their living conditions—and they were never willing to break with structures like private property.

Varieties of capitalism

The diversity of positions and practices in the face of capitalism makes it very useful to rescue the notion of the **varieties of capitalism** advanced by Hall and Soskice (2001). This notion provides tools to address this heterogeneity while allowing for economic considerations and other dimensions such as the role of institutions and corporations. That original study was followed by other contributions, including analysis focused on Latin America, such as Boschi (2011a), Bizberg (2014) and Fernández and Ebenau (2018), that enriched it.

From this perspective it could be proposed that much of the Latin American debate was actually grappling with different types of capitalism, including some varieties that progressives presented as socialists. This was admitted on more than one occasion. For example, then-President Rafael Correa said that 'we are basically doing things better with the same pattern of accumulation, rather than changing it, because it is not our desire to harm the rich, but it is our intention to have a fairer and more equitable society'.[2] It shows that no alternatives to capitalism were sought or achieved, but reforms that could reduce some of its negative effects without putting it at risk were explored. In other words, they were confusing the idea of a more benevolent capitalism as if that were enough for a socialist alternative. Thus, these positions ended in agreeing with policies that promote economic growth and foreign investment (as recognised, for example, by Boschi, 2011b; see also Gaitán and Boschi, 2015), although these policies were implemented differently. There were also clashes over the surplus between those who wanted to secure its benefits, especially economic ones, and those who sought to avoid economic, social and environmental damage.

From the reversal of economic expansion, progressive capitalisms had faced growing questions from much more conservative varieties of capitalism, including the return of neoliberalism. For example, in Brazil, *Lulaists* and proponents of neodevelopmentalism clashed with conservative sectors that no longer seemed willing to support the prior political pact regarding the sharing of power and the surplus (see, for example, Boito Jr., 2018), and so the far-Right extreme of Jair Bolsonaro has come to pass. Similar processes, although in different times and each with their particularity, were also lived in Argentina and Uruguay with the exit of the progressivists governments through elections; in Ecuador by a break within Alianza PAIS, and in Bolivia with the fall of the MAS government.

Notwithstanding the pendulum swing and turn to the right, it can be postulated that progressivism in its diverse forms is superior to governments and policy regimes of conservative or neoliberal inspiration, and this is important as can be witnessed in the case of Argentina's return to progressivism in 2019 after four years of increasingly neoliberal policies with Mauricio Macri. But there was also an abuse of the positive features under progressivisms when they were depicted as virtually a socialist revolution. The issue is that those administrations in most cases will bet on the Left when compared with political opponents like Ivan Duque in Colombia or Jair Bolsonaro in Brazil; the centre as a reference is shifting to the right.

But this fact should not prevent us from understanding that the progressive regimes, including the newly installed regime in Argentina, were and are still engaged in arrangements design to preserve some kind of capitalism, and that in this circumstance words such as socialism, oligarchy, autonomy and sovereignty, have lost the consequences of their original meanings to remain no more than rhetorical slogans. In this context the common sense meaning attached to the idea of alternatives has become increasingly confusing.

Varieties of development

The concept varieties of capitalism still has some limitations as an analytical framework, two of which can be linked to the analysis advanced in this chapter. On the one hand, it provides a perspective on capitalism and not on any other options presented as non-capitalist; and on the other, it has difficulty in considering cases where the controversies over capitalism are supplanted by development disputes. To overcome these problems, and associating it with various contributions of Critical Development Studies, it is possible to advance the concept of **varieties of development** (Gudynas, 2016).

These varieties can looked at analytically by using criteria derived from different theoretical perspectives, such as classical political economy (capitalism, socialism), or by focusing on particular content or purposes (e.g. human, local, endogenous, sustainable development, etc.), or political philosophy (liberal, conservative, socialist, etc.), and so on.

Applying this perspective view to Latin America there arises at least four situations. First, we see varieties that defend conventional capitalism. Then we see those progressives that sought or seek reforms to achieve a more benevolent capitalism, that sought to reject capitalism with some successes and many failures, and then finally we have the case of state socialism in Cuba. Following this analysis, there are overlaps between these groups, and in turn they are heterogeneous within them. Thus, any classification of varieties of capitalism is limited and can be supplanted by another based on different criteria.

But the concept 'varieties of development' has another analytical utility: it allows us to identify components found in all cases. For instance, it is necessary to question why political actors such as J.M. Santos in Colombia and José 'Pepe' Mujica in Uruguay, who are at opposite extremes in their political ideology, around the same time defended mega-mining in their countries. Similarly, it is shocking how all these regimes, and so many economists and even social movements, time and again, argue the need for more economic growth and an increase in exports, or celebrate the rise in consumerism. The differences here are relevant but so are coincidences, as many of the possibilities and obstacles to thinking about alternatives are played out there. It is astonishing that across and beyond so many different paths almost identical ideas are repeated as to how to understand development.

The constants and similarities between all varieties correspond to concepts and sensibilities that are found in the basement of development thought and practice (defined as the 'zero' level in the Critical Development Studies approach referenced in Gudynas, 2018). These foundations of development thought and practice are not entirely rational or objective, but are embedded in affectivity; they have a long history and are thus deeply rooted in different national cultures. The particularity of the Latin American case, and especially in regard to the emergence of progressivism, is that all this was evident in a limited period of time in which despite the variety of experiences some ideas were repeated over and over, and different problems resembled one another.

This basic way of thinking and feeling includes, among other things, conceiving of development as linear progress from situations that are considered inferior to others viewed as superior or advanced. Progress is achieved by the engine of economic growth, an indispensable factor of progressive social change. Society is conceived of as separate from nature, and therefore the intensive appropriation of natural resources is not only accepted but required. Development is understood as essentially linear, universal but in the image and likeness of Western evolution.

Valuations are anthropocentric; only humans are subjects and the rest are objects, and it is also patriarchal. It promotes utilitarian positions that explains the dominance of economic valuation and the proliferation of reductionisms such as human or natural capital, and accepts the idea that issues of justice can be resolved in the market.

With this framework and worldview images are constructed that oppose modernisation to primitivism, advancement to backwardness, civilised to savage, and so on. Progress is achieved through Cartesian-based science and technology with the promise of a total management and control over society and Nature.

Development as it is understood here does not operate as a program obeyed by all actors at the same time; in fact, between groups and sectors there are coincidences such as clashes, certainties and doubts. Development is neither homogeneous nor deterministic but it is a shared belief, and within this realm it is discussed, sometimes fiercely, as to how to organise and bring it about. The previous sections describe these disputes between different ways of organising and instrumentalising development from conservative extremes as in Colombia to invocations of socialist revolution in Venezuela.

Disputes about varieties of development

A focus on varieties of development makes it possible to point out the existence of two types of disputes in the first step. Type I refers to controversies related to varieties in the same tradition, such as capitalism. Type II are discussions between varieties located in different fields, such as socialism versus capitalism (this typology is based on Gudynas, 2016). The Latin American debates of type I in this scheme correspond to discussions about varieties of capitalist development, such as those that engage conservative and reformist progressives. When these capitalisms are opposed to different versions of socialism we classify the debate as Type II. That is, the discussions here take place between perspectives rather than within them. An example would be an exchange or opposition of ideas between proponents of Colombian capitalism and Venezuela's Bolivarian Revolution aka twenty-first-century socialism.

Typologies should not be interpreted rigidly as grouping may follow different perspectives, and also because there are always overlaps between different postures even in type II disputes. But this make clear why calls for reforming or even abandoning capitalism actually reinforced development ideas. What was presented was an alternative but only in the sense of proposing another instrumentalisation of development without altering its foundations.

In the shared field of development (represented by the largest dotted ellipse in Figure 10.1) can be found generally accepted or thinkable rules and arguments that condition all varieties. But beyond those limits there is nothing; there would be no disputes, as they would be unacceptable issues or procedures, and that there might be a world beyond development is even unthinkable. Different discussions and debates about 'development' take place within operative although undefined limits that relate to the search for 'best practice' ideas or different ideas about how to emerge from 'underdevelopment'. But this also raises a consensus regarding the senselessness, for example, of a world without economic growth. Similarly, a discussion about the role of the state in extractivisms is tolerated, but a world without extractivisms is almost unthinkable.

This situation is repeated in Latin American debates, and so it is not surprising that, for example, alternatives to current development practice or processes in Brazil were presented as a 'new' development, or that Bolivia's communitarian socialism is described as a 'integral development'. Essential elements such as economic growth, or, for that matter, capitalism, are taken for granted (as domain assumptions) and not the subject of dispute, inasmuch as the dynamics of capital accumulation and economic growth are sought and will be found in all varieties of capitalism and non-capitalist alternatives. Critics of capitalism might question whether the dynamics of economic growth have been appropriately supported or whether the benefits of growth have been maldistributed, but there is no questioning its need or importance.

During the phase of high commodity prices [2002–2012], progressives were able to deploy policy instruments that could be understood as heterodox attempts at conventional capitalism, with some good results that allowed them to

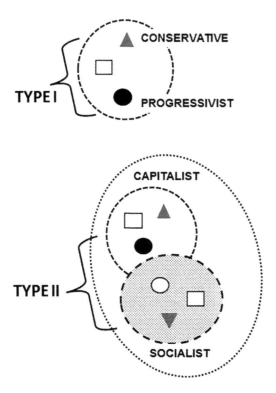

Figure 10.1 Disputes between development varieties. Type I corresponds to clashes within the same group (in the scheme are different types of capitalisms). Type II corresponds to clashes between varieties located in different sets (in the scheme they are socialist or capitalist). The grouping of varieties can follow different criteria but must be applied consistently in all cases. Both types are within the concepts and sensibilities of development (dotted line ellipse).

argue that there are different pathways towards economic growth—different engines, as it were. Under these conditions (in the context of progressive cycle in Latin American politics) the state was particularly active in mediating the dispute over surpluses, managing to use economic compensation as a mechanism for reducing poverty and to pacify the citizenry (Bolivia's communitarian socialism raised this in all sincerity). That is why at the time it seemed that type II disputes were proliferating. But when those prices began to fall, fiscal resources were drastically reduced and compensatory cash transfers to the poor and reparations declined; the state's ability to arbitrate the distribution of the economic surplus was significantly reduced—all conditions that contributed to the exhaustion of progressivism. Second-tier disputes began to wane and began to manifest as type I clashes, especially because of a reorganisation of parties on the political Right that began to attack progressivism (e.g. in Argentina and Brazil).

This brief explanation allows to reconsider some bizarre situations that are not always properly analysed. This is the case with the repeated defence of extractivisms by progressivisms despite the contradictions it implied with its rhetoric and civil society resistance. One of the most striking defences was in Ecuador where the government of Rafael Correa proposed to increase extractivism so as to leave them behind sometime in the future. The justification was that the extraction and appropriation of natural resources was the main source of capital accumulation that would allow the country to move forward to other stages of development—a justification presented without irony as a part of the 'socialism of *buen vivir*' (Ecuador, 2009). But behind this defence of extractivism were ideas of conventional capitalism as a dynamic of capital accumulation which would allow the country to move or leap forward into other supposedly more advanced stages (the final phase of that model was to expand tourism, new industries and the exportation of bio-knowledge). These ideas, regarding the accumulation of capital as a means of jumping into more advanced stages of development, were almost identical to those proposed in 1960 by W.W. Rostow. The irony is that Rostow defended the capital accumulation dynamics of economic growth as part of a 'non-communist manifesto' while Ecuadorian progressives presented it as a socialist alternative. The same logic can be found in the position taken by the MAS government in Bolivia (on this see García Linera, 2012, in his defence of extractivism in the Amazon).

What was lost sight of here was that the maintenance of extractivist strategies meant that there was no choice but to participate in capitalism. Conservative governments always understood this and defended it, but because some progressives rightly criticised globalisation on this score they faced numerous difficulties and contradictions in sustaining the correspondence between discourse and actions, and were thus forced to appeal to tortuous explanations such as those in the example above.

In this context, many in the debate about development stopped questioning capitalism in general to focus on one of its varieties: neoliberalism. In this way a radical anti-capitalist and ant-imperialist rhetoric could be maintained while remaining within the bounds and parameters of development under the rubric of some sort of reformed or humanised capitalism (inclusive development). For some, this was justified as a transitory stage until a revolution on a planetary scale occurred (see, for example, Borón, 2012). For others, this stance (invisiblising capitalism and its contradictions) allowed them to shift the location of an alternative horizon to more precise issues such as reducing poverty or securing well-being by improving access to consumption. Under these conditions, these alternatives aligned with the goal of a benevolent capitalism that could reduce the most severe impacts of extractivism and the inequalities that are generic to capitalism in all of its varieties. This meant that many type II discussions became type I disputes among varieties of capitalism.

Alternatives to development and *buen vivir*

There are many other perspectives that question capitalism and propose alternatives. For example, beyond the question of how to define capitalism, there is a rich literature in the Marxist tradition that has had a lot of influence in Latin America (for an assessment of these contributions see Wright, 2010). Others, that are more recent and originate in the global north, explore varieties of so-called post-capitalism that turn out to be stronger and more effective in criticism but weaker in determining precise alternatives (for example, Mason, 2016; Rogers, 2014; Harvey, 2014). A more detailed contribution can be found in the 'real utopias' described by Wright (2010), although these possible alternatives, like those previously mentioned, are located within the type II disputes and thus still remain within the field of development. Other contributions along the line of 'alternatives' appear under the term 'degrowth', which is aimed directly against the concept of 'growth', one of the basic ideas of development. But there is no consensus on contents and practices among degrowthers and the efforts to link it to some Latin American alternatives, as those facing extractivisms, did not offer specific policy and management programs (Acosta and Brand, 2017). In contrast, a more precise discussion of alternatives to growth is given by Jackson (2009) in his proposal for 'prosperity in a steady state economics'.

All of this questioning assumes a rational analysis in which the accumulation of evidence is sufficient for understanding the evils of capitalism. But as noted above, this is not the case, and the foundations of development (and thus those of capitalism) also include affectivity and irrational dynamics. A discussion of alternatives should therefore incorporate these aspects as well. An example of this is the notion of post-capitalism advanced by Gibson-Graham (2006), who proposes the need for changes in our 'modes of thinking and feeling, in the self, and even in the understanding of the world'.

Such a change in perspective has occurred precisely in Latin America with the uchronia of *buen vivir* discussed by Ramiréz in the previous chapter. In its original formulation as *sumak kawsay* or *suma qamaña,* promoted more or less simultaneously in Bolivia and Ecuador, and partly in Peru, the notion of *buen vivir* allowed for and led to exploring other ways of understanding and feeling (see for example Chuji et al., 2019). These explorations have resulted in ideas and proposals that mix some contributions of indigenous peoples and elements of certain critical currents of Western knowledge such as those that provided by some ecologies and feminisms. *Buen vivir* is more than the Western idea of living well, as in all its versions defend the integrity and continuity of Society–Nature, and they include a redefinition of communities that are inhabited by both humans and non-humans; and significantly, none of these proposed alternatives endorse the anxiety for progress of both orthodox and heterodox economists, or the widely shared idea that there are universal models that should or must be followed (as an illustration of the diversity of this way of thinking in regards to Bolivia, for example, see Yampara, 2011; Torrez, 2012; Burman, 2017; Ranta, 2018).

This explains the fact that in its original versions, *buen vivir* questioned development in all of its varieties. It was a critique that pointed to shared domain assumptions and basic concepts, promoting alternatives beyond any kind of development. Thus, the concept of living well generated disputes that did not correspond to neither type I nor type II debates. Thus, it is necessary to identify type III disputes in those situations where any of the varieties of development are questioned, bringing into focus both ideas within and beyond development and the possibility of thinking and feeling the possibility of 'another' or 'other worlds' (Figure 10.2). These disputes at the same time point to various post-capitalist and post-socialist alternatives, something which is not always understood.

Indeed, for believers in development, alternatives that do not accept their domain assumptions and share their basic concepts and their sensibilities are inconceivable. Thus, they generally do not accept or understand type III disputes, and react to them in several ways. In many situations, they reinterpret them as if they were type II debates. Then, when progressives listened to the questionings of *buen vivir* they were labelled as allies of the conservatives or propagators of extreme leftist infantilism, as was heard repeatedly in Bolivia and Ecuador (the then vice-president of Bolivia offered many examples, as in García Linera, 2012). The intellectuals who supported them added arguments such as imperialist domination and the impossibility of an alternative to capitalism until we have a planetary revolution, resulting in shielding development beliefs (in Borón, 2012, for example, such rationalities can be found).

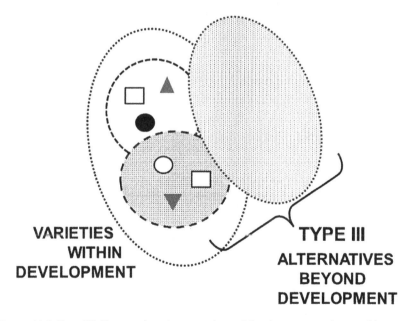

VARIETIES WITHIN DEVELOPMENT　　　　**TYPE III ALTERNATIVES BEYOND DEVELOPMENT**

Figure 10.2 Type III disputes that pit any variety of developments against positions that challenge or reject their bases and postulate alternatives beyond them.

These postneoliberal progressives also set about the complex task of redefining *buen vivir* in order to achieve a version that was both socialist in form and functional for development. In Ecuador a 'socialist *buen vivir*' was launched while in Bolivia progressives conceived and talked of 'communitarian socialism' and integral development' in order to *vivir bien* (Ecuador, 2009; Bolivia, 2016). For many activists and activist scholars who worked alongside and with the social movements, these new formulations were meaningless because *buen vivir* rejected the contents and practices in these conceptions.

Indeed, *buen vivir*, for example, does not include or accept the goal of economic growth, and strategies such as extractivism violate its essence as it destroys mixed communities of humans and non-humans. In other words, a serious fulfilment of living well would force progressives to abandon all their extractivist projects in mining, oil or monoculture. But adherence to this type of development was so powerful and so deeply entrenched that progressives felt and still feel compelled to reformulate that alternative.

Type III disputes are not new, but have always been around us. What happens is that these disputes depart from shared domain assumption that impose a certain fixed idea of development, and those within this field almost always understand them as type II disputes. This was evident in many encounters between progressive intellectuals and politicians, on the one hand, and indigenous peoples and movement leaders on the other; and, for example, in the face of the demands of indigenous people, peasants or local NGOs, against extractivisms, demands which even the most progressive governments regarded as an expression of political opposition, environmental terrorism, or radical infantilism.

Buen vivir is anti-capitalist, although at times this is understood to be insufficient. Similarly, it incorporates some elements that can be considered socialist, but that on their own can also be considered as insufficient. For example, it does not reject changing the ownership and labour rules proposed by the post-capitalism of Mason or Rogers, or, as proposed by David Harvey, to dismantle the infrastructure and superstructure of financialisation. But these alternatives are partial and in practice do not ensure a process of transformative change, inasmuch as they would inevitably fall back into a form of development that would once again result in social and environmental injustices. The limits of all kinds of developments, from the most reactionary neoliberalism to the most radical socialism, have been experimented with and tested in Latin America over the past several decades. But none of them have managed to solve the demands of social and ecological justice.

Progressives have posed alternatives in reformulating the capital–labour relation, but without changing the ways of assigning values or understanding that the development idea is at the core of this relation. Redistributive policies do not change how value is conceived, nor do they allow for a resolution of disputes over surpluses; at most they can change the actors involved in the struggles over the surplus.

On the other hand, *buen vivir* leaves the field of development as it recognises multiple valuations, including intrinsic values, in the non-human and Nature.

Value is no longer tied to work or human agency; it assumes multiple forms. In this way, the alternatives of *buen vivir* go far beyond seeking a balance between use and exchange values, as in Harvey (2014) or as proposed by ecosocialists such as Lowy (2011), presenting a plurality of values and including the non-human. This would necessarily cross one of the boundaries that encompasses development: anthropocentrism.

The concept of *buen vivir* crosses this boundary and also breaks with the other foundations of development built by modernity, such as adherence to progress or the privileged status of Cartesian knowledge (Yampara, 2011; Torrez, 2012; Burman, 2017). It is always plural, anchored in ecological, historical and cultural contexts, and therefore unable to offer a universal guide.

Beyond all this, unlike other alternatives those associated with *buen vivir* have wide support in some social groups and offer concrete alternatives in both policy and action. This partly explains the enormous effort of progressives to control and marginalise these alternatives. They challenge and put at risk the development programs and projects that they need to sustain their governments and themselves in power.

Buen vivir has had the enormous merit of highlighting the limits of the field of development, fracturing these limits and producing openings to other possible alternatives that were previously unthinkable. It operates as an opening mechanism. In that sense, it has shaped the next step in the transformations initiated by the left and some progressives, although the same progressivism has sought to nullify this potentiality. This was not because these progressives prefer capitalism, but because of the inability of progressivism to escape the closed box of development.

Exhaustions and alternatives

At the beginning of 2020, the Secretary General of ECLAC confessed that the 'economic model has been exhausted'.[3] Despite the gravity of this diagnosis something was somehow admitted that almost everyone acknowledges but few say openly: none of the development trials were successful; there are several years of stagnation and even setbacks in some countries; and the coronavirus pandemic is accelerating the deterioration in living conditions.

The confession of development depletion must be placed in historical perspective. It cannot be hidden that at the political climax of progressivism, in 2008, they simultaneously ruled in seven of the 12 countries of South America, encompassing just over 300 million people. Wall Street at the time was collapsing under the weight of a severe financial crisis that hit industrialised countries,[4] and all the political pundits n experts on capitalism were questioned. Marx's works became bests sellers and citizen mobilisations demanded changes.

It was a very favourable scenario for change, and even for conditions that many old militants had dreamed of, as, on the one hand, a number of governments with a progressive agenda (inclusive development, poverty reduction) had won power by democratic means, and on the other, the capitalism faltered under the weight of its diverse contradictions. They were ideal conditions for advancing new alternatives, and the original *buen vivir* options were already available. But the anticipated substantive transformations did not happen. The foundations of development were not changed, and some of these progressive regimes fell and were replaced by far-right governments pursuing a neoliberal policy agenda.[5]

It is necessary to learn from these circumstances. A first lesson is to assume that the classical understanding that alternatives are transitions from capitalist to non-capitalist options (usually described as socialist), may be incomplete or not enough to ensure substantive changes in social and ecological justice.

A second lesson is the need to improve analytical rigour in handling terms or concepts. For example, progressives do not constitute neoliberalisms, but they are not a socialist revolution either. Similarly, labelling any regime that is to be criticised as populist does not improve an understanding of what is happening; concepts like oligarchy deserve to be bailed out because they continue to be meaningful. Words and their meanings remain important.

A third lesson is that we should assume that development ideas and sensibilities precede the dominant currents in political and economic thinking today. They are deeply rooted and explain that the clashes are actually between varieties of development while this thinking persists. Thus, there are two very different perspectives regarding alternatives, some between varieties of development, and others beyond any development. To contest ideas in this area requires expanding the content under discussion; for example, considerations of Capital and Labour in the development process should be expanded by adding, for example, affectivity. It is also crucial to approach different ways of conceiving values in order to break with anthropocentrism.

A fourth lesson is a warning that there are blockages for alternatives beyond development such as those suffered by proposals for *buen vivir*. In many cases these proposals, as embodied for example, in Ecuador's National Plan for *buen vivir* (2009–2013), were not even understood and interpreted as a conventional political party platform, or they were reconfigured so as to make them functional for development.

A fifth lesson is to recognise the enormous importance of these issues that should no longer be restricted to academic encounters or intellectual dreams in the transition of dystopia to utopia; they should be expressed in the political arena involving multiple social actors. Widespread citizen participation is indispensable to further explore alternatives to the current crisis. Indeed, the persistence of problems such as poverty, the worsening ecological collapse on the continent and on the planet, together with the coronavirus pandemic, require new alternatives. We know that trying to solve these and such problems by means of a new variety of development that remains based on material growth is unsustainable. The horizon of alternatives is elsewhere; the discussions about *buen vivir* show it.

Finally, these experiments show that the threshold to be crossed is to overcome development, but at the same time, the direction in that exit is to the left since the commitment to justice is indispensable if the social and ecological crisis is to be resolved. The concept of *buen vivir* prefigures this change in conceiving and feeling the world.

Notes

1 For example, in Ecuador, poverty rose from 36.7 per cent in 2007 to a low of 21.5 per cent in 2017, to rise again since 2018; income-based indicator according to the National Institute of Statistics and Census, www.ecuadorencifras.gob.ec.
2 Interview in *El Telégrafo*, 15 January 2012.
3 "América Latina ha perdido el tren de la política industrial y la innovación" I. Fariza interviews A. Bárcena, *El País*, Madrid, 7 February 2020.
4 Editor's note: The crisis was billed as 'global' ('the global financial crisis') although, unlike the cycle of financial crises in the 1990s that impacted primarily countries on the periphery of the world system, the 2000 crisis primarily hit countries at the centre of the system. This was reflected in an essay by the economist Arturo Porzecanski (2009) that, with reference to Latin America, raised the question 'Crisis. What Crisis?'.
5 Editor's note: On these dynamics, and the left-right swing of the pendulum of electoral politics, see Veltmeyer and Petras (2019).

References

Acosta, A. and U. Brand (2017). *Salidas del laberinto capitalista. Decrecimiento y postextractivismo*. Barcelona: Icaria.

Acosta, A. and J. Cajas Guijarro (2018). *Una década desperdiciada. Las sombras del Correismo*. Quito: CAAP.

Alvarez R.V. (2009). Venezuela: *¿Hacia dónde va el modelo productivo?* Caracas: Centro Internacional Miranda.

Alvarez R.V. (2013). "Transiciones logradas y transiciones pendientes," pp. 221–315, In: *Promesas en su laberinto. Cambios y continuidades en los gobiernos progresistas de América Latina*. La Paz: CEDLA.

Arze Vargas, C. and J. Gómez (2013). "Bolivia: ¿El "proceso de cambio" nos conduce al vivir bien?" pp. 37–137, In: *Promesas en su laberinto. Cambios y continuidades en los gobiernos progresistas de América Latina*. La Paz: CEDLA.

Bizberg, I. (2014). *Variedades de capitalismo en América Latina: los casos de México, Brasil, Argentina y Chile*. Mexico: El Colegio de México.

Boito Jr, A. (2018). *Reforma e crise política no Brasil. Os conflitos de classe nos governos do PT*. Campinas, UNICAMP.

Bolivia (2016). *Plan de desarrollo económico y social en el marco del desarrollo integral para vivir bien. 2016–2020*. La Paz: Ministerio Planificación Desarrollo.

Borón, A. (2012). *América Latina en la geopolítica del imperialismo*. Buenos Aires: Luxemburg.

Boschi, R.R. (ed.) (2011a). *Variedades de capitalismo, política e desenvolvimento na América Latina*. Belo Horizonte: Editora UFMG.

Boschi, R.R. (2011b). "Introdução. Instituições, trajetórias e desenvolvimento. Uma dicussão a partir da América Latina," pp. 7–27, In R.R. Boschi (ed.), *Variedades de capitalismo, política e desenvolvimento na América Latina*. Belo Horizonte: Editora UFMG.

Burman, A. (2017). "La ontología política del vivir bien," pp. 155–173, in K. de Munter, J. Michaux and G. Pauwels (eds), *Ecología y reciprocidad: (Con)vivir bien, desde contextos andinos*. La Paz: Plural.

Campanini, O., M. Gandarillas and E. Gudynas (2020). *Derechos y violencias en los extractivismos. Extrahecciones en Bolivia y Latinoamérica*. Cochabamba: La Libre.

Carneiro, R. (ed.) (2006). *A supremacía dos mercados e a política económica do governo Lula*. São Paulo: UNESP.

Chávez, H. (2007). "El socialismo del siglo XXI," in N. Kohan (ed.), *Introducción al pensamiento socialista*. Bogota: Ocean Sur.

Chuji, M., G. Rengijo and E. Gudynas (2019). "Buen Vivir," pp. 111–114, in A. Kothari, A. Salleh, A. Escobar, F. Demaria and A. Acosta (eds), *Pluriverse. A Post-Development Dictionary*. New Delhi: Authors Upfront.

Cuvi, J. (ed.) (2014). *La restauración conservadora del correismo*. Quito: Montecristi Vive.

De Azevedo, A., C. Feijó and D. Arruda Coronel (eds) (2013). *A desindustrialização brasileira*. São Leopoldo: UNISINOS.

Dieterich, H. (2005). *Hugo Chávez y el socialismo del siglo XXI*. Caracas: Instituto Municipal de Publicaciones de la Alcaldía de Caracas.

Ecuador (2009). *Plan Nacional para el buen vivir 2009–2013. Construyendo un Estado plurinacional e intercultural*. Quito: SENPLADES.

Ermida Uriarte, O. (2007). "La política laboral de los gobiernos progresistas," *Nueva Sociedad*, 211: 50–65.

Fernández, V.R. and M. Ebenau (eds) (2018). *Variedades de capitalismo entre centro y periferia. Miradas críticas desde América Latina*. Buenos Aires: Miño y Dávila.

De Moraes, W. dos Santos (2011). "Capitalismo sindicalista de conciliação e "capitalismo de las calles. Brasil e Venezuela no pós-neoliberalismo," pp. 347–372, in R.R. Boschi (ed.), *Variedades de capitalismo, política e desenvolvimento na América Latina*. Belo Horizonte: Editora UFMG.

Gaitán, F. and R. Boschi (2015). "State-Business-Labour Relations and Patterns of Development in Latin America," pp. 172–188, in M. Ebenau, I. Bruff and C. May (eds), *New Directions in Comparative Capitalisms Research. Critical and Global Perspectives*. New York: Palgrave.

García Linera, A. (2012). *Geopolítica de la Amazonia. Poder hacendal-patrimonial y acumulación capitalista*. La Paz: Vicepresidencia del Estado Plurinacional.

Gervasoni, C. and E. Peruzzotti (2015). *¿Década ganada? Evaluando el legado del Kirchnerismo*. Buenos Aires: Debate.

Gibson-Graham, J.K. (2006). *Postcapitalist Politics. Minneapolis*: University of Minnesota Press.

Gudynas, E. (2018). "Post-development and Other Critiques of the Roots of Development," pp. 84–93, in H. Veltmeyer and P. Bowles (eds), *The Essential Guide to Critical Development Studies*. London: Routledge.

Gudynas, E. (2016). "Beyond Varieties of Development: Disputes and Alternatives," *Third World Quarterly*, 37(4): 721–732.

Gudynas, E. (2020). *Extractivisms. Politics, Economics and Ecology*. Halifax: Fernwood.

Harvey, D. (2014). *Seventeen Contradictions and the End of Capitalism*. New York: Oxford University Press.

Hall, P. and D. Soskice (2001). "An Introduction to Varieties of Capitalism," pp. 1–68, in P.A. Hall and D. Soskice (eds), *Varieties of Capitalism: The Institutional Foundations of Comparative Advantage*. Oxford: Oxford University Press.

Jackson, T. (2009). *Prosperity without Growth. Economics for a Finite Planet*. London: Earthscan.

Kerner, D. (2017). *Del modelo al relato. Política y economía durante el Kirchnerismo*. Buenos Aires: Biblos.

Kulfas, M. (2016). *Los tres kirchnerismos. Una historia de la economía argentina 2003–2015*. Buenos Aires: Siglo XXI.

Lavinas, L. (2017). *The Takeover of Social Policy by Financialization. The Brazilian Paradox*. New York: Palgrave Macmillan.

Lowy, M. (2011). *Ecosocialismo. La alternativa radical a la catástrofe ecológica capitalista*. Buenos Aires: El Colectivo and Herramienta.

Mason, P. (2016). *Postcapitalism. A Guide to our Future*. London: Penguin.

Munck, R. (2018). "Rethinking the Left: A View from Latin America," *Global Discourse*, 8(2): 260–275.

Ospina Peralta, P. (2013). "Estamos haciendo mejor las cosas con el mismo modelo que antes que cambiarlo. La revolución ciudadana en Ecuador (2007–2012)," pp. 139–220, in *Promesas en su laberinto. Cambios y continuidades en los gobiernos progresistas de América Latina*. La Paz: CEDLA.

Philip, G. and F. Panizza (2011). *The Triumph of Politics. The Return of the Left in Venezuela, Bolivia and Ecuador*. Cambridge: Polity.

Porzecanski, A. (2009). "Latin America: The Missing Financial Crisis," *Studies and Perspectives* 6. Washington DC: ECLAC.

Pucciarelli, A. and A. Castellani (eds) (2017). *Los años del Kirchnerismo. La disputa hegemónica tras la crisis del orden neoliberal*. Buenos Aires: Siglo XXI.

Ranta, E. (2018). *Vivir Bien as an Alternative to Neoliberal Globalization. Can Indigenous Terminologies Decolonize the State?* Abingdon: Routledge.

Rogers, C. (2014). *Capitalism and its Alternatives*. London: Zed Books.

Serrano Mancilla, A. (2014). *El pensamiento económico de Hugo Chávez*. Quito: IAEN.

Singer, A. (2012). *Os sentidos do lulismo: reforma gradual e pacto conservador*. São Paulo: Companhia das Letras.

Singer, A. and I. Loureiro (eds) (2016). *As contradições do Lulismo. A que ponto chegamos?* São Paulo: Boitempo.

Torrez, M. (2012). *Suma qamaña y desarrollo: el t'hinkhu necesario*. La Paz: Programa Nacional Biocultura.

Valencia Lomelí, E. (2008). "Conditional Cash Transfers as Social Policy in Latin America: An Assessment of Their Contributions and Limitations," *Annual Review of Sociology*, 34(1): 475–499.

Veltmeyer, H. and J. Petras (2019). *Latin America in the Vortex of Social Change: Development and Resistance Dynamics*. London: Routledge.

Wainer, A. (2018). "Economía y política en la Argentina kirchnerista (2003–2015)," *Revista Mexicana Sociología*, 80(2): 323–351.

Wanderley, F. (2013). *¿Qué pasó con el proceso de cambio? Ideales acertados, medios equivocados, resultados trastocados*. La Paz: CIDES UMSA.

Webber, J. (2011). *From Rebellion to Reform in Bolivia. Class Struggle, Indigenous Liberation, and the Politics of Evo Morales*. Chicago: Haymarket.

Wright, E.O. (2010). *Envisioning Real Utopias*. London: Verso.

Yampara, S. (2011). "Cosmovivencia andina: Vivir y convivir en armonía integral – suma qamaña," *Bolivian Studies Journal*, 18: 1–23.

Index

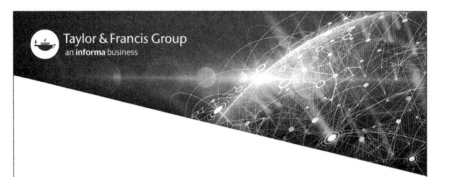

Taylor & Francis eBooks

www.taylorfrancis.com

A single destination for eBooks from Taylor & Francis
with increased functionality and an improved user
experience to meet the needs of our customers.

90,000+ eBooks of award-winning academic content in
Humanities, Social Science, Science, Technology, Engineering,
and Medical written by a global network of editors and authors.

TAYLOR & FRANCIS EBOOKS OFFERS:

A streamlined
experience for
our library
customers

A single point
of discovery
for all of our
eBook content

Improved
search and
discovery of
content at both
book and
chapter level

REQUEST A FREE TRIAL
support@taylorfrancis.com

Printed in the United States
By Bookmasters